DARK GENIUS

THE INFLUENTIAL CAREER OF LEGENDARY POLITICAL OPERATIVE AND FOX NEWS FOUNDER ROGER AILES

KERWIN SWINT

UNION SQUARE PRESS
An imprint of Sterling Publishing Co., Inc.

New York / London
www.sterlingpublishing.com

STERLING and the distinctive Sterling logo are registered trademarks of
Sterling Publishing Co., Inc.

Library of Congress Cataloging-in-Publication Data Available

10 9 8 7 6 5 4 3 2 1

Published by Sterling Publishing Co., Inc.
387 Park Avenue South, New York, NY 10016
© 2008 by Kerwin Swint
Distributed in Canada by Sterling Publishing
c/o Canadian Manda Group, 165 Dufferin Street
Toronto, Ontario, Canada M6K 3H6
Distributed in the United Kingdom by GMC Distribution Services
Castle Place, 166 High Street, Lewes, East Sussex, England BN7 1XU
Distributed in Australia by Capricorn Link (Australia) Pty. Ltd.
P.O. Box 704, Windsor, NSW 2756, Australia

Sterling ISBN-13: 978-1-4027-5445-6
        ISBN-10: 1-4027-5445-0

For information about custom editions, special sales, premium and
corporate purchases, please contact Sterling Special Sales
Department at 800-805-5489 or specialsales@sterlingpublishing.com.

To Professor Bill Thomas

And, of course, my incredibly supportive family

Contents

Introduction

There's no getting around it—Roger Ailes is an amazing man, of singular achievement and worldwide impact. After all, how many individuals have influenced the direction of the two most important institutions in the world—politics and media—for forty years? From Richard Nixon to Bill O'Reilly, Ailes has been there—shaping the message, managing the performance, staging the images, and perfecting the "stylistic" approach that has appealed to so many Americans, whether in presidential campaigns or television news networks.

He is an immensely talented and driven individual—a creative and organizational genius in the opinion of many, including this author. But in his long career he has too often used his talents to demean his adversaries, to camouflage his clients' intentions, and to obfuscate the truth.

Ailes is such a fascinating subject for a book because he is, in a way, the Forrest Gump of American politics. Like Tom Hanks's mythical character in the popular movie, Roger Ailes has been actively involved in most of the big political media moments of the last generation. There is no other single figure in American society who has been a key player in, first, syndicated daytime television talk and variety programming, then Richard Nixon's conquest of television in 1968, the birth of the New Right in the 1970s, Ronald Reagan's reelection in 1984, George Bush's 1988 presidential campaign, Rudy Giuliani's first political campaign, Rush Limbaugh's television show, programming for NBC as one of the network's executives, the transformation of cable television news as the founder and president of Fox News, and finally, the continued growth of Rupert Murdoch's worldwide multimedia empire.

This author is no psychologist, but Roger Ailes the man actually presents the world with a very interesting conundrum. He is a very moralistic person, dedicated to preserving the principles of what he sees as the "traditional" American way of life. Yet in achieving those ends he has used his abilities and his talent in some very questionable and cynical ways, which seems to undercut those all-American principles. His friends say he is warm, charming, reliable, and has a great sense of humor—all the qualities one would want in a neighbor. Yet, in this author's opinion, he has engineered some of the most duplicitous, misleading, and occasionally vitriolic and mean-spirited, political campaigns in American history.

What is undeniable, though, is that he has had enormous success. Since the 1960s, Ailes has been at the center of a slow-motion, decades-long conservative Republican march on American culture—pushing the political and media center of the country toward the right. How has he done it? Quite simply, the man understands television better than any other person on the planet. And in the service of ideologues interested in pushing a political philosophy, he has been very adept at using TV to cast favorable images on candidates and causes he supports, while trashing the opposition—often using, in this author's opinion, deceptive and misleading TV programs and advertising in his political campaigns, and perfecting the use of catch phrases like "fair and balanced" as the president of Fox News.

It's a monumental achievement, really—it has long been an article of faith among conservatives that the main obstacle, really the only obstacle, to the widespread acceptance of conservative political thought and the long-term victory of its political strength is the liberal mass media. A firm believer in Richard Nixon's Silent Majority, Ailes believes he has given a voice to that majority. This book will examine his role in this cultural, political, and media transformation as it has unfolded over the last four decades.

Roger Ailes grew up in a relatively comfortable working-class family in Warren, Ohio, in the 1940s and '50s and was taught the traditional values of small-town America: hard work, self-reliance, and faith in country. His polit- ical and media career has been very much focused on serving these traditional ideals (that he has interpreted through a conservative political philosophy) and working for those in power whom he believes share those ideals—politicians like Nixon, Reagan, and the elder Bush, and the media mogul Rupert Murdoch, the chairman of News Corporation and Fox Broadcasting.

Interestingly, one of the traits these leaders appear to have shared is the conviction that Americans, or at least honest, decent, freedom-loving people, are in a historic struggle against forces that seek to undermine the conservative, tradi- tional America to which Ailes has dedicated his life. For Nixon, that evil force was Communism; for Reagan, it was a combination of big government, high taxes, and Communism. For Rupert Murdoch and for Ailes, it is the perverse and corro- sive influence of the liberal, anti-American, anti-Western mass media.

For his part, Ailes felt strongly enough about these convictions and the political ideas behind them to work in politics for a quarter century. He likes to say that he has never been all that political, but nobody would spend twenty-five years working in partisan politics only because it was a good job opportunity. Ailes never completely abandoned the media and television business during his political consulting career, continuing to do various media consulting as well as other ventures, but politics and ideology have maintained a constant presence in his life.

The Roger Ailes story of the last forty years is very much linked to the rise of television since the 1960s and its domination of politics. His career has paralleled the dramatic ascension of TV and its ability to shape our environment. Ailes is one of the primary architects of that environment. In a way, this book is about the political communication history of the modern era, warts and all—from the vantage point of one of its master craftsmen.

What the world needs to understand about Roger Ailes is that he is not so much a newsman as he is a showman. First and foremost, he is an entertainment producer and is very good at teaching his clients (in politics, business, and broadcasting) how to put on a great show and win over an audience.

As an early pioneer of political television, he saw its potential to influence Americans' attitude toward ideas and individuals. He also understood that TV is about images and performance—seeing is believing—and that good, effective TV programming could be used to alter public opinion. He would use this knowledge over the next several decades to recast the political and media universe in a more conservative direction.

Ailes would say he has used TV to educate, inform, and present views that were misrepresented or shut out of the traditional mainstream media. His critics say he has used TV to deceive and manipulate. He is seen by many as the Wizard behind the curtain in an electronic Oz, using TV to cast spells and create false images. What is without question, though, is that his made-for-TV imagery and his mastery of style over substance have made him arguably the dominant political media figure of the age.

But like many ideologues and visionaries throughout history, his critics accuse him of gross exaggeration, sweeping away inconvenient facts and details, misrepresenting the views of those he supports and those he opposes, the use of images to distract attention, and the use of emotional hot buttons to achieve his ends. To visionaries, after all, the ends do justify the means.

The book opens with the historic television encounter between Richard Nixon and John F. Kennedy in 1960—the moment when television imagery began to eclipse the substance of ideas and policy in modern American politics. As we have all learned together over the last forty years, television truly is a Pandora's box. In the fall of 1960, that box was opened.

Roger Ailes absorbed the lessons of televised communication, and became a television producer and director in the mid-'60s. It was while working as the director of *The Mike Douglas Show* that he met Richard Nixon and struck up a conversation about politics and TV. The rest is history. Ailes helped Nixon conquer TV by tailoring his television appearances around staged question-and-answer sessions that looked an awful lot like the kind of television shows Ailes had been producing for entertainer Mike Douglas.

Afterward, Ailes became a consultant for media organizations and for Republican political candidates. By the 1980s he had become known as something of a communications guru. A member of the advertising team feeding ideas to the Ronald Reagan reelection campaign in 1984, he helped Reagan recover from his disastrous opening debate with Walter Mondale by working with him to refocus on his core beliefs. And in 1988 came the big one: Ailes was the communications and media consultant for the George Bush presidential campaign, one of the best-conceived media campaigns in history, and also one of the most negative and hostile. Notably, Ailes's name surfaced in a preliminary Federal Election Commission inquiry into illegal coordination between the George Bush campaign and the independent organization that ran the notorious Willie Horton TV commercial. The Willie Horton ad injected racial fears into the presidential campaign by showing menacing photographs of the African-American Horton while suggesting that the Dukakis campaign was too soft on violent criminals. Horton had fled from authorities while on a weekend furlough from a Massachusetts state prison and committed rape and armed robbery.

The '88 Bush campaign, considered the high-water mark for negative campaigning in the last quarter century, had lasting aftereffects. For one, it made it more difficult for Ailes to work in politics. He was credited, rightly or wrongly, with the nastiness of the Bush effort, particularly with regard to the Willie Horton affair. Every candidate he worked for from 1989 to 1992 had to deal with Roger Ailes as an albatross around his neck—and most of those candidates lost. Once again, Ailes was at a career crossroads.

The book then covers Ailes's transition away from political campaigns and back toward television news, including CNBC and Fox News. His experience in TV programming and production were put to use in the early '90s as a consultant for 20th Century Fox Television and Paramount Television, working for shows like *Hard Copy* and *Entertainment Tonight*. Then in 1993 he was hired to run CNBC. While there, he developed innovative talk and entertainment programming, such as America's Talking—in a way, the forerunner of the Fox News Channel. But NBC had other plans. When they paired with Microsoft to create MSNBC, Ailes wasn't part of the picture.

As it turned out, Ailes had other plans too—big plans. His association with Rupert Murdoch, the chairman of News Corporation and Fox Broadcasting, changed not only his life but American television news forever. Murdoch and Ailes shared the vision of creating a news network free from what they considered liberal bias. But what they created instead was the world's first news network to have a conservative bias. Even so, within seven years of its birth, Fox News had surpassed rival CNN in the ratings war and was redefining the media landscape. The book also covers the movement of Rupert Murdoch and Roger Ailes into the future—Internet platforms, integrated media, the acquisition of the *Wall Street Journal,* and the launch of the Fox Business Network. How did they do it? The book will explore the communication and entertainment formula Ailes brought to Fox News, how it is similar to his approach with political candidates, and how he has impacted the news business, the business of politics, and American culture.

1

Dawn of the TV Age

With the coming of television, and the knowledge of how it could be used to seduce voters, the old political values disappeared. Something new, murky, undefined started to rise from the mists.

—Joe McGinniss, author of *The Selling of the President 1968*

On the evening of September 26, 1960, after his historic debate with John F. Kennedy, Dick Nixon said his good-byes and then walked to his waiting car. He felt good about how he had responded to the panel's questions and how he had engaged Senator Kennedy on the issues, but he couldn't shake the feeling that he had missed something. *Something was wrong.*

Perhaps Nixon's postdebate exit didn't happen exactly that way, but the description above may be close. The televised 1960 debate between John Kennedy and Richard Nixon made history. And it made history in ways that no living person in 1960 could have imagined.

First, it was historic in some obvious ways. It was the first debate in American history that featured the two presidential nominees of the major parties. Presidential candidates didn't really campaign as we know it until late in the 1800s. Actively campaigning for one's self for public office was considered undignified and best left to others. And candidate debates at any political level were very rare until the second half of the twentieth century.

Prior to the Kennedy–Nixon face-off, the most famous political debates had been between Abraham Lincoln and Stephen Douglas, who ran against each other for U.S. senator from Illinois in 1858. Lincoln and Douglas met in a series of seven debates across the state, each lasting three hours, which helped frame the political dialogue around the issues of slavery, states' rights, and the Union. These famous encounters became, and still are for the most part, the model for honest, forthright political debate. There were no such debates in 1860 or, for that matter, the next hundred years.

According to the bipartisan Commission on Presidential Debates, the only other such events were a 1948 radio debate between Republican presidential candidates Thomas Dewey and Harold Stassen, and a 1956 television debate between Democratic presidential candidates Adlai Stevenson and Estes Kefauver. Before JFK came along, television was still in its infancy. TV would grow into rebellious, devilish adolescence in the 1960s. To politicians and political parties in the 1950s, television was an interesting toy. In the '60s, it would become an instrument of mass political destruction.

It is fitting that Roger Ailes was born around the same time that television was born. In fact, the year of his birth, 1940, was the very year that Peter Goldmark developed the first color television system for CBS laboratories. Television would change the world, and Roger Ailes would help change television.

To most observers of politics, media, and history, the 1960 debate between Kennedy and Nixon is historic for other reasons. It is considered by many to be the very moment when television began to take over American politics. It was the first time that anyone could say with any reasonable amount of confidence that TV had a decisive effect on the outcome of a political campaign.

Before the 1960s, Americans were accustomed to getting most of their political information from newspapers and radio. Not enough homes were equipped with TVs yet for the new medium to make a significant impact. When Dwight Eisenhower's 1952 campaign revolutionized presidential campaigning with its emphasis on selling its candidate with TV ads, only 34 percent of American homes had televisions. By 1960 that number was up to 87 percent. The Kennedy–Nixon debate, and the intense media coverage throughout the 1960 campaign and afterward, helped drive up those numbers even more. By the end of the 1960s, for the first time in American history, more Americans were getting their news from television than from newspapers or radio. That fundamentally changed our society, for better *and* worse.

It was also an important cultural shift to many. To air the debate, CBS bumped one of the most popular shows on television, *The Andy Griffith Show*. Itself a cultural icon, featuring a small-town sheriff doing his best to raise his boy, *The Andy Griffith Show* has been cast by more than one observer as a program "that teaches you most of the lessons you need to know in life."

"The innocence of the 1950s ended with the bumping of *The Andy Griffith Show*, and the seriousness of the 1960s began with the first Kennedy–Nixon debate," claims Bruce Dumont, president of the Museum of Broadcast Communications.[1] Dumont noted that until 1960, television was largely defined by comedies, variety acts, and game shows, but not hard news. The 1960 debate was "the turning point from retail politics—glad-handing and meeting everyone face-to-face—to the politics of the mass media," according to author Alan Schroeder.[2]

It seems obvious now why this televised confrontation between Kennedy and Nixon made such an impact, but the reasons were not so evident at the time. Part of the reason is the expectations game. Nixon was much better known than Kennedy, and as Dwight Eisenhower's vice president, had earned a reputation for toughness and confrontation. He had impressed many with his "kitchen debate" with Soviet leader Nikita Khrushchev only one year earlier. And, ironically, it was Nixon who had helped demonstrate the potential power of television back in 1952 with his performance in the Checkers speech, his nationally broadcast talk defending himself against charges of campaign finance irregularities, which was credited with saving his spot on the ticket as Eisenhower's running mate. Kennedy was the underdog. With much less experience and less public recognition than Nixon, he seemed to have an uphill challenge in besting the incumbent vice president in open debate.

There were actually four debates between the two in September and October 1960 but it was the first, September 26, that mattered most. For it was the first time ever that American citizens had the opportunity to see the two nominees for president side by side, live, answering questions, and putting forth their case for election to the most powerful office in the world. And Kennedy made the most of it.

On that September night, Roger Ailes most likely tuned in to the debate from his parents' living room at their home in Warren, Ohio. Ailes was a student at Ohio University, where to pay the bills and stay in school, he worked as the morning disk jockey at the college radio station. He enjoyed being on the air, but he was even more drawn to the creativity of broadcasting—the scripting, the deadlines, the energy and enthusiasm of putting on a show. The college radio experience had a definitive impact on his career choices and the very direction of his life.[3]

It is by now an often-told story of how Kennedy's charisma and charm overpowered Nixon's sweaty, shifty-eyed performance. Those who only heard the debate on the radio thought that Nixon had won, while those who saw it on TV thought that Kennedy had prevailed. Kennedy had been campaigning in California and came into the TV studio with a deep tan and wearing a dark suit. Nixon by contrast was quite pale, having recently been ill, and his charcoal-colored suit blended in with the background of the studio set. Equally important, Kennedy seemed to have an instinctive grasp of what the television audience was looking for—when responding to Nixon, he looked directly into the camera and reassured the voters at home that the country would be safe in his hands. In the words of Don Hewitt, who produced the Kennedy–Nixon debate for CBS and went on to produce 60 Minutes for the next quarter century, "We didn't even have to hold the election … John Kennedy walked out of the studio that night the next president of the United States." Well, the election turned out to be a lot closer than Hewitt remembers, but his point is still valid.[4]

What's important here is what came next. Due to the growing importance of television advertising in American society and the impact of the Kennedy–Nixon debate, politics and television embarked on a torrid romance in the '60s. After all, they were made for each other. Politics has all the drama that good television requires, a fact that Roger Ailes and countless other political operatives have used throughout their careers. Political campaigns have great characters—heroes, villains, and fools—with flaws, strengths, and back stories. Politics provides great theater, sometimes through confrontations such as debates and sometimes through advertising and news coverage. And sometimes there is comedy, thanks to such politicians as Spiro Agnew and Dan Quayle.

Of course, due to the perceived thrashing that Nixon took at the hands of Kennedy in 1960, there would be no more presidential debates until Gerald Ford met Jimmy Carter in 1976. But by the mid-'60s American politics and television were married to each other, and TV would find many ways to influence the course of national events. For example, TV journalism came of age in the 1960s. The two major networks, CBS and NBC, expanded their evening news broadcast to a full half hour from only fifteen minutes. And the bread and butter of national news coverage became politics, because as noted above, it makes great television. Some forty years later, Roger Ailes and Fox TV would make political theater and television nearly an art form.

By the early '60s the role of the TV news anchor had also become institutionalized, giving the TV networks a recognizable, authoritative voice to help Americans understand the daily news. Walter Cronkite of CBS became "the most trusted man in America," according to media accounts. And the traditions of political news coverage were also established—the TV networks had their correspondents for the White House, Capitol Hill, the Pentagon, the State Department, and so on.

The significance of the transition of politics from newsprint and radio to television cannot be overstated. It changed everything. To many, for example, the main lesson taken from the Kennedy–Nixon debate was that how you look is as important, as if not more important than, what you say. This was the beginning of the "style over substance" approach that has framed so much of our political dialogue over the last several decades, and continues to drive political communication and media coverage today.

Politicians had to be concerned with appearance, which mattered little before television but now became crucial. For better or worse, the era of the political consultant was born. Candidates needed coaching about their hair, their complexions, their clothing styles, and later, when color TV became the norm, the color of their ties or dresses. And most important, they had to be concerned about their performances—how they came across on television. Authoritativeness of voice, correct grammar, good eye contact, appropriate hand gestures: Image became everything. *Style became substance.*

In 1962 CBS launched the *CBS Evening News with Walter Cronkite*, which dominated television news for the next two decades. That was also the year in which Roger Ailes graduated from Ohio University. He had two job offers: one from a radio station in Columbus and one from a television station in Cleveland.[5] He chose the TV job, and a star was born. The station had just started a local TV talk and entertainment program starring Mike Douglas, a former big band singer. After a stint in the navy, Douglas broke into show business with *Kay Kyser's Kollege of Musical Knowledge*. He became a popular voice on the nightclub circuit, crooning to a largely female audience in his light pop style. (He provided the singing voice for Prince Charming in Disney's cartoon classic *Cinderella*.) As a TV host, he was affable and likeable. He would chat with his guests and encourage them to perform if appropriate—famously getting Judy Garland to sing "Over the Rainbow" at one of the points in her life when she was reluctant to do so.[6]

Ailes was hired as a production assistant by the station's program manager, Chet Collier, whom Ailes would hire thirty-four years later to help him build Fox News. Ailes wrote cue cards, fetched sandwiches, and picked up guests at the airport. It turned out that he had a natural ability for staging, lighting, and scripting for television. In the words of Collier, "he had the drive, the energy, the smarts to know what should make the show work."[7] Ailes quickly became indispensable, and began directing and producing segments, then whole programs.

In 1963 *The Mike Douglas Show* was syndicated by its corporate sponsor, Westinghouse, to all five of its owned and operated TV stations. In 1965, to be closer to New York City and the celebrities on the East Coast, Westinghouse moved the show to new studios in Philadelphia. Ailes, who had been the creative force behind much of the show's success, was made executive producer and won an Emmy Award for the show in both 1967 and 1968. *Mike Douglas* became a popular stop for many of the top music, TV, and movie performers of the day. By 1967 the show was available in 171 media markets and had over 6 million viewers a day.

Suddenly, Roger Ailes, still in his mid twenties, was rubbing shoulders with the likes of Bob Hope, Red Skelton, Marlon Brando, Ray Charles, and others. With Douglas's easygoing style and Ailes's talent for TV production, the program was a welcome hit in the relatively weak daytime entertainment lineup. By the late '60s and early '70s, pretty much everyone who was anyone in show business or politics appeared on the program.

One of the show's signatures, and an Ailes innovation, was Douglas's use of cohosts, who would sit by his side for the entire week and help question the other guests. Most memorably and least typically, perhaps, was the week in 1972 when John Lennon and Yoko Ono filled the role, helping the studiously non-hip Douglas connect to such guests as George Carlin and Jerry Rubin.

Early on, Roger Ailes had displayed a gift for two things that would characterize his entire career: thinking big, and making ordinary people look and sound great on television. Mike Douglas was a product of the 1940s and '50s whose style was big band and swing. Ailes helped him connect to the changing world of the 1960s. He and Chet Collier assisted Douglas in adapting his style to a changing social and political culture in a way that worked for him. Similar to John Kennedy, Ailes had an instinctive feel for what the television audience wanted. Douglas never quite became hip, but Ailes helped him develop a show that appealed to a broad daytime audience. Ailes also produced crowd-pleasing thematic programs, such as *Armed Forces Week*, in which Douglas would meet with servicemen and "give a little pat on the back to our guys in uniform." Mike Douglas was a performer, but Ailes helped him become a TV star and would later help another product of the

'40s and '50s, Richard Milhouse Nixon, to connect to television. Then even later, he helped an Australian media mogul named Rupert Murdoch conquer cable television news.

Ailes was onto something. Television and politics changed together in the 1960s, and they changed quickly. Many of the changes are forever and inexorably tied to the Kennedy years—the1960 debate, definitely. But there was much more to it than that. Kennedy became the first TV president. The camera loved him. The camera also loved his wife, Jackie, who broke the mold of the traditional, matronly first lady.

The growing audience for television news in the 1960s was drawn to the attractive, sophisticated, debonair couple. They helped usher in the age of celebrity political journalism. It was in the early '60s that the nation first became intimately acquainted with the everyday lives of its presidents. We knew where Kennedy went on vacation, who his close friends were, what football team he rooted for on Sunday, and so on.

And the Kennedy administration shrewdly made the most of television's ability to reach the nation and shape the political landscape. Kennedy's men knew that television had played a large role in getting him to the White House, and they knew that TV could play a role in his success or failure as president. Foreshadowing the Ronald Reagan White House media machine some twenty years later, the Kennedy team used TV to their advantage. Early in 1961, Kennedy's press secretary, Pierre Salinger, announced that they would begin televising presidential press conferences. This had never been done before, and it was seen as a great leap forward in the media's ability to cover the president and in the public's access to information.

Of course, it was also a way to smooth Kennedy's relationship with the press and boost his visibility. And the White House knew that he was a good media performer; they were searching for ways to take advantage of his public appeal and his ability to appear presidential and authoritative on television.

Ultimately, though, it may have been the coverage of Kennedy's assassination in 1963 that permanently bound Americans with their TV sets. The country watched in horror as CBS newsman Walter Cronkite announced, with moist eyes, that the president was dead. Record numbers of American viewers watched, in shock, the live TV coverage of the assassination, the bizarre series of events leading to the live broadcast murder of Lee Harvey Oswald, and finally, the somber funeral procession of the slain president. History and television had never before come together so poignantly.

TV commentators and social historians have theorized that after Americans gathered around their television sets to mourn the death of their beloved leader, TV, especially TV news, was never the same. Television had become the "Global Village." It had become "America's campfire," around which the family sat to hear stories, see comedy, and learn of the day's events.

The civil rights struggles of the 1960s also gained prominence through the growing national audience for television news. The issue of civil rights and race relations was yet another area that Nixon would later have to finesse in his 1968 run for the presidency. Roger Ailes, Pat Buchanan, and others would help show him how.

In the spring of 1963, Americans watching the news saw scenes that were surely taking place in some faraway foreign country. Police in riot gear were setting attack dogs on peaceful protestors and using fire hoses as water cannons to try to disperse the crowds. But it was happening in America. What had started as protests at whites-only lunch counters had exploded into full-scale civil unrest as events spun out of the control of the Birmingham, Alabama, police. Network news coverage had given the protestors national attention and had swollen their ranks.

Television had helped to create the modern civil rights movement, and to frame the political and social themes that would form the basis of much of the political dialogue between the two major parties and between future presidential candidates. Johnson, Goldwater, Nixon, and Humphrey would feature prominently in that dialogue as Roger Ailes and other political advisors played supporting roles.

If the 1960 election year cemented the relationship between television and politics, then 1964 set the tone and direction that relationship would take—a tone that Roger Ailes would later hone into a sharp instrument. The 1964 presidential election is best known for the "Daisy Girl" ad of Lyndon Johnson's campaign. The ad, now considered a classic of political advertising, shows a little girl counting daisies in a field, when suddenly an announcer begins a missile launch countdown. As viewers see a nuclear mushroom cloud, President Johnson's voice is heard in a plea for peace. The ad was rather shocking to 1960s audiences and was controversial, but it relayed perfectly the Johnson campaign's message that the world is too dangerous a place to put the "extremist" Barry Goldwater in charge.

But the Daisy Girl spot was just one piece of a coordinated TV strategy by the Johnson team to paint a picture of their opponent, Arizona senator

Barry Goldwater, as so distasteful and unacceptable that he had to be rejected. They were successful. In 1964 negative campaigning moved full force into television and began its path of destruction. And the Daisy Girl spot is indeed what this author has called in an earlier work "the mother of all attack spots."[8]

First of all, LBJ was no JFK. The popular, charismatic Kennedy was a product that by and large sold itself. Johnson was a different kind of commodity. Overtly ambitious, rough around the edges, he was used to pushing people around to get his way. He was actually more like Nixon than Kennedy. He was more at home on the floor of Congress, where he served as senate majority leader, than he was running a national campaign for the presidency.

As a candidate, Johnson had a number of things going for him; personality just wasn't one of them. But he was carrying the torch passed to him by JFK, which gave him immense credibility with a large segment of the public. Civil rights, the space program, better health care, the cold war, and other unfinished items on the Kennedy agenda were his platform. His biggest advantage in the race, though, was that his opponent was considered by most to be an extremist. Extremism may not be a vice, to paraphrase Goldwater, but it sure is hard to sell on TV.

The Johnson campaign decided to focus its strategy on hammering away at Goldwater's unfitness for office. They would use TV's growing reach as a weapon to bludgeon their opponent. Johnson didn't use TV as a blunt instrument, however. His TV advertising campaign was a sharp, well-oiled precision attack aimed right at Goldwater's jugular. The Johnson campaign's advertising was handled by one of the best-known Madison Avenue advertising agencies, Doyle Dane Bernbach.

Lyndon Johnson, his advertising team, and especially the man who produced most of his TV spots, Tony Schwartz, helped to create the negative television ad. But to Schwartz, it wasn't "going negative" in the sense that we have today. He believed the campaign was simply using television to "activate" feelings and attitudes the voters already had about Barry Goldwater. Schwartz maintained that ads do not have to change fixed beliefs or political philosophies in order to be effective. In fact, they can't, he said. But what they can do is touch certain impressions or emotions in the voters that influence their voting behavior. The trick, he said, is to choose the proper images and sounds to mobilize these feelings in the direction you want them to go.

The '64 Johnson campaign is remembered not only for the Daisy Girl spot, which played on voters' anxieties about nuclear war and Goldwater's hawkish military views; there was much more. A different ad featured another little girl licking an ice-cream cone while an announcer frets about the effects of strontium 90, a toxic chemical present in nuclear fallout. The ad closed by suggesting that by voting against the Nuclear Test Ban Treaty, Senator Goldwater was not protecting America's children from strontium 90.

There were also ads about Goldwater's domestic stands. One well-known spot showed a man on the street literally tearing up his Social Security card because Goldwater and his running mate, William Miller, had voiced concerns over the funding and the structure of the Social Security program. Another ad took advantage of the Arizona senator's critical comments about the "eastern political establishment" by showing a giant saw cutting through the continental United States, as the entire eastern seaboard drifts off into the Atlantic Ocean. Taken together, these cleverly thought-out and brilliantly produced TV spots helped make Barry Goldwater an "unacceptable" candidate for president.

Surely, Roger Ailes is a student of Tony Schwartz's as much as he is a student of Marshall McLuhan's or Niccolo Machiavelli's. Ailes has likely read Schwartz's book *The Responsive Chord*, just as he has likely read McLuhan's work and Machiavelli's *The Prince*. Actually, the student may have exceeded the teacher. Ailes used "images" and "sounds" in 1988 against Michael Dukakis to the same devastating effect as Schwartz did for LBJ against Goldwater in 1964.

But before destroying the image of Dukakis, Ailes helped improve that of Richard Nixon in 1968. Nixon running for president again? How could one sell *that?* In '68 the Republican Party would have to move forward, not backward. Richard Nixon was from yesterday—the nation had previewed his act already and was not impressed. The problem for Republicans was that their supply of potential presidential candidates had been depleted. The party hadn't recovered from tearing itself to pieces in 1964.

After his heartbreaking, razor-thin loss to Kennedy in 1960, Nixon had gone sulking back to California. He planned to start his political comeback by running for governor of California in 1962. If America didn't want him, well, by God he would run America's biggest state and then force himself on the American people again in 1968. Only it didn't work out that way. He lost the California governorship to Edmund G. Brown, the Democrat. Nixon was yesterday.

The morning after his humiliating loss to Brown, when he told the national media basically to go jump in a lake, all indications are that he actually meant it. He'd had it. Fed up with politics, Nixon moved back east to New York, formed a law firm with some established litigators, and started making some real money.

But in New York he kept meeting people who thought he really was presidential material. Len Garment, a partner in the law firm, was one. Garment and other Nixon allies introduced him around New York City, and Nixon (with wife Pat) hit Manhattan's social scene. He was still a big name—former vice president, presidential candidate, and all that. In New York he found the potential money and support to start thinking about politics again. And Goldwater and Rockefeller's self-immolation act in 1964 had actually made room for him again as a presidential candidate.

It was in this environment that Ailes met Richard Nixon in 1967, when Nixon appeared on *The Mike Douglas Show*. The guests on the show that day were Nixon and a belly dancer called Little Egypt, who was accompanied by her pet boa constrictor. Ailes told one interviewer, "I didn't wanna scare Nixon and I didn't wanna scare the snake, so I stuck Nixon in my office ... If I'd put Little Egypt in there, I'd be managing belly dancers right now."[9]

Nixon, who had learned to loathe TV, struck up a conversation with the twenty-seven-year-old Ailes, who had grown up with TV and knew that it was the future. It was the TV atheist versus the TV prophet. "It's a shame a man has to use gimmicks like this to get elected," said Nixon, who really did think TV was some kind of passing fad. Joe McGinniss, author of the influential book *The Selling of the President 1968*, believes TV's role in politics "offended" him. "It had not been part of the game when he learned to play," said McGinniss. "And he could see no reason to bring it in now. He half suspected it was an eastern liberal trick: one more way to make him look silly."[10]

For his part, Ailes was fascinated to learn that Nixon thought so little of the power of television and that he believed its significance might even pass. Taken aback by the comment, he told Nixon that TV was no gimmick, and that if he thought that way, he would lose again. Ailes made it clear he believed Nixon's lack of TV savvy was the reason he lost to Kennedy. Nixon and his campaign staff must have decided that if they were going to have to use television to win, they would have to do it well—and they needed the help of someone who understood television production and who saw its potential value. Someone like Roger Ailes—because several weeks later, Nixon had his campaign staff call Ailes and offer him a job. Ailes says he wasn't particularly political at the time, but jumped at the opportunity because he saw it as a great challenge. An Ohio Republican himself, he undoubtedly saw in Nixon the kind of leader he believed America needed. Thus, Roger Ailes began a twenty-three-year on-again, off-again sojourn into political media production. It was the way for him to merge his two passions—television and politics.

2

The Image Is the Message

*Boy, is he going to be pissed . . . He'll think we
really tried to screw him. But critically it was the
best show he's done.*

—Roger Ailes after one of the Nixon TV shows[1]

In 1988, the same year that he directed George Bush's scorched-earth television campaign against Democratic nominee Michael Dukakis, Ailes wrote a book called *You Are the Message: Secrets of the Master Communicators*. A guidebook for improving one's communication skills, it is filled with anecdotes and advice, such as "Try Listening" and "The Four Essentials of a Great Communicator." It is all about putting one's best foot forward and making the best "presentation" one can.

The title of the book is a tribute to author-visionary Marshall McLuhan's famous statement: "The medium is the message." But one can argue that it also reveals Roger Ailes's approach to political communication and to news production: *Image is everything—Perception is reality*. Everything Ailes has done in politics and TV news has been about creating the right environment through staging, lighting, and scriptwriting, then coaxing the perfect performance from his characters. He understands that TV is an emotional medium, and that TV performers must communicate likeability and confidence—whether in politics or in broadcasting.

In politics, Ailes created TV personas for Richard Nixon and for George Bush Sr. that were largely media creations. They were TV characters that were heavily scripted, coached, and directed. This is what he specializes in, the creation of "reality" through imagery. He was also brought in by Ronald Reagan's campaign in 1984 to coach the incumbent president after his disastrous opening debate with Democrat Walter Mondale. Reagan had fumbled over his answers and looked tired and confused during much of the debate. Ailes worked with Reagan on rebuilding his confidence, and reconnecting with his sense of humor and his faith in his worldview.

Later Ailes replicated the formula in the development of the Fox News Channel. By focusing on personality and performance, Fox drew an audience. And the market positioning of Fox as the only news channel not dominated by liberals built on that audience and instilled loyalty in its viewership. Ailes and Fox CEO Rupert Murdoch are conservatives who were interested in building a conservative news operation—but it also made good business sense.

Tuesday, October 7, 1984, Louisville, Kentucky—the Gipper was in trouble. Here was the most charismatic, the most unflappable political TV performer of his generation, in his first debate with Democratic nominee Walter Mondale sounding like he had just been hit in the head with an iron pipe. His speech was halting, and he often paused and rambled. And when he recycled his big applause line from his 1980 debate with Jimmy Carter—"There you go again!"—Mondale was ready and waiting, and pounced on the opportunity. "You remember the last time you said that?" Mondale asked. "You said it when President Carter said you were going to cut Medicare, and you said, 'Oh, no, there you go again Mr. President.' And what did you do right after the election? You went right out and tried to cut $20 billion out of Medicare."[2] Through much of the debate, especially the second half, President Reagan was struggling for answers, almost to the point of panic. He even admitted just before his closing statement that he was "confused." Half of America was squirming in their armchairs with each painful syllable.

Reagan was so far ahead in the polls that the election seemed like it was over before it ever got started. But would Reagan's dismal, confused debate performance against Mondale so unnerve people that it could actually make it a competitive race again? That's what Reagan's men—Ed Rollins, James Baker, and Mike Deaver—had to be wondering. After the debate, when the inevitable questions started flying about Reagan's age and mental sharpness, the campaign went into crisis management mode. Everyone vaguely familiar with public relations or political campaign management understands what this means. A client's success is threatened by a single event or issue that comes along, promising to upset the applecart, after months (or even years) of careful planning and hard work. The crisis has to be managed in such a way that disaster is averted. Sometimes a specialist is called in or other professionals are consulted. In this case, the Reagan reelection campaign had someone in mind to help them deal with this particular emergency.

By the early 1980s Roger Ailes was a well-established media consultant, having worked for a number of Republican candidates for Congress and statewide office. This, in addition to his consulting work for corporations and trade groups, had made him known in Washington and New York as something of a communications specialist. He was already part of the Reagan reelection effort. In 1983 he was hired as a consultant to the loose confederation of advertising agencies that was working for the Reagan campaign, known as the Tuesday Team. This group was responsible for some of the most acclaimed political campaign ads ever, including the "Morning in America" spots, which focused on Norman Rockwell–type images of firefighters, boys and girls playing, and the virtues of small-town life. These ads helped to reinforce the Reagan campaign's message that America was back on track and that life was getting better.

Ailes, Reagan's men figured, was particularly good at media coaching—working with an individual to improve his performance in front of the cameras. After all, Ailes had helped Nixon and countless other political candidates and corporate types to "be all they can be," so to speak. Not that President Reagan needed to be trained—this was the Great Communicator. But he needed at least a tune-up. Maybe he just needed a pep talk—something, anything, would be better than what they got in Louisville.

The consensus of some political analysts and media commentators seemed to be that the president was overcoached. His advisors had drilled him on policy specifics, economic forecasts, nuclear weapon tonnage and throw weights, and so on. They wanted him to be prepared to answer Mondale's challenges with specifics. But Reagan was never that kind of leader. His approach to governing was to envision and communicate broad policy goals, while relying on his team to handle the specifics. And, let's face it, in 1984 he was no spring chicken. He was seventy-three, the oldest president in American history, which is, of course, why all the questions about his abilities were resonating. In the Louisville debate, he seemed to be trying to remember what statistic to recite and which studies to quote, and he got all confused and tangled up over his words. Reagan's longtime friend Senator Paul Laxalt complained that the president had been "brutalized" by his handlers, Jim Baker and Richard Darman—an assessment shared by Nancy Reagan, according to Reagan's campaign manager Ed Rollins.[3]

Ailes was asked by the White House to come down to Washington and listen to Reagan's prep sessions for the second debate, and offer any advice that he could. Ailes believed that what the American people wanted from President Reagan was "some reassurance that he wasn't too old for the job, and given that, they would reelect him."[4] In the debate practice session that Ailes watched, he thought Reagan's aides were hectoring him and badgering him to get the right answers. Here we go again, he thought.

Ailes told Mike Deaver and Jim Baker that everyone needed to get off Reagan's back and help him rebuild his confidence. Ailes knew instinctively that television debates are about imagery and performance, not about providing textbook answers to specific questions. It's sort of like the M*A*S*H* TV episode where a colonel barges in and interrupts a press briefing when reporters are too persistent, shouting, "This is a military press conference, for heaven's sake! The last thing we want to do is answer a bunch of questions!"

Ailes asked for some private meeting time with the president. He told Reagan that for the second debate he needed to stop playing defense and reconnect to the images and themes that defined his presidency and his leadership. He urged him to be more "thematic" in his answers and to connect debate questions with his "vision" for the country's future.

In what is called the "pepper drill," Ailes fired questions at the president and encouraged him to go with his gut. What do your instincts tell you about this issue? he asked him. Forget the minute details of issues, why are they important to you? Ailes was trying to help him regain his confidence, but also get him into a positive mindset, and start a certain rhythm and beat going.

Of course, the elephant in the room was the president's age. This was what was on the nation's mind. Was he past his prime? Could he still handle the rigors of the job? According to Ailes, he was told by Reagan's men not to mention it. But, Ailes being Ailes, *he* went with *his* gut and mentioned it anyway. It was too important. At the end of the final meeting, the day before the second debate, he matter-of-factly asked, "Mr. President, what are you going to do when they say you're too old for the job?" As Mike Deaver choked on his coffee, Reagan stopped and thought for a minute. "Well, there's an old line I've used before," the president said. Ailes listened to him, and then said, "That's perfect. Just use that line and don't say anything else. Don't get drawn into a discussion about age. Just say your line and then stand there."[5]

Tuesday, October 21, 1984—Kansas City—Reagan was doing much better against Mondale. Not quite the old Reagan, but his answers were crisper and more confident than they had been in Louisville during the first debate. Then came the moment everyone had been dreading. One of the panelists, Henry Trewhitt of the *Baltimore Sun*, brought up the age issue: "Mr. President, many Americans wonder if at your age you are still up to the rigors of being president." Without missing a beat, Reagan said that he was very much up to the job, and, with his trademark grin, he added, "and I want you all to know that I will not make age an issue in this campaign. I am not going to exploit for political purposes my opponent's youth and inexperience." The audience erupted in laughter; even Mondale laughed. The debate was over. The election was over. The Gipper was back.

But it was with Richard Nixon in 1968 that Roger Ailes "made his bones," as they say in the mob. Joe McGinniss, in *The Selling of the President 1968*, asserts that Richard Nixon's campaign staff used television to create an entirely new Nixon—a made-for-TV, thoughtful, insightful, self-deprecating, phony Nixon, with a sense of humor and a quick smile. Others have disputed the transformation claim, questioning if it is even possible to create something like that if it doesn't already exist. The noted communications researcher Kathleen Hall Jamieson takes McGinniss to task for "overstepping the evidence." She believes that he wrote the book from a biased point of view, selectively using quotes and events to support a preconceived view of Nixon and his campaign.[6]

The truth lies somewhere in the middle, where it is usually found. One thing that's clear is that Nixon and his advisors had learned a lesson from 1960, and this time around they were determined to use TV in a way that worked for their candidate. Nixon's own words add weight to McGinniss's approach—in 1967 he told his staff, "We're going to build this whole campaign around television. You fellows just tell me what you want me to do and I'll do it."

Ironically, McGinniss and Ailes are friends; they have been for forty years. McGinniss was a reporter and columnist in Philadelphia at the same time Ailes was there producing *The Mike Douglas Show*. So they were quite familiar with each other's work, and their paths had crossed on a number of occasions. Mr. McGinniss told this author that Ailes is one of the funniest people he knows and in reality is a very nice person. He said Ailes has a rapier-like wit and can even turn it on himself on occasion. "We always enjoyed each other's company and could make each other laugh."

Just to be clear, McGinniss "abhors" his friend's politics. "I've wished for almost forty years that he would have put his brilliance in the service of humanity, not its oppressors. But we've long since stopped discussing that." At the time, said McGinniss, Ailes knew how he felt about Nixon from his columns in the *Philadelphia Inquirer*. According to McGinniss, "Roger told me, 'I wouldn't have let you within a million miles of this campaign,' but because I'd been cleared by guys higher up the chain, he was one hundred percent open from start to finish."

The Selling of the President 1968, caused quite a stir when it was published in 1969. From their vantage point, the Nixon campaign (now the Nixon White House) felt they had been misled by McGinniss about his intentions. They had cleared him to observe some of the campaign's planning and media preparation, but they claimed at the time they had no idea he was working on a book. Yet he insists that he told them about the book contract up front and that he made no attempt to hide his intentions. A spokesman for the Nixon administration accused McGinniss of selectively using quotes and events from the campaign in an effort to make Nixon look as bad as possible.

McGinniss said that Ailes "never said a negative word about the book, publicly or privately, even when pressured to do so. His position was sort of that 'it was all true and it wasn't my fault they let the guy observe all that.'" Ailes has said that McGinniss pretty much got it right, but that he now wishes, for his mother's sake, that he (Ailes) had used cleaner language.

In some interviews, Ailes has been rather modest, saying that he was a minor figure in the campaign, taking directions from Nixon's advertising honchos. But if only half of what Joe McGinniss said in his book is true, then there is absolutely no way Ailes was a minor character. Roger Ailes played a huge role in the redevelopment, the refinement, the remodeling of Richard Nixon as a presidential candidate.

And that is what is important for this story. Regardless of whether McGinniss was biased, or how much of Nixon's true character and personality was on display, the fact is that Ailes and Nixon's admen (Harry Treleaven and Frank Shakespeare) redefined modern presidential campaigns. Obviously, it wasn't the first campaign to emphasize advertising and marketing to sell a presidential candidate. But it was the first example, and still one of the best, of how a campaign organization built its candidacy around the skillful manipulation of television.

Ailes was brought in to produce and direct Nixon's television appearances. This time there would be no debates with the Democratic nominee. And Nixon would limit his TV appearances on news programs such as *Meet the Press* and *Face the Nation*. Instead, the campaign would create the TV environments in which Nixon could excel and then buy broadcast time on local TV stations in selected markets around the country. Ailes was perfect for the job—he was an Emmy Award–winning producer who had been writing, staging, and directing TV programs for Mike Douglas, starring some of the biggest celebrities in the world. He was up to the challenge of making Richard Nixon look good.

And he definitely saw it as a challenge. "Let's face it," he told his team over lunch. "A lot of people think Nixon is dull. They think he's a bore, a pain in the ass … Now you put him on television and you've got a problem right away. He's a funny-looking guy. He looks like somebody hung him in a closet overnight and he jumps out in the morning with his suit all bunched up and starts running around saying, 'I want to be President.' I mean this is how he strikes some people. That's why these shows are important. To make them forget all that."[7]

Ailes, Treleaven, and Shakespeare all agreed that the content of these TV shows was secondary. The content wasn't going to be all that different from 1960 anyway. What mattered most was the image that viewers received about Nixon. Not many observers at the time understood the significance of how image and performance were transforming American culture, particularly television and politics—but Ailes sure got it.

Joe McGinniss has said that citizens don't so much vote for a candidate as make a "psychological purchase" of him. At least on this point, he is indisputably correct. In general, for someone to be elected president in the modern era of mass communications the voters must, on some level, like the candidate—or at least be comfortable with the candidate. After all, the president will be in America's living rooms for the next four years.

Al Gore would probably be president today if he came across as more likeable. And, possibly John Kerry—if he had gone windsurfing one less time. Let's face it, most modern presidents, from Kennedy to Reagan to Clinton were likeable people—the kind of person one wouldn't mind having a drink with or going to a ball game with. Nixon could never quite get there, but in 1968 he became tolerable.

Ailes certainly works from this philosophy of likeability, and considering the success he has had, the viewpoint merits considerable attention. He calls it the "like vote." For example, he told a reporter for the *New York Times* in 1980, "I'm convinced that a lot of people vote for what I call the 'like' vote. You go into the voting booth, pull the drape, and you're not overwhelmed with any of the candidates. You stand there and you reach for a lever because you may like one guy slightly more than the other."[8] It sounds so simple. But if it were that easy, every political candidate would achieve likeability.

With Nixon it was never easy. Survey research commissioned by the Nixon campaign had shown that a "personality gap" existed between Nixon and Hubert Humphrey, the Democratic nominee. Nixon was perceived by most voters as cold, while more voters perceived Humphrey as warm. So it was essential that Nixon's communication efforts warm him up. Hence, the emphasis on warmth, personality, and showmanship in the 1968 campaign.

For the Nixon campaign, Ailes produced ten one-hour television programs and Nixon's election eve telecast. The programs were to be taped in front of a live audience to provide energy and so that Nixon could feed off of the applause. In fact, that's how Ailes saw the audience, as "applause machines." That was their main purpose. His assistant would go out before the show and instruct the audience on how to behave, when to applaud, and so on. Then, at the end of the show, they were supposed to "rush the stage" and surround Nixon with warmth and enthusiasm, conveying the impression that here is an important, substantive man, saying important things, and attracting all these fans.

For what it's worth, this is a format roughly followed today at many events by most presidential campaigns. Stock the audience. Have them rush the stage, or at least approach the stage, and seek autographs from their hero—it makes for great TV. Bill Clinton, at one of the debates with Bush in 1992, stayed around a good half hour or so, signing an autograph for every single Democratic operative who asked.

The Nixon TV programs would run from early September through late October in ten cities selected for maximum geographic and electoral impact— Chicago, Philadelphia, Boston, New York, Los Angeles, and so on. The audience of roughly 300 was recruited from local Republican Party organizations to provide a friendly crowd. There would be a panel of citizens asking Nixon questions to provide spontaneity. Of course, it was sort of a "planned" spontaneity—the panel of questioners was carefully screened in each city and selected to provide a preferred balance of race, occupation, gender, and ideology. Ailes and his team apparently gave this a great deal of thought. According to McGinniss, "This meant a Negro. One Negro. Not two. Two would be offensive to whites, perhaps to Negroes as well. Two would be trying too hard. One was necessary and safe … Texas would be tricky though. Do you have a Negro and a Mexican-American, or if not, then which?"[9]

The set for the program featured a round, carpeted platform where Nixon would stand. He would take questions from the panel members, who were seated in a semicircle around him. The audience of course filled the bleachers in the studio. It occurred to Ailes later that it reminded him of being in an arena, and he dubbed the programs the "Man in the Arena." Ailes thought the arena concept had "guts," and made Nixon look bold to the audience at home.

Ever the director, Ailes was in charge of the details: "Tell Nixon he should play more to the at-home audience by looking at the camera more often; an effort should be made to keep him in the sun occasionally to maintain a fairly constant level of healthy tan [Ailes should have been around for the 1960 debate with Kennedy]; in the briefing tell the panelists not to ask two-part questions; to jazz up the opening of the program, add some music, or cue the applause earlier."[10]

Ailes is something of a perfectionist, who has high expectations of a product that has his name associated with it. Those who have worked with him might even say he is a control freak, which of course wouldn't be all that unusual for a producer. During the taping of the program in Philadelphia, he became incensed that the floor director couldn't get the right close-up of Nixon. So he fired him and directed the last five programs himself. He also fought constantly with the other Nixon staff about the size and composition of the panel of questioners for the programs. No farmers, he insisted, because they ask dull questions about farm subsidies no one else understands or cares about. And a panel of eight was too large, Ailes said. Seven, or even six, would be much better. If the panel was too big, it would be impossible for Nixon to establish personal relationships with the members in just one hour. And "interpersonal relationships were the key to success," he insisted.

Anyone who watches Fox News for more than a few hours realizes that Roger Ailes understands how to make good, engaging TV. It's been the key to his success all these years. He didn't want the Nixon TV programs to appear too "canned" or predictable—that would be boring and run counter to the whole idea of doing the programs in the first place. He knew it would make for better

TV if there were some sparks flying on occasion. For one thing, it would make Nixon look more authentic and real. "I'm convinced we need legitimately tough panels to make Nixon give his best."[11] And after all the briefings and rehearsals, he thought Nixon could handle it—he knew his material.

For example, Ailes thought Nixon's best performance from a critical standpoint was the Philadelphia program. That's because Nixon was pressed hard by one of the panelists, a controversial Philadelphia radio talk show host named Jack McKinney. Ailes had wanted a journalist on the panel, and when a "Negro" reporter with the *Philadelphia Inquirer* was unavailable, McKinney's name came up. During the program, McKinney hit Nixon hard with questions about Vietnam and Korea, and "Why are you refusing to appear on the news shows like *Meet the Press*? Why will you face the public only in staged settings such as this?" At first Nixon was unsettled, but he pasted on a smile, fought his way back, and didn't back down. And the crowd was on his side. "I've done those quiz shows, Mr. McKinney," Nixon fired back. "I've done them until they were running out of my ears."[12] McKinney went on to challenge him about statements he had made about Vietnam, but Nixon, feeling the support of the crowd, defended his positions forcefully. They cheered his every response, building his confidence—McKinney, after all, was outnumbered roughly 300 to 1. After the show, Ailes was jubilant. "Boy is he (Nixon) going to be pissed," he said. "He'll think we really tried to screw him. But critically it was the best show he's done."[13]

For the election eve telecast, the Nixon team wasn't taking any chances. The telephone operators who would take calls from viewers with questions for Nixon were recruited from local Republican organizations. The same was true for the several hundred spectators. And the Nixon staff toyed with the telephone call-in questions. When asked by a technician how the questions would work, Ailes joked in his usual dry wit, and said, "Well, what's going to happen is all of the questions are going to come through the operators over there, and then runners will bring them down to the producer's table, and from there they will go to a screening room where the Nixon staff will tear them up and write their own. Then they'll go to Bud Wilkinson (the announcer) who will cleverly read them, and Nixon will read the answers off a card."[14]

He was exaggerating, but not by much. What actually happened was that the Nixon staff had prepared questions Nixon wanted to answer, and when a caller's question sounded similar, they substituted the staff-written question to make sure it was properly worded. Ailes called it "semi-forgery."

The cumulative effect of the TV programs accomplished what Ailes and the Nixon staff had hoped. It made the candidate seem more engaging, more human, and in control of his world. And combined with the campaign's paid advertising spots, it created an unstoppable Nixon bandwagon that carried him to the White House. It also made it easier that Hubert Humphrey had an uphill climb. The voters were in a mood to punish the Democratic Party over Vietnam (similar to Iraq War–weary voters' attitude toward Republicans in the congressional elections of 2006). Many people wanted to vote for Nixon, but were uneasy about it—the programs Ailes produced made them feel better about it.

The Nixon TV strategy was historic in its effects and very controversial to this day. But the bottom line is this: Nixon, in his 1968 campaign appearances, and particularly in the Man in the Arena TV programs, did *exactly* what Roger Ailes later prescribed in his 1988 book, *You Are the Message.* Nixon was the perfect client for a consultant. He was motivated. He considered his strengths and weaknesses, he put his best foot forward, he worked hard at it, and he knocked it out of the park.

George Bush (the forty-first president) was another matter. He was Nixonian in a sense—old school, pretelevision, stiff as a board; but with a lot of differences—patrician, eastern, old money. And when Bush was running for president in 1988, his image problem was opposite that of Nixon's in some important ways. If Nixon was too strident, cold, and overtly political, then Bush's image was too soft and too preppy—almost nerdy.

Bush found himself in the strange position of having been one of the youngest fighter pilots in World War II, shot down in the Pacific, and decorated for bravery—but being perceived by voters as something of a wimp. But as Ailes told him, a lot of his problems had to do with perceived weaknesses in how he came across to voters—primarily his goofy, incomprehensible speech patterns, his tinny voice, and his tendency to say things like "neat" and "golly."

Another large part of the elder Bush's problem was the fact that he had to follow a very tough act. Ronald Reagan remade the political stage in terms of connecting with the public and using mass communication. And Bush seemed to play no significant role as Reagan's vice president. It's become somewhat of a cliché, but it is nonetheless true, that one of Bush's primary responsibilities seemed to be representing President Reagan at the funerals of foreign heads of state. And unlike Reagan, he seemed to have no sense of purpose about why he even wanted to be president. To this day, his administration's goals remain largely undefined. He seemed to acknowledge this, without really dealing with it, saying, "I know I'm not big on the vision thing, but . . ."

So from a candidate image and public relations standpoint, Bush really had to be rebuilt from the ground up. Luckily for him, his campaign's director of communications was one of the best image-makers and TV producers to be found anywhere—Roger Ailes. Ailes became Bush's personal performance coach, advising him on everything from what shirts to wear to how to slow down his distractingly rapid eye movements.[15] Just as he had done with his corporate clients, Ailes told Bush that one of the keys was to practice speaking, using the tips and guidance Ailes had given him. He also wanted Bush to stick closely to his written text and not speak off-the-cuff. Even though Bush hated the idea (just as Nixon did), and thought it beneath him (just as Nixon did), he worked at getting better (Nixon worked harder at it).

Ailes was also in charge of the Bush campaign's advertising, which will be examined in subsequent chapters. The Bush TV ads played a significant role in redefining his image to the American people and setting up the contrasts between him and his Democratic opponent, Michael Dukakis, on which the Bush campaign wanted the public to focus. But it was always the live campaign appearances in which Bush was most vulnerable. Even though he had improved under Ailes's tutelage, he still flubbed one-liners, talked over applause lines, mispronounced people's names, and was generally known for uttering bizarrely uncommon words and phrases.

Some in his campaign feared that his problem went deeper than diction. "Privately," according to *Time* magazine, "some aides worried that he lacked the single-minded obsessiveness that seems necessary to win the presidency. They fear that Bush is perhaps too nice or a bit lazy. 'I know there are limits to what a coach can accomplish in speechmaking,' says Ailes frankly, 'unless the subject is a diligent student of himself.'[16] Ailes added that Bush's attitude is "'I am what I am.' He's not a narcissistic person and he refuses to become one." Presumably, that's one of the biggest differences between Nixon and Bush.

Ironically, Nixon thought very little of Bush's political abilities. In a conversation in 1981 with Republican political consultant Ed Rollins, Nixon said Bush was a "mediocre" campaigner. Rollins, who had managed Reagan's landslide reelection victory in 1984, emphatically agreed, as did many Republicans. According to Rollins, Bush "ran a terrible race in 1980, and had performed erratically for us in 1984 against a demonstrably weaker and less experienced Geraldine Ferraro . . . From start to finish, Bush acted like a candidate who didn't really care if he won. Without a doubt, he was the worst campaigner to actually get elected president in modern times."[17]

And the Bush campaign team had stumbled into another disaster of their own making that no public relations genius or campaign coach could do much about: Dan Quayle. This was absolutely the worst choice of a running mate a presidential candidate had made in the last hundred years. And it was so unnecessary. The decision to choose Quayle was driven by a combination of Bush's insecurity as a candidate (he didn't want to be upstaged), his campaign team's lack of homework on Quayle, and their assumptions that the youthful senator from Indiana would be a bridge to the future for the GOP.

Even Ailes was taken in. Or at least he tried to make the best of a dreadful situation. He advised the campaign to portray Quayle as a "charismatic, Kennedy-like figure" who would appeal to a younger generation. He even suggested that Quayle's handlers "set up a deal where he'd be in a convertible and girls would tear off his cufflinks."[18] Ailes and other campaign advisors tried to teach Quayle how to walk and talk like a candidate, how to read from a TelePrompTer, and how to debate, but it was no use.

Yet even with all these problems, Bush and Quayle won. Why? Enough voters gave Bush the benefit of the doubt because he was Ronald Reagan's vice president, and the Bush advertising campaign, led by Ailes, destroyed Michael Dukakis's credibility.

3

Fairness Is for Sissies

Wedge Issue: noun. Def: A sharply divisive political issue, especially one that is raised by a candidate or party in hopes of attracting or disaffecting a portion of an opponent's customary supporters.

—American Heritage Dictionary

Some observers consider Ailes to be the Muhammad Ali of political TV. The two men do have similarities—they're both tough, smart, and opportunistic. But they are opportunistic in different ways. Ali took advantage of an opponent's weaknesses, while Ailes takes advantage of society's weaknesses. As one of the top political consultants in the land, his natural instincts were to look for openings—areas of concern or fragmentation in the American political and moral landscape that could be exploited—and then go after them. When the name of the game is winning, and little else, this leads to some pretty crass and shallow activities on the part of campaigns, consultants, and sometimes political party officials. For example, Ailes is one of the old masters of the use of the notorious "wedge" issues that Republicans were famous for in the latter part of the twentieth century. And one of the biggest and most successful wedge issues is *race,* which goes back to Nixon's "Southern Strategy" of 1968.

For the last forty years, Republicans just haven't quite known what to do with black people. Politics can be a nasty business. The pressure to win—the seduction of winning—makes people do things they ordinarily wouldn't. A succession of candidates and consultants (Republican and Democrat), going all the way back to Barry Goldwater in 1964, have been tempted to use racial fears and anxieties for no other reason than just to win a political campaign.

In a way, Republicans—or conservatives, rather—are in a bind. Modern conservatism is defined by limited national government, limited federal spending, and a reliance on state government authority and private sector initiatives. So in opposing big government, many conservatives were ideologically obliged to oppose federal civil rights policies. The trouble for the GOP has often been that there were just enough real racists in the mix who sided with them, tarring them with the same hateful brush. And this trouble has been compounded by GOP candidates, staffers, advisors, and consultants who have cynically used the race issue to help them win elections.

To his credit, Barry Goldwater renounced that kind of politics. Goldwater was no racist; indeed, he was a cofounder of the Arizona chapter of the NAACP. But many racists jumped on the Goldwater bandwagon because his ideology-based opposition to federal power and big government also meant opposition to civil rights and other social causes. Because he voted against the Civil Rights Act, Goldwater's candidacy was endorsed by the Ku Klux Klan, much to the delight of the Lyndon Johnson campaign, which watched gleefully as Goldwater was forced to renounce that endorsement. To make matters much worse, an independent group called Citizens for Goldwater produced a half-hour film called *Choice* that prominently used images of blacks as symptomatic of America's problems, notably crime. The film was universally declared racist, and Goldwater felt compelled to issue a public statement renouncing it.

Both the Goldwater campaign and the Nixon campaign four years later found that significant numbers of voters were watching and listening for clues about their intentions toward civil rights and integration. Segregationists, along with openly racist elements such as the KKK, were drawn to their campaign because their opposition to federal power fit the segregationists' agenda of resisting civil rights.

When Kevin Phillips, a Nixon advisor in 1968, wrote *The Emerging Republican Majority* in the late 1960s, he saw demographic trends developing that would help to define American politics for the next forty years. One of these trends was that the natural cultural conservatism of the South—promilitary, antifederal government, antitax—was making the region hospitable to Republican candidates for the first time ever. For more than one hundred years, to a significant degree, the Republican Party had been the party of the North and the Democratic Party had been the party of the South. But that was changing. By the 1960s the Democrats had become the party of federal government action—what many southerners saw as big government, higher taxes, welfare programs, and civil rights policies for African-Americans.

This gave an opening to those who opposed the use of federal power and wanted to maintain the status quo of state power and local decision making. Along came George Wallace and the American Independent Party. Similar in some ways to Louisiana's Huey Long three decades earlier, George Wallace portrayed himself as a populist to his followers, a defender of ordinary people against the rich and the powerful. However, Long's crusade was built on class warfare, while Wallace's agenda was built on race and the federal government's imposition of policies that ran counter to people's long-held beliefs about race relations. Wallace appealed to those southerners who feared the cultural and spiritual loss of the America they had known. He claimed to speak for the disaffected, those who were fed up with the political establishment and with federal government "interference." But he also appealed to the worst fears of those who mourned the political and social changes that were taking place as a result of integration and civil rights enforcement.

But the changes taking place in the South also gave an opening to the Republican Party, and Richard Nixon and his advisors were politically savvy enough to see it. The Vietnam War had weakened the Democrats nationally, and the Democratic Party's support of activist federal government policies had made them particularly vulnerable in the South. Supporting George Wallace became an outlet for many southerners to voice their displeasure with the direction the Democrats were taking the country. Yet at the same time, many southerners also knew that it was like siding with the devil, giving in to one's worst instincts, giving in to fear.

But there was a compromise position. Southerners could punish national Democrats and state their preference for less federal government by supporting Richard Nixon. Unlike Barry Goldwater, Nixon and his advisors seemed to relish the opportunity to harness the cultural and political resentment brewing in the southern states. When Nixon spoke of his concern for states' rights in campaign appearances and statements to the press, he knew exactly what he was doing. He was pushing a button.

He and his advisors focused on running a law-and-order campaign, a promise to quell the street violence and civil disobedience that had so unnerved many Americans in the '60s. But to many, law and order implied a commitment to do something specifically about the civil rights demonstrations and protests that had garnered so much attention and led to crucial changes in the law. Nixon voiced his opposition to busing, a divisive issue not only in the South, but in many northern cities as well. Nixon had both the opportunity and the will to push buttons that, just four years earlier, Goldwater never really had a chance, nor a desire, to push.

Although Nixon was not a conservative in the modern political sense (after all, this is the man who created new federal agencies and advocated government control of wages and prices), he had campaigned for years against Kennedy's and Johnson's reliance on the federal government to solve the nation's problems. In 1968 most voters, and especially southern voters, understood that a Nixon presidency would be less hospitable to the kinds of big government programs that had become so prevalent from 1960 to 1968.

It's just a stone-cold irony that Goldwater was actually a much stronger believer in states' rights than was Nixon. But Goldwater was fighting the extremist label that had been attached to him; thus, he was forced to run as fast as he could away from any association with racist propaganda. From a policy and governing standpoint, Nixon wasn't that concerned with states' rights—he had other fish to fry. But he and his advisors knew that the issue could move votes in some of the key southern states—move them away from supporting the Democratic nominee and toward the Republican side. Nixon finessed the issue. He didn't actively promote segregation or attack civil rights—he didn't have to.

So Richard Nixon and George Wallace became competitors for the votes of southern whites. Even after he was elected president, Nixon felt threatened by Wallace's appeal as a candidate in the South—so much so that when Wallace ran for governor of Alabama again in 1970 (to use the position as a launching pad for another run at the White House in 1972 no doubt), the Nixon White House funneled money to Wallace's opponent, incumbent governor Albert Brewer. But electability was always an issue for Wallace, the nominee of the amorphous, suspicious-sounding American Independent Party. And where Nixon handled race relations and sensitive political issues with nuance and practiced professionalism, Wallace handled them with blunt-force trauma. That may have appealed to many southerners at the time, but enough of them knew that it spelled trouble in the long run. Wallace was risky. Nixon was the safer choice.

And conveniently for Nixon, many in the South believed that the national media had become an enemy to their way of life. The media were pushing the cultural changes in movies, television, and literature that many considered antifamily, pornographic, and violent. It was the media that were pushing the civil rights issue and exposing the problems in southern cities. And the media were losing the war in Vietnam, and so on. A good many southerners simply felt that the national media were against them and everything for which they stood.

It so happens that Nixon had a problem with the media too. He blamed them for his loss to Kennedy in 1960, his loss of the California governorship in 1962, and his ongoing image problems as he struggled to regain political power. So he had an enemy in common with large segments of the South. If Nixon was suspicious and distrustful of the national media, so was a growing majority of voters—in the South and elsewhere.

The Man in the Arena programs managed by Roger Ailes were structured to go over the heads of the media and communicate directly to the voters, so that Nixon's message couldn't be edited down and interfered with. Nixon's men wanted the programs to send just the right message and use the right symbols. When it came to the so-called Southern Strategy and race issues in general, they wanted the Man in the Arena programs to make Nixon appear reasonable and open, but not overly sympathetic to blacks and to civil rights. That's why Ailes and his team emphasized demographic balance on the panels, and often seemed to be obsessed with finding the right kind of "Negroes" they could use.

Sometimes the search ran to the comical or bizarre, as these political calculations often do. In one conversation Ailes had with his staff, they were looking for a black panelist for one of the programs. According to McGinniss, Ailes said, "On this one, we definitely need a negro. I don't think it's necessary to have one in every group of six people, no matter what our ethnic experts say, but in Philadelphia it is. *U.S. News & World Report* this week says that one of every three votes cast in Philadelphia will be a negro. And goddammit, we're locked into this thing anyway. Once you start it's hard as hell to stop, because the press will pick it up and make a big deal out of why no negro all of a sudden."

"I know one," said a local Republican staffer. "He's a dynamic type, the head of a self-help organization, that kind of thing. And he is black." "What do you mean, he's black?" "I mean he's dark. It will be obvious on television that he's not white." "You mean we don't have to put a sign around him that says, 'This is our negro'?" Ailes asked. "Absolutely not." "Fine. Call him. Let's get this thing going."[1]

Politics in the TV age: The fate of the free world was at stake in 1968, and campaign members strategize over the shade of skin color of a potential panelist. But it's that kind of attention to detail that defined the new kind of television politics born in the 1960s. And it's the kind of production detail Ailes is famous for nailing.

It seems that in the modern political era, the race card is always on the table. In a separate conversation about a panel in a different city, Ailes, in what has to be an eerie foreshadowing of the racial undertones of the 1988 Bush campaign, famously said, "You know what I'd like? A good, mean Wallace-ite cab driver. Wouldn't that be great? Some guy to sit there and say 'Awright, mac, what about these niggers?'"[2]

Republican consultants like Ailes didn't invent wedge issues, but they have sure spent a lot of time talking about them and working on them. Republican campaigns, beginning with Nixon's in '68, have intently focused on maximizing and mobilizing white, moderate-to-conservative voters. This has involved a balancing act—voicing support for basic fairness, justice, and equal rights, but without going too far and alienating whites. For example, Pat Buchanan—media commentator, political adventurer, and longtime Nixon aide—strongly urged Nixon not to visit Martin Luther King's widow, Coretta Scott King, in 1969, because he felt "it would outrage many, many people who believe Dr. King was a fraud and a demagogue, and perhaps worse … It does not seem to be in the interests of national unity for the president to lend his national prestige to the argument that this divisive figure is a modern saint."[3] For what it's worth, Buchanan still argues that it is a mistake for the Republican Party to reach out to minorities, because it will damage their white male base.

While Roger Ailes, Pat Buchanan, or any Republicans for that matter may not be racist, the cynical manipulation of race relations and the use of painful social divisions for the purpose of winning political campaigns is one of the things that has made the general public disgusted with the political process over the last thirty to forty years.

The above examples of Ailes's cynicism and use of race as a political weapon might be forgiven if the Nixon campaign were a lone, isolated example. But it isn't. It was merely the first in a long, multidecade history of pushing racial tensions as a wedge issue to help his political campaign clients. Unfortunately, he has plenty of company, as a number of consultants from both major parties have used race to further their political causes. But Ailes is a man whose current career is marked by the credo "Fair and Balanced."

The Willie Horton ad has its own chapter a little later on, but it's worth mentioning here, if for no other reason than the huge impact it has apparently had on Roger Ailes's life and career. One could make the argument that the Willie Horton issue helped drive Ailes out of politics in the early 1990s. There is also considerable evidence to suggest that much of Ailes's career since then has been at least partly based on an effort to exorcise the Willie Horton demon out of his past. Consider this, from the *New York Times Magazine* in early 1995, a year before he was edged out at CNBC and made the jump to Fox: "For Ailes, success in television will mean freedom from the past, from the stain of Willie Horton, the defining moment of his career thus far. 'Roger's nightmare,' says David Garth, the political strategist to whom he is most often compared, 'is that some idiot might write an obit that calls him the man behind the Willie Horton commercial. He's out to make sure that doesn't happen.'"[4]

Roger Ailes, it appears, may have the "Alfred Nobel Syndrome." It is by now a well-known story that Nobel, the inventor of dynamite and a number of other applied chemical products, woke up one morning and saw his obituary in a newspaper (a mistake obviously) that identified him primarily as the inventor of modern explosives used in warfare. Horrified at the thought of his epitaph being that he was the creator of a weapon of mass destruction, he established and funded the Nobel Prize as a means of recognizing and rewarding the best in human endeavors from the arts to the sciences.

To complete the logic here, Ailes's equivalent to the Nobel Prize is the Fox News network—or more broadly, his list of achievements in television producing and news broadcasting since the early 1990s. He likely wanted to leave his political baggage behind and be remembered for Fox News and his role in helping to build the Murdoch media empire. Or he might say his legacy is the development of a new and better way to cover news and world events, rather than relying on what he considers the old, tedious, left-leaning news media.

Speaking of the media, by the 1980s the media were firmly entrenched as the enemy of the Republican Party, at least in the opinions of most people in the GOP. George H. W. Bush the candidate shared with Richard Nixon the candidate a desire to run against the media. ANNOY THE MEDIA, VOTE FOR BUSH was a popular bumper sticker among Republicans, and Bush even uttered it himself on several occasions on the campaign trail.

In one sense, the Willie Horton saga is a return to the Southern Strategy. The record suggests that the spiritual father of the Willie Horton ad is actually

Lee Atwater, the combative political strategist behind George H. W. Bush's 1988 campaign. It was he who said, "We're going to make it look like Willie Horton is Michael Dukakis's running mate."[5]

Atwater was from South Carolina. He came of age during the tremendous period of growth for the Republican Party in the southern states, and he was a driving force in his home state's embrace of Ronald Reagan and later George Bush Sr. He probably understood southern politics better than anyone else alive at the time, which may be why he was so excited about the discovery of Willie Horton. He understood what the effects would be of an ad campaign showcasing the image of Horton, along with the horrific story of his crimes. All voters would be shocked by the Willie Horton story, but many southern voters would be outraged.

As Chapter 7, "Hatching Willie Horton," details, commentators have suggested that the Bush campaign designed a two-track strategy whereby the official Bush campaign produced ads about the Massachusetts furlough program and Michael Dukakis's deficiencies in fighting crime, while independent groups not affiliated with the campaign would produce ads aimed at provoking fear and hostility from voters everywhere.[6]

Evidence does not prove that Lee Atwater, Roger Ailes, or anybody else told others to make a Willie Horton ad, suggested anyone make a Willie Horton ad, or requested anyone to make a Willie Horton ad. But the reality is, by the spring of 1988 the case of Willie Horton had been researched, focus-grouped, and widely disseminated in GOP circles. Maybe it was simply an incredibly happy "coincidence" for Atwater and Ailes that a group surfaced out there and made a Willie Horton ad.

But the plot thickens. A similar pattern occurred in two other races Ailes ran in 1989, the year after Willie Horton. And in these instances, the TV ads were not produced by independent groups. It seems that Roger Ailes's political consulting clients are always running against opponents who coddle and support "kidnappers." It became a predictable formula for Ailes's campaigns.

Rudy Giuliani is the Prince of the City. Actually, for several years he's been Prince of the Country after his performance on 9/11. He's "America's Mayor." But in 1989 he wasn't yet nationally known. He was known in New York, of course, as a tough federal prosecutor appointed by Ronald Reagan, who had made a reputation of going after organized crime and filling jail cells with mafia dons, drug dealers, and white-collar criminals.

When he made the decision to go into elective politics by running for mayor of New York City, he knew it would be tough. New York is a Democratic city. Registered Democrats outnumber Republicans by 5 to 1. No Republican had been elected mayor as long as anyone could remember. New York was not seen as a friendly place for Republicans, especially after two terms of the acerbic, anti-Reagan street-fighting style of incumbent mayor Ed Koch. And Giuliani would be facing a popular local Democratic politician, the Manhattan borough president David Dinkins. Actually, there was a good deal of excitement surrounding Dinkins's candidacy because, if elected, he would be the city's first African-American mayor, a source of pride to many Democrats.

Giuliani started the race behind in the polls, and he stayed there through Election Day. It was rough going from day one. His campaign message was muddled, according to journalists and other political observers. His fund-raising lagged. He appeared to waffle on key issues. He remained the front-runner in the Republican primary, but his lack of political campaign experience showed. To try to steady the ship, Giuliani shook up his campaign team by bringing in the man who was by then probably the most feared political gunslinger in the country, Roger Ailes. Ironically, in explaining the move, Giuliani's campaign manager, Peter Powers, said his candidate had "had trouble communicating a positive message ..."[7] One is not sure if Mr. Powers really thought Roger Ailes was going to help Rudy Giuliani deliver a "positive" message or if he was just searching for something to say to the press. The campaign between Dinkins and Giuliani became one of the most negative the city of New York had ever seen.

Ailes brought his attack-dog reputation with him to the campaign, and the Dinkins staff was put on edge, as were the New York media, who anticipated that something nasty was coming. While acknowledging that David Dinkins was a "nice fellow," Ailes suggested that Dinkins was being given a pass by the media because he was African-American.[8] The Willie Horton controversy from 1988 had stoked emotions in New York City as it had elsewhere, and many local politicians, as well as voters, were on a hair trigger. Some Democrats cried foul, accusing Ailes of trying to exploit racial fears in the city. But they should have waited; Ailes and Giuliani were just getting started.

Ailes was going to adapt Michael Dukakis's 1988 playbook for New York City and David Dinkins. As Richard Nixon did against the Democrats in 1968, and as George Bush did against Dukakis in 1988, Giuliani and Ailes ran against David Dinkins as irresponsibly soft on crime. They were going to make him the issue. Nixon's law-and-order campaign and Bush's Massachusetts prison furlough campaign became a template for Ailes's attacks on many of his clients' opponents. "The only thing Dinkins has said about crime until now is that he wants to set up a commission to investigate police brutality," complained Ailes.[9]

Apparently, Ailes even thought he had found a New York City version of Willie Horton—Robert "Sonny" Carson. Carson was a convicted kidnapper who was African-American. He and several others were convicted in 1974 of kidnapping a man they suspected of stealing money. The kidnapped man was shot in the head, but Carson was acquitted of murder and attempted murder. After his prison term, Carson became a community organizer and led many of the protests in New York City relating to police and community issues. After the killing of a black teenager in Brooklyn's predominantly white Bensonhurst section, Carson led a "Day of Outrage" protest at the Brooklyn Bridge that left forty-four police officers injured.[10] And now he was on the Dinkins campaign payroll; the campaign hired Carson's group, the Committee to Honor Black Heroes, to help get out the vote in the September Democratic mayoral primary.

Ailes pounced. He said the Dinkins campaign's payments to Carson's group amounted to "Walking Around Money,"[11] a notorious and controversial practice involving political campaigns that pay community organizations, and sometimes churches, to get their members out to vote on Election Day. It's considered, essentially, buying votes. As proof, Carson's organization, said Ailes, had no address and few receipts showing how the money was spent.[12]

The Giuliani campaign released a TV ad produced by Ailes: "It's becoming a pattern. First, David Dinkins failed to file his income taxes for four straight years [in the early 1970s]. Then he failed to accurately report campaign contributions required by the law ninety-nine percent of the time. Next, he hid his links to a failing insurance company. Now his campaign has paid a convicted kidnapper through a phony organization with no members, no receipts, and no office. David Dinkins—Why does he always wait until he's caught?"

Dinkins flatly denied the charges about Carson. He said that he had been unaware of the kidnapping conviction, but that Carson's community group did have an office and did have members. Ailes charged that the Dinkins campaign knew they had a PR problem with Carson's involvement in his campaign and that the payment to his organization was a "payoff" to keep Carson quiet until after the election.[13] Giuliani fit the Carson issue into his anticrime platform: "Imagine if this fellow Dinkins is sitting in City Hall, and he starts hiring Sonny Carsons on us, and he starts paying out $8,000 to $10,000 without receipts," he told audiences.[14]

The Dinkins camp responded by making public a letter it sent to the Giuliani campaign deploring "gutter" politics. Dinkins singled out Ailes as the source of the campaign's negative tone. "You and Mr. Ailes have bullied people in the past. But I will not be bullied … I am determined not to let your consultant, Roger Ailes, do to me what he has done to other Democrats in other races, slandering their records and playing upon fear," the letter said. Dinkins went on to warn the Giuliani campaign to halt its negative attacks "in the next 24 hours" or face retaliation. "I am challenging you one last time to stop the gutter politics."

The comparisons to Willie Horton came fast and furious. A *Washington Post* headline read, "With Ailes's Aid, Convict Becomes 'Willie Horton' of N.Y. Campaign." Ailes answered back with his typical indignation. "They're both felons and they're both black, but that's not my fault," he said of the parallels to Horton. "I didn't bring Sonny Carson into the race. If a guy breaks the law and hires a kidnapper and pays him secretly, I would be remiss if I didn't make it an issue."[15] He kept the pressure on Dinkins, in what many saw as an intensely personal charge after vowing not to attack Dinkins personally. "We have at least six cases where Dinkins has broken the law," Ailes said. "He apparently feels stealing a little bit is okay."

One New York Democratic consultant said, "You're now in Ailes's ballpark. . . This is where he makes his money. If you go into the alleyway with him, he comes after you with a bottle and a brick."[16]

Far from backing off from the mud bath, Ailes exulted in it. Just before the election, with Giuliani still trailing in the polls, his campaign released another Sonny Carson ad. This one showed Carson leading a demonstration and reminding viewers of his criminal past and his connection to the Dinkins campaign. Dinkins called the ad a "scurrilous attack," and his media advisor, Robert Shrum, called it "one last roll in the mud." "Some of this will be counterproductive," added Shrum. "Maybe I have more faith in human nature than Roger Ailes, who obviously has none."[17]

Dinkins won the election, though by only two percentage points—a much closer margin than the campaign polls had suggested. The Giuliani campaign's ads produced by Ailes, along with the turmoil it created, put Dinkins on the defensive and made the outcome close. Dinkins benefited from a parade of heavyweight Democratic names campaigning for him in the closing weeks—Mario Cuomo, Ted Kennedy, incumbent mayor Ed Koch, and others. That and the overwhelming advantage Democrats have in New York City may be the only things that carried the election for him.

That same year Ailes used similar tactics in Jim Courter's race for governor of New Jersey. It was a different kind of race, though. Unlike Dinkins, who ignored Giuliani for much of the race, Representative Jim Florio, the Democratic nominee for governor, was very willing to engage in a negative campaign war. This race is covered in some detail in a later chapter, but once again, Roger Ailes was looking for a Willie Horton or a Sonny Carson to use against the opposition.

This time the best he could do was David Teti. He wasn't African-American, but he was a kidnapper. On behalf of Courter, Ailes tried the same strategy he had used against Dukakis and Dinkins. TV ads run by Courter's campaign accused Florio of fighting to keep drug dealers out of jail and asking New Jersey parole officials to release a "dangerous kidnapper." Some of the charges stemmed from Florio's work for his law firm, which handled criminal defense cases.

The charge of coddling convicted kidnappers referred to a letter Florio had written while serving in the U.S. House. The mayor of Runnemede, New Jersey, David Vanella, asked Florio to assist him in the parole hearing of a personal acquaintance, David Teti. In 1985, Teti had pleaded guilty to charges of kidnapping, conspiracy, and the possession of an unlawful weapon. He was sentenced to ten years.

Vanella, who knew Teti's family, asked Florio for his help in early 1988, describing Teti as a "fine young man." Florio didn't know Teti, but said he respected Mayor Vanella and his opinion. "I would appreciate any consideration you might afford David Teti in his request for parole," Florio wrote to the administrator of the courts.[18] He wrote a similar letter to the chair of the parole board. Teti's parole hearing was held that May, and he was paroled in July 1988.

Courter and Ailes's campaign to paint Florio as dangerously irresponsible wasn't nearly as successful as Ailes's efforts against Michael Dukakis, or even David Dinkins. For one thing, the race was never close and didn't become competitive. And for another, David Teti was no Willie Horton. He wasn't even a good Sonny Carson. He was apparently a model prisoner and even took the opportunity to improve himself. While an inmate at

Annandale state prison, he enrolled in courses offered by Mercer Community College. He made the dean's list and began tutoring other inmates enrolled in courses.

Florio's press secretary, Jon Shure, called Courter's TV ad disgusting and beneath New Jersey voters. He said Jim Florio "did not ask that he (Teti) be paroled, but that they give him any consideration … For Jim Courter and Roger Ailes to try and turn this person into the Willie Horton of New Jersey simply will not wash. It's offensive for them to take this person and turn him into a pawn for their game of political distortion."[19]

Another reason that Ailes's work for Courter wasn't as successful as for previous clients was that Courter's campaign had its own problems. Two of his consultants resigned in the summer of 1989 due to their ties to a firm involved in accusations of influence peddling at the U.S. Department of Housing and Urban Development. Greg Stevens, who at the time of the campaign was a senior vice president at Ailes Communications, and GOP consultant Roger Stone left Courter's campaign because they were afraid the scandal would harm his candidacy. Courter accepted their resignations as "selfless and courageous," but it did further damage to his already long-shot bid to defeat Florio.

And Courter himself had to answer questions about his ties to the scandal-plagued Wedtech Corporation. He had written a letter in 1981 to the secretary of the army on behalf of Wedtech, which was seeking army construction contracts. Wedtech collapsed in 1986 following a major bribery scandal. Courter said he had merely toured the facility in the early '80s and encouraged federal officials to consider the company because of the jobs it would create. "I wouldn't have written the letter if I had known," he said.[20]

And Ailes wasn't through yet with Rudy Giuliani. In the spring of 1991, as Giuliani was preparing another run for mayor of New York and Roger Ailes was performing his death spiral in his last days as a political consultant, he wrote a speech for Giuliani's appearance at a legislative event. Giuliani was invited to give the Republican rebuttal at the annual state Legislative Correspondents Association roast in Albany, New York. According to journalists present, Giuliani "laid a 40-minute egg."[21]

He began with a gravel-voiced mafioso imitation, followed by several tasteless jokes, which may or may not have been of his own creation, for example, how he and his wife, a television reporter, had a "Chinese wall arrangement," whereby she handled the press and he handled the politics, to which he added that he should be careful because the "Asiatics" were getting powerful in these parts. The audience, including some of the state's biggest political operators, mostly sat in embarrassed silence as he plunged on.[22]

By the time of Giuliani's 1993 campaign for mayor, Ailes was done with politics. Rudy hired David Garth, who had managed a number of successful campaigns in New York, including those of Ed Koch and John Lindsay. This time the outcome was different.

4

Machiavelli's Love Child

*You don't have to be a patsy, you don't have to
sit there and allow people to kick you and then
edit your remarks so that you look like an idiot.*[1]

—Roger Ailes

In the movie *The Boys from Brazil*, Gregory Peck's character tries to clone Adolf Hilter, using DNA samples he took from his führer in the 1940s. Imagine that it would be possible to have similar samples taken from Niccolo Machiavelli, the legendary sixteenth-century politician and author of the world's best-known handbook for political cunning and treachery, *The Prince*. It might have produced a character such as our hero, Roger Ailes.

Is there a better student of Machiavelli than Ailes? After all, Machiavelli advised that there was a difference between public ethics and private ethics, and that political goals and ethical considerations are not related. He described the importance of establishing a reputation of strength, and stressed the importance of subterfuge and deception. In a way, he is the father of political consulting.

Ailes's career has been truly Machiavellian. The very goal of the TV programs Ailes created in 1968 was to camouflage Richard Nixon's true nature and showcase a "prince" that didn't really exist to the American public. Ailes performed a similar role for George Bush.[2] As discussed in Chapter 2, "The Image Is the Message," Ailes helped the Bush campaign develop an image and a persona for their candidate that was more "Reaganesque"—tough, determined, and principled. Of course, the problem for President Bush, as well as the American people, is that it was only an image, a mirage. George Bush Sr. is a good man. But he was no Ronald Reagan. Yet for a while, because of Roger Ailes, many people thought he was.

Ailes and Bush strategist Lee Atwater were determined to make Bush "get tough" and show Republican voters that he had what it takes to be the Republican leader in a post-Reagan world. He had hit back pretty hard against opponents in some of the early Republican debates, tweaking Bob Dole on his record and jabbing back at Alexander Haig's barbed comments. Bush famously put Delaware governor "Pete" Dupont in his place by calling him by his given name, Pierre. It takes a certain amount of chutzpah for a man with four names (George Herbert Walker Bush), and who himself is a notorious blue-blood rich kid, as is Dupont, to venture into those waters. But he pulled it off. "My friend, Pierre, let me help you on some of this," he said. It was the most memorable line of the debate and was the sound bite most people heard on the news.

In helping Bush to dispel the wimpy image that dogged him through the Reagan years and in the early stages of his 1988 campaign, some commentators have suggested that Ailes's master stroke was to prepare Bush to pick a fight on the air with CBS anchorman Dan Rather and then coach him through that hostile (and now historic) confrontation. The timing was crucial for Bush; it was two weeks before the Iowa caucus, and he was neck and neck with his main opponent for the nomination, Kansas senator Bob Dole. Rather and the *CBS Evening News* staff intended to focus the interview on Bush's role in the Iran-Contra scandal, knowing that it would be a very tense encounter and possibly very controversial.

But Bush won the battle before it was ever fought—because Ailes had insisted that the interview be done live instead of on tape. CBS had done taped interviews with the other Republican presidential candidates, such as Bob Dole and Jack Kemp, and they proposed a taped interview to the Bush campaign. But the Bush people stood their ground—it will have to be live, take it or leave it, they said.

Ailes knew that a taped interview gives too much control to the reporter and the editors in the newsroom, who can slice it and dice it to achieve the effect they want. Countless politicians and public figures have complained about taped interviews being edited to alter their impact and statements that were taken out of context through the editing process. But in a live interview, there is no removing comments from their context. What you see is what you get. The interviewee has the control. Ailes himself advised live interviews in his 1988 book *You Are the Message*. It's Communications Consulting 101.

According to *Newsweek*, "CBS was uncomfortable. Live interviews, particularly on the Evening News, are unpredictable ... a live interview gives the subject a chance to manipulate the conversation."[3] The *Evening News* staff knew it was risky, but to get the vice president one-on-one with Rather, they thought it was a risk worth taking. From their standpoint, they couldn't afford to lose the interview. With the Bush campaign's ultimatum, CBS had no choice but to agree to a live interview. So the tactical victory went to Roger Ailes. To quote another master strategist, the ancient Chinese military tactician Sun Tzu, "The smartest general fights on the terrain of his choosing, not his opponent's" and "a wise general plans in such a way that the battle is won before it is fought."

Both sides had planned the encounter for weeks—like two opposing armies plotting strategy and making sure the battlements were in place. "We knew it was going to be a brawl," said Richard Cohen, senior executive producer of the *Evening News*. "We prepared with that expectation."[4] Rather prepared for the interview like a candidate getting ready for a debate. In the days leading up to the event, he had a series of one-hour rehearsals with stand-ins playing Vice President Bush. In the meantime, Ailes had prepared Bush for combat. From the moment the Bush camp got the invitation to appear and knew that the interview would be conducted by Rather, they began prepping for a high-stakes affair.

But apparently the Bush campaign was holding some cards up its sleeve. According to Robert Garcia of ABC News, the Bush campaign had a mole at CBS who tipped them off as to the nature of the interview. And according to Garcia, Bush himself admitted this in an interview with ABC's Sam Donaldson in 2000, saying that the Republicans had a mole on the inside at CBS who gave them advance word "of the questions that Rather was going to ask."[5] This was confirmed to *Newsweek* by Bush's chief of staff, Craig Fuller, who said, "We kept getting reports that it was going to be an ambush ... CBS was leaking so badly that if they'd been Dutch they'd have been underwater."[6] By the way, in Sun Tzu's masterpiece of strategy *The Art of War* there is a whole chapter devoted to the use of "spies."

The interview was not face-to-face; Rather was on the set at CBS headquarters in New York, and Bush was on camera in his vice presidential office at the Capitol. Bush was accompanied by Craig Fuller and Roger Ailes, who were off-camera. The CBS crew had set up a TV monitor so that Bush could see the five-minute intro piece Rather had prepared, which focused almost exclusively on Iran-Contra. When the interview started, Bush was steaming. Ailes had prepared him to be direct, forceful, and not to back down. Bush came out swinging. "I find this to be a rehash and a little bit, if you'll excuse me, a misrepresentation on the part of CBS, who said you're doing political profiles on all the candidates."[7] Of course, with Ailes's prepping for combat and the advance word from the "mole" that Rather was going to come at him hard on Iran-Contra, Bush knew very well what to expect, so his surprise and outrage were obviously premeditated. But it was effective, as it caught Rather and his crew a little off guard.

The interview was like a battle or a heavyweight boxing match—pick your analogy. Both men weighed in, both men frustrated and angry. *Newsweek* suggested that during the interview Rather "crossed the line between objectivity and emotional involvement. From the start, Rather was peremptory, as though time were running out even before the clock began ticking; he seemed on the edge of explosion … Bush never relinquished his tone of tinny, aggrieved militancy," reported *Newsweek*'s Richard Stengel. "I don't want to be argumentative, Mr. Vice President," said Rather. "You do, Dan. You absolutely do," complained Bush.[8]

The thing is, during the actual interview, Bush had plenty of help. According to a number of sources, including CBS producer Howard Rosenberg, Ailes was standing just off to the side where Bush could see him as he held up cue cards prompting the vice president to use certain phrases. It must have seemed like an old *Mike Douglas Show* flashback— Ailes was stage-managing Bush's performance on live TV! In response to Rather's questions, Ailes would furiously scribble down pithy comebacks and hold the card up for Bush to see. As Rather pressed, the encounter turned into more of an argument than an interview.

Then came the *coup de grâce* that Ailes and Bush had worked on. They had decided they would try to turn the tables on Rather and mention his most embarrassing moment: the time he walked off the set of his *Evening News* broadcast in a huff when the network's sports coverage cut into his news time. According to *Congressional Quarterly* columnist Craig Crawford, who claims to have gotten the information firsthand from a CBS cameraman,[9] as Rather continued to press Bush about his role in the Iran-Contra scandal, Ailes held up a cue card that read NOW ASK! Then Bush let fly with the zinger: "It's not fair to judge my whole career by a rehash of

Iran … How would you like it if I judged your career by those seven minutes when you walked off the set in New York? Would you like that?"

A visibly angry Rather asked Bush if he was willing to hold a news conference before the Iowa caucus and answer questions. Bush replied he had "been to eighty-six news conferences and I …" Rather, running out of time, cut him off, saying, "I guess the answer is no … thank you very much for being with us, Mr. Vice President, we'll be back with more news in a moment."

The Bush campaign was jubilant. The postshow atmosphere at CBS was "grim," according to *Newsweek*'s Stengel. But Ailes wasn't quite through with CBS. That evening, the network switchboard received approximately 6,000 calls, most of them negative. According to Robert Garcia of ABC News, who was with CBS at the time, it was believed that Ailes orchestrated a telephone call-in operation and had Bush supporters voice their outrage over Rather's treatment of the vice president. "The phone-calling onslaught was so effective it brought the CBS New York switchboard to a grinding halt for nearly three days," claims Garcia.[10]

Bob Dole wasn't impressed. "If you can't stand up to Dan Rather," he said sharply, "you've got to deal with Gorbachev and a few other people."[11] He also told reporters that the interview was proof that Bush's role in Iran-Contra would be an issue that would haunt the vice president through the fall campaign. But the event seemed to galvanize Bush and his supporters, and is seen as a turning point in his presidential campaign.

"It was an extraordinary nine or ten minutes on national television," Ailes said. "I think more people should realize that you don't have to be a patsy, you don't have to sit there and allow people to kick you and then edit your remarks so that you look like an idiot."[12]

But these are strange comments for a man who in 2006 reacted angrily when the tables were turned during the now famous on-air clash between former president Bill Clinton and Fox News host Chris Wallace. The circumstances were similar. Just as with Bush in '88, Clinton thought he was being taken advantage of and that the network was ambushing him. Wallace asked him why he hadn't done more as president to stop Osama Bin Laden. Clinton felt it wasn't so much a question as an accusation, so he lashed out at Wallace, as Bush had against Rather.

> CLINTON: *So you did Fox's bidding on this show. You did your nice little hit job on me.*

WALLACE: *Well, wait a minute sir . . . You don't think that's a legitimate question?*

CLINTON: *It was a perfectly legitimate question, but I want to know how many people in the Bush administration you asked this question of.*

WALLACE: *We asked, we asked . . .*

CLINTON: *I don't believe you asked them that.*

WALLACE: *We ask plenty of questions of . . .*

CLINTON: *You didn't ask them that, did you? Tell the truth, Chris.*

WALLACE: *With Iraq and Afghanistan, there's plenty of stuff to ask.*

CLINTON: *Did you ever ask that? You set this meeting up because you were going to get a lot of criticism from your viewers because Rupert Murdoch's supporting my work on climate change. And you came in here under false pretenses and said you'd spend half the time talking about what we did out there to raise $7 billion plus in three days from 215 different commitments. And you don't care.[13]*

But this time it was Ailes crying foul. He accused Clinton of a "wild over-reaction," and said that it was proof that the former president had a "hatred for all journalists."[14] Well, these are some more very strange comments coming from a man who has spent the better part of the last forty or so years criticizing journalists as being lazy, partisan, and unfair. This is the man, after all, who designed Richard Nixon's 1968 television programs to go over the heads of those same journalists he now so passionately defends, and who questioned the motives and the professionalism of journalists who criticized him both during and after the Willie Horton affair.

There is one difference, though, between the 1988 Bush–Rather interview and the Clinton–Wallace confrontation. And this was pointed out by MSNBC's Keith Olbermann: Whereas Bush's outrage was premeditated and planned out in advance as part of a media strategy, Clinton's anger appeared to be genuine and spontaneous. "I saw President Clinton immediately before the Wallace interview," Olbermann said, "and I interviewed him immediately after it, and he was still visibly upset." [15]

In any case, how deliciously ironic it is that Roger Ailes played such an interesting role in both events.

The 1968 Nixon campaign had introduced Ailes to presidential politics, and his role in that campaign was substantial. But by 1988 he was a star in the Republican Party, and unlike in 1968, he was in complete control of his candidate's media and communications strategy. He likes control, which fits his management style and organizational philosophy, but it also happens to be a necessary ingredient in a political campaign—someone has to be in charge and make decisions. In directing the Bush campaign's media efforts, Ailes has said, "From the beginning, I basically announced that we were not a democracy."[16] Political scientist Kathleen Hall Jamieson suggests that by the spring of 1988 it was clear that Ailes was in charge. After the Dan Rather interview, she says, "Ailes's claim to control was uncontested ... In the general election, Ailes shaped the Republican news, advertising, and debate strategy."[17]

Bush's new Ailes-crafted public image had helped secure the nomination, but it was the fall advertising campaign that won the election and put this one in the history books. In the summer of 1988, polls showed Dukakis with a double-digit lead, and at least one poll had him up eighteen points over Bush. For the first time in a long time, Democrats could smell victory. So the Bush campaign started the fall campaign as an underdog—not always a bad place to be in politics.

Under Ailes's guidance, the Bush campaign created one of the most devastatingly effective negative ad campaigns in history, following Bush strategist Lee Atwater's stated goal of "stripping the bark off of Michael Dukakis."[18] The three most memorable spots were the "Revolving Door" ad, the Boston Harbor spot, and the tank ad. The Revolving Door spot was, of course, the official Bush campaign ad blasting Michael Dukakis's record as governor of Massachusetts. Bush and the Republicans went after Dukakis as "soft on crime," with exhibit A being the prison furlough program that he (and a number of other governors around the country) administered in the 1980s. This ad, together with the Willie Horton spot created by an independent non-Bush campaign group, made Dukakis look like a felon-hugging, irresponsible "liberal." More on these two ads in the next chapter.

The Boston Harbor ad is now considered a classic. Part of its notoriety stems from its sneak attack strategy. No one saw it coming. And as a political strategy it was simply brilliant. For more than a generation, Democrats have been the "environmentally responsible" party. Their candidates have run campaigns on protecting the environment, cleaning up pollution, and safeguarding the planet's natural resources. And they have seen many legislative victories in these efforts—the Clean Water Act, the Clean Air Act, and automotive emissions standards.

Going into the 1988 campaign, Democrats certainly had the upper hand when it came to the environment as a political issue. Polls showed that voters trusted the Democrats far more on environmental issues than they did the Republicans. The Reagan presidency did not have a distinguished record on environmental issues in most people's eyes. Reagan's appointments to the leadership of the Environmental Protection Agency—James Watt, then Ann Burford—were public relations disasters, which fed the public perception that Republicans were apathetic at best, or even hostile, to environmental protection.

As vice president, Bush had chaired a Task Force on Regulatory Relief, which recommended among other things, delaying the removal of lead from gasoline, temporarily suspending the federal program for toxic waste control, and delaying the implementation of fuel efficiency standards. Bush was not the environmentalists' friend, to say the least. But Michael Dukakis was. His commitment to changes in hazardous waste disposal, more rigid enforcement of the Clean Water Act, a national attack on acid rain, and developing renewable energy sources won him plaudits from the environmental lobby. His presidential campaign was endorsed by most of the national environmental groups, such as the League of Conservation Voters and the Audubon Society.

All of the campaign how-to books and seminars, and the advice from the experts say to play from one's strengths and attack the opponent's weaknesses. Most campaigning literature refers to military doctrine and usually quotes some well-known army strategist (usually it's von Clausewitz)—"concentrate your forces in a mass to take advantages of your strengths and attack your enemy where they are weak." It's classic political strategy and has become conventional wisdom. And it's usually effective.

But Roger Ailes is neither classic nor conventional. If anything, he's anti-conventional. He's a paradigm-buster. The Boston Harbor ad was different from most political advertising strategies, because it took a perceived weakness (Bush's environmental record) and attacked the opponent on what was supposed to be his strength. The Bush campaign went into Michael Dukakis's backyard and attacked him on the environment.

The ad showed the pollution-clotted harbor of Boston, which had been fouled by industrial pollution and commercial shipping since the 1800s, as an example of Dukakis's hypocrisy. The ad opens with the words: "The Harbor." Then viewers see a sign warning RADIATION HAZARD: NO SWIMMING. A dark, dramatic voice then says, "As a candidate, Michael Dukakis called Boston Harbor an open sewer. As governor, he had the opportunity to do something about it. But he chose not to. The EPA calls it one of the most expensive public policy mistakes in the history of New England. Now Boston Harbor, one of the dirtiest harbors in America, will cost residents six million dollars to clean. And Michael Dukakis promises to do for Americans what he has done for Massachusetts!"

It was one of the ads that dominated the airwaves in September and October, and it helped the Bush campaign sow doubt in many voters' minds about Michael Dukakis. The news media also found it to be newsworthy in a strategic political sense, and thus the ad was repeated on newscasts as analysts oohed and aahed over it. It was extremely effective. It's also an example to many observers of how advertising can be technically accurate, but misleading. Jonathan Alter of *Newsweek* has said that truth in advertising and accuracy in advertising sound like they're the same thing, but they're not. He believes the ad "misleads both through what it says and what it shows."[19] The facts of the harbor ad are accurate, but carefully selected. For example, Dukakis was the first Massachusetts governor to actually try to do something about pollution in Boston Harbor, but found no assistance at all from the Reagan/Bush EPA or Interior Department. Through the skillful use of images and the careful parsing of facts, Ailes and Bush were able to take a signature issue for the Democrats and turn it on its presidential nominee: by Election Day, polls showed that Bush and Dukakis were evaluated by the public almost evenly on environmental issues.

As serious as the environmental issues were in the harbor ad, the tank ad just made people laugh. There's an old saying in politics: "Don't wear funny-looking hats." When running for office, candidates are often called upon to do some cornball, goofy things and ham it up in front of the cameras for the locals. Flipping pancakes for the folks in Iowa, sampling ethnic foods in New York or Los Angeles, for example. But one should always keep in mind how such images may be used. What today appears to be a great way to connect with the folks and seem down-to-earth might be tomorrow's embarrassing photo that ends up in the opponent's TV ad or direct-mail flyer. Candidates are always looking for a way to make their opponent look foolish and amateurish anyway, so why help them?

Michael Dukakis obviously wasn't thinking about this when he took that ride in the tank. It might still have been dignified if it hadn't been for the helmet. But he and his team decided that, since he was a governor with no foreign policy experience, a perceived weakness, they needed to convey the image that he was engaged and knowledgeable about military issues and foreign affairs. He didn't want to fall into the Mondale trap of looking weak on national defense. While he was calling for reducing America's arsenal of nuclear weapons, he also wanted to emphasize his calls for strengthening conventional military defense, like tanks, artillery, and aircraft. So being filmed riding in an M1 tank at a General Dynamics facility in Michigan prob-ably made some strategic sense. After all, politicians, notably Vice President George Bush, posed with military units all the time, even tank units.

But it didn't go well. For one thing, the visual effect was all wrong. Instead of being filmed talking to tank commanders and asking questions, Dukakis climbed inside the tank and took a tourist's ride, looking like a fish out of water. Donning a helmet, he failed to even remove his tie (remember Nixon on the beach?). It didn't help that he smiled and waved at the camera, like someone on a Ferris wheel at the local carnival. The media covering the affair obviously felt it was a jokey event, because that's essentially how they reported it. Instead of a message about Dukakis's commitment to building up conventional military forces, the dominant story line was of a politician trying to patch over a weakness by staging a photo op with the troops. The Dukakis campaign's message got lost in the unflattering visuals.

Roger Ailes was licking his chops. He knew that, just like the Willie Horton case, something golden had just fallen into their laps. "I was trying to define Mike Dukakis in terms of foreign policy and he defined himself," Ailes told *Advertising Age*. "Here was a guy who was opposed to almost every defense system in the world and then he rides around in a tank with a silly hat and tie on."[20] Ailes and his team used the Dukakis tank footage to make an ad mocking the Massachusetts governor's attempt to look strong on defense. In the Bush ad, the tank is circling around showing Dukakis smiling at the camera. An announcer says:

Michael Dukakis has opposed virtually every defense system we developed. He opposed four missile systems, including the Pershing Two missile deployment. Dukakis opposed the Stealth bomber and a ground emergency warning system against nuclear attack. He even criticized our rescue mission to Grenada and our strike against Libya. And now he wants to be our commander in chief. America can't afford that risk.[21]

It was a very successful ad for the Bush campaign in terms of using television to achieve your campaign strategy. The ad helped them make their point that the country's national defense would not be in good hands with Michael Dukakis. And the memorable visuals in the ad guaranteed it would be noticed by voters and by journalists. Hardly anyone noticed that the Bush ad got its facts wrong; it was simply good television. Dukakis did not oppose "virtually every defense system" as the ad claims. He opposed two proposed missile systems (the MX and the Midgetman), not four as the ad says. And he did not oppose building the Stealth bomber, but favored using it as a bargaining chip in negotiations with the Soviet Union.[22]

Dukakis and his campaign were understandably livid. The candidate filmed an ad to rebut the claims made in the Bush campaign ad. Dukakis is shown turning off the tank ad on a television monitor, then saying, "I'm fed up with it. George Bush's negative TV ads are full of lies, and he knows it. I'm on the record for the very weapons systems his ad says I'm against." But by this time the impression of Dukakis as weak on defense was already set, and Dukakis could not get the journalists covering the campaign to refocus on what he was actually saying about conventional defense forces. TV images had once again triumphed over facts.

That same year Roger Ailes also worked for some very good friends of his in the tobacco and cigarette industries to try to defeat an antismoking referendum in California. The group he went to work for was called Californians Against Unfair Tax Increases (CAUTI). Their opponent was the Coalition for a Healthy California, which endorsed a referendum calling for an increase in the tobacco tax.

The increased tobacco tax would raise approximately $600 million a year to fund hospital care for the poor, medical research of tobacco-related diseases, and an antismoking campaign aimed at young people. To the tobacco companies it was like a bad dream—it would surely cut consumption of ciga-rettes by making them more expensive, and the tobacco companies would essentially be paying for an advertising campaign against themselves.

Ailes's company produced several TV ads to attempt to sway public opinion against the measure. His strategy was basically to convey the impression that the tax proceeds would enrich doctors and that a higher cigarette tax would lead to organized crime's smuggling black market ciga-rettes, which would mean more guns on the street, and those extra guns would endanger our kids.

Here is what one of the ads looked and sounded like: A rugged-looking man walks up to a van with its side doors open. "California police officer 19 years," says a subtitle. Crates inside the van overflow with handguns. The man looks into the camera and says, "How much money could a street gang make from smuggling cigarettes? With a van like this, a gang could make enough money to buy 185 handguns. Every week. In the past year gangs have killed over 200 people, many of them innocent children." Then the scene changes to a jungle gym with children. As the man talks, the kids disappear and are replaced by white silhouettes. "More guns might not cause more murders, but is it worth taking the chance that even one more innocent person may be killed? Proposition 99 would create major crime. California doesn't need any more crime. Vote No on Proposition 99."[23]

So you see, according to this logic, Californians could save their kids' lives by keeping cigarettes cheap! But as over-the-top as it sounds, the ad actually played pretty well on television. Polls showed that many Californians were concerned about crime and guns, so the ad tapped into a fear that was already there.

Ailes and big tobacco might have won if not for an oversight on one of their other TV ads. "I'm an undercover cop," says the man in the ad. "I risk my life every day out here. But if Proposition 99 passes, I can spend my time chasing cigarette smugglers." The man really was a police officer, but he did not work undercover, he had an administrative job with the department. He was also a part-time actor, with bit parts in movies from time to time. He blows away two Secret Service agents in the movie *To Live and Die in LA*.

When someone recognized him from one of his movies, the Coalition for a Healthy California began hitting the airwaves. They held press conferences announcing that the man in the ad was not an undercover cop but was in fact an actor. They showed videotapes juxtaposing the TV ad he did for Ailes with his performance in *To Live and Die in LA*. The publicity around the controversial ad called into question the credibility of the CAUTI advertising campaign. In the end, Proposition 99 passed, and its sponsors believe much of the credit goes to this ad, which essentially blew up in the faces of the tobacco companies.

According to the Center for Media and Democracy, Ailes's biographical profile submitted to the congressional Energy and Commerce Committee for hearings on tobacco and tobacco-related illnesses, stated that "in 1992, Ailes retired completely from political and corporate consulting to return full-time to television." But according to internal Phillip Morris documents, Ailes advised the company until at least 1994—after he had begun working as a network executive for NBC. A memo from the Phillip Morris Washington, D.C., office provides an outline of supplementary monthly budget expenditures on consultants, listing "Roger Ailes contract" with a figure of $15,000 under the heading "General Media Strategy."[24] A June 1993 letter from a Phillip Morris VP sent to Ailes laments the fact that in the pro-smoking battle "we are losing support."[25] And a June 1994 e-mail lists some possible speakers for a meeting, "some possibilities: Roger Ailes who we pay 5k a month to be available."[26]

Ailes may have been introduced to the tobacco and cigarette folks by another good friend of his, the current Republican leader in the U.S. Senate, Mitch McConnell. Senator McConnell is probably the most powerful ally the tobacco lobby has in Congress. He is one of the "big money" senators in Congress and is very loyal to the Political Action Committees that fund his campaigns. "Senator Cigarette" has raised over a quarter of a million dollars from tobacco and cigarette interests, second only to Representative Richard Burr of North Carolina.[27] Senator McConnell's importance to the tobacco industry is summed up by looking at an internal memo from the RJ Reynolds tobacco company: "As we have done during his previous elections, we will provide maximum help very early … The Senator is our strongest supporter on the product liability and the effective date issue for punitive damages …"[28]

Roger Ailes helped bring Mitch McConnell into national politics. He was McConnell's political consultant in 1984 when he narrowly defeated incumbent Democratic senator Dee Huddleston. This is one of the campaigns that helped launch Ailes to political consulting stardom in the 1980s, as it showcased his wicked sense of humor and showed that political attacks can also be funny and entertaining.

Students of political campaigns will remember the famous "bloodhound" ad, where a pack of tenacious hound dogs are on the trail of the "missing" Dee Huddleston. Ailes hired an actor to portray Senator Huddleston fleeing from the hounds—through woods, across a beach, into a pasture, and up a tree. As the chase is occurring, the man guiding the bloodhounds is recounting Huddleston's alleged missed votes in Congress. The ad enabled McConnell to make an issue of Huddleston's votes, or lack thereof, on key issues. But the format was friendly and funny—it was one of the first national TV spots in the 1980s to use humor in a political attack, and it helped reignite the trend of humorous attack ads. The spot won a national advertising award and is now considered a classic.

From George Bush and Dan Rather to cigarettes and bloodhounds, Roger Ailes has used his knack for strategy and unconventional attacks for the benefit of his clients. But as the next chapter shows, as early as the 1970s, he had put his talent to use for those who would inject conservative Republican ideology into television news coverage.

5

Coors to You

Do you see that tugboat out there? Did you ever see the way a tugboat turns an ocean liner around? It doesn't do it in one swift motion. It pushes and nudges the liner slowly. That's the way we want to put our philosophy in the news: gradually, subtly, slowly. It must be subtle.

—Jack Wilson, President of Television News, Inc.[1]

"We tell both sides of the story when it comes to reporting the news."

"Traditional network news is slanted to the liberal left and is not objective."

"We try to offer a more 'balanced' presentation of the news."

"We play it straight down the middle."[2]

Typical slogans and catch phrases from Fox News? Sound bites from Roger Ailes about Rupert Murdoch's News Corporation? No, that would be about three decades off. The above quotes are from the first effort by Roger Ailes to establish a conservative news organization and steer the mass media toward the political right. The year was 1975, and Roger Ailes was hired as the news director of Television News, Inc., or TVN.

TVN was a national news service established in 1973 by beer magnate and right-wing political activist Joseph Coors. Coors provided the money for the news operation and relied on associates from some of the other conservative political organizations he was supporting, such as the Heritage Foundation, to develop and manage the news product. Coors and his associates believed that the news media in America overwhelmingly consisted of knee-jerk liberals from the East Coast who held an elitist, left-wing view of American politics and society. TVN was an effort to provide a conservative presentation of national news.

Joe Coors was deeply concerned about the moral direction of the country and what he saw as the liberal domination of American society. "Coors is the most important right-wing ideologue in the state," said one Colorado Coors watcher. "He's the anchorman of the right-wing point of view."[3] Coors himself said that he started TVN and the other conservative political organizations he funded "because of our strong belief that network news is slanted to the liberal left side of the spectrum and does not give an objective point of view to the American public."[4] If that sounds familiar, it's because some twenty years later, Rupert Murdoch and Roger Ailes used almost identical language in announcing the launch of the Fox News Channel.

Striking parallels exist between TVN and Fox News today. Consider this quote from the president of TVN in 1973: "The one thing that we try desperately to do is to get both sides of an issue. We don't feel it's our responsibility to make up anyone's mind for them ... but rather to give the American public ... which is a very intelligent group of people ... both sides of a story and enough information about both sides in an honest factual way so that they can make up their own minds."[5] Sounds a lot like "We Report, You Decide," one of the main slogans of Fox News, right?

The TVN president who made the above statement was Jack Wilson, the main political assistant to Joseph Coors, and one of the founders of the Heritage Foundation. And it would be a very nice sentiment and a very helpful news product if only it were true. But all available evidence points to an ideologically driven organization that produced a politically slanted newscast, trying desperately to camouflage its work by using words like "fairness" and "balance," much like Fox News today.

The idea for a conservative television news service like TVN originated with Robert Pauley, a Boston investment banker.[6] Pauley shared Coors's opinion that the media exhibited a "disgraceful liberal bias," and he wanted to restore some balance by having a conservative alternative to the news.[7] Coors put up $1 million to start TVN and committed another $2.5 million for annual operating costs. Coors and Pauley envisioned a visual equivalent of a wire service: They would produce video packages and distribute them to subscribers of the service. Their target audience was the potentially vast number of local television stations that were independent—not affiliated with any of the Big Three networks. It was viewed by Coors and Wilson as a stepping stone to the creation of a "fourth TV network."[8] They were twenty years ahead of Rupert Murdoch and Fox; they just didn't have Murdoch's ability to take financial losses, his distribution network, or his political connections with the FCC.

At the time, United Press International was the only other independent news film service, delivering features and sports reels to TV stations by truck. Coors and Pauley made the video service available using telephone transmission lines, which was quite expensive. Coors's eventual goal was to transmit the service using emerging satellite technology, but those plans never got off the ground, for financial and regulatory reasons.

Joe Coors was a crucial player in the emergence of the New Right in the 1970s and '80s. Basically, he provided the money. Beginning in the 1960s, the Coors family became one of the most prolific and generous underwriters of conservative and right-wing political causes in the country. Coors either created, or helped to fund, dozens of the best-known conservative political organizations in America, including the Christian Broadcast Network, the Heritage Foundation, the Hoover Institution, the Manhattan Institute, the Ethics and Public Policy Center, and the Free Congress Foundation. And according to author Russ Bellant and other sources, Coors's largesse didn't stop with the "respectable" conservative organizations—he also helped to support the John Birch Society, as well as individuals with links to racist organizations, former Nazi collaborators, and neofascist groups.[9]

TVN came into being around the same time as the Heritage Foundation, the most prestigious and the most ideologically driven conservative political think tank on the political right. The Heritage Foundation was begun by Joseph Coors, his assistant Jack Wilson, and by conservative activists Paul Weyrich and Edward Feulner. Along with Jack Wilson and Roger Ailes, Paul Weyrich was a prominent force at TVN. Coors and Wilson met Weyrich in the early '70s when Weyrich was an aide for Senator Gordon Allot of Colorado. Coors was looking for conservative political groups and projects to support. Weyrich convinced him that what conservatives needed was a research and policy center they could rely on and that would provide a counterweight to established liberal organizations like the Brookings

Institution. Coors donated a quarter-million dollars plus a commitment for millions more down the road, a breathtaking amount of money in 1973. Thus, Heritage was born.

The next year, Coors also provided the money for Weyrich to establish another group, the Committee for the Survival of a Free Congress (CSFC). This later became the Free Congress Foundation (FCF). This group engages more in direct political advocacy, organizing forums and seminars in Washington, lobbying, and funding political candidates through a political action committee. These two organizations provided crucial institutional support for conservative political activism in its early days.

Weyrich's CSFC embarked on a national fund-raising campaign to "defeat 100 radicals in 1976."[10] Coors was the group's largest contributor. Weyrich targeted one hundred Democratic members of Congress for defeat in the next election. One of the fund-raising letters said in part: "If we can (gear up) in 100 congressional races we will deal the liberals a staggering defeat and turn this country away from socialism and prevent a Communist defeat of America."[11]

TVN was part of a long-term political strategy, laid out by Weyrich, Coors, and other supporters, to create conservative political institutions that would influence public policy and politics in America. As reported by the *Washington Post* in 1974, "TVN is one of several projects Coors is financing in his effort to move the United States to the right politically."[12]

Weyrich is a controversial figure. He put the "right" in right-wing. Some sources, notably the Anti-Defamation League, even link him and the Free Congress Foundation to a radical ideology known as "dominionism," which advocates religious control of American political institutions and cultural centers. Weyrich has dismissed these accusations, calling them "bigoted."[13] Statements attributed to Mr. Weyrich and the Free Congress Foundation at least reveal a plan to wage war with the political left, which dominates American culture, according to Weyrich. He believes we must develop a network of parallel cultural institutions existing side by side with the dominant leftist cultural institutions. He has defined the New Right as "radicals working to overturn the present power structures in this country."[14] It seems that a certain conservative television news service (TVN) was a part of this long-term plan.

The first year of TVN's existence was characterized by battles between Coors management and the professional news staff he hired to produce the news packages. Charles Gibson, who is now the anchor of ABC's *World*

News Tonight, was on the original news staff. Coors and Jack Wilson, who eventually held the title of president at TVN, were constantly pushing the news staff to produce stories that catered to the political right. This created tension in the newsroom, as reporters and editors realized that Coors and Wilson simply wanted a conservative news operation, not the mainstream news service that had been discussed. In its brief life span, TVN went through four news directors—two were fired and one quit—and one mass firing of news staffers.

In hindsight, one could conclude that Coors management held views that were not only conservative, but extremist. For example, the following correspondence to Joseph Coors equates an American civil rights icon with Fidel Castro or Che Guevara:

> To: Joe Coors
> From: Jack Wilson   July 26, 1973
> Subject: Critique of Daily News Feed
>
> Martin Luther King was an avowed communist revolutionary. It is not necessary for us to cover him or any of his subordinates (Abernathy) just because the other networks do so. We are going to be different—if we are going to be the same then we are going to continue to cover all of the communist stories and carry all of their lines.[15]

The first news director hired by Coors and Wilson in January 1973 was Dick Graf, a former newspaperman and writer for NBC News. When he was hired, Graf told Coors that the news he was going to put on was going to be straight down the middle. "As long as it is down the middle—okay," Coors told him.[16] But apparently, one man's "middle of the road" is another man's "communist conspiracy." Within weeks after TVN began production, Coors's office issued a statement to the staff that company policy "requires a more 'balanced' presentation of the news than the service has thus far exhibited."[17] It soon became clear to Graf and his reporters that they had a very different conception of the word "balance" than Coors and TVN management.

Soon Jack Wilson was bombarding Graf and the TVN Washington bureau chief, Bob Frye, with suggested story ideas. It has been reported that former TVN staffers have said that these story ideas came directly from Republican government officials and legislators that Wilson talked to on a weekly basis.[18] Many of them also came from Paul Weyrich. Wilson deluged Graf and Frye with memos suggesting ideas for stories and critiquing how TVN was covering certain issues and political figures. Graf resisted this pressure and complained to Coors about Wilson's interference—setting the stage for conflicts to come.

The disputes between Graf and TVN management continued into the summer of 1973, and so did the partisan political pressure from Jack Wilson. He fired off a series of memos to Coors outlining his concerns and offering editorial guidance. These memoranda reveal a concerted effort to push a partisan political agenda onto the news. A sampling of his memos:

> June 1, 1973
> Agnew speech. Very good. Clip showing Agnew in a relaxed and human fashion. This was one of the stories we could be proud to show our friends.

> June 20
> Summit meetings … by referring to Brezhnev as the "Soviet leader" we put the man in the same category as Nixon … Brezhnev is not elected, but our President is. Brezhnev is actually a party boss and should be so identified …This subtly obscures the fact that there is a real difference in our systems. With all of the media doing the same thing, we gradually break down the barrier and create a climate of equality between the Russian and the American systems. The end result is that they are upgraded and we are downgraded and everyone is equal.

> June 21
> … Smut. This is ABSOLUTELY OUTRAGEOUS!! TVN has made me explode on several occasions and this has got to rank in the top three. Our announcer says nothing about the problems of smut or in any way supports the Supreme Court of the United States, but rather picks out a fellow who says smut is ok and is allowed to give his reasons … In my opinion no one in the news department has learned one thing, and on this issue alone several people should be fired!

June 27
Cambodia bombing veto ... How in the @#$% can our autocratic, professional journalists swear on the shrine of Walter Cronkite that they would be mortally wounded if anyone from the outside tried to make them less than balanced in reporting news? How can they ... put out a story about the bombing veto with the perfectly balanced, wonderful reporting of Jerry Ford, who supports the President, then the balance of Hubert Humphrey, Thomas Eagleton, and Alan Cranston? Something like that is the most flagrant display of contempt that I can imagine.

July 5
David Rockefeller. Nothing like this should ever be allowed on our air. Rockefeller took a Communist public relations tour, the same as Ramsey Clark did in Hanoi when he reported our prisoners were all well fed, healthy, happy men . . . We are not providing this service to give voice to that kind of propaganda.

Mysteriously, copies of these memos from Wilson to Coors and the rest of the TVN board found their way to the news staff and were circulated among reporters and editors. These memos had a crushing effect on the morale of the news team; a number of resignations followed. The memos also reveal a sizeable gap between the intentions of TVN management and the goals of most news professionals. Stanhope Gould, a journalist and author who chronicled the experiences of TVN in a *Columbia Journalism Review* article called "Coors Brews the News," suggests there wouldn't be anything wrong with a news network designed to promote conservative views "if its product were clearly labeled." Gould goes on to say that there is something in TVN's actions that contradicts the basic idea of a news network—covering the news. "It is one thing to argue that certain kinds of stories don't get balanced treatment from the networks, and to insist that an alternative, independent news service provide the balance," said Gould. "It is quite another thing to argue that certain kinds of movements and ideas should simply be KEPT OFF THE AIR. There is no balance—or journalism—in that."[19]

Fast-forward to Fox News and Roger Ailes. One of the criticisms of Fox News is that Fox management tries to push a conservative political agenda through its newscast, not unlike TVN. And one of the main complaints of Fox critics and of journalists who formerly worked at Fox is that management openly encourages and actively suggests story ideas and reporting angles that are ideological in nature, and support conservative Republican policy goals. In circumstances eerily reminiscent of Jack Wilson's memos at TVN, the executive vice president of Fox News, John Moody, routinely sends memos to Fox news staff directing them to emphasize certain story angles and ignore others. These memos have been characterized by former Fox News employees and Media Matters and by others who have seen them as overtly political and designed to provide a conservative spin on the national news.

A sampling of Moody's memos to the Fox newsroom as posted on the Media Matters Web site:

May 22, 2003
The tax cut passed last night by the senate, though less than half of what Bush originally proposed, contains some *important victories for the administration. The D.C. [Fox News] crew will parse the bill and explain how it will fatten—marginally—your wallet.*

June 3, 2003
President Bush is doing something that few of his predecessors dared undertake: putting the U.S. case for mideast peace to an Arab summit. It's a definitely skeptical crowd that Bush faces. *His political courage and tactical cunning are worth noting in our reporting through the day.*

March 12, 2004
John Kerry may wish he'd taken off his microphone before trashing the GOP. Though he insists he meant Republican "attack squads," his coarse description of his opponents has cast a lurid glow over the campaign.

March 24, 2004
The hotel where our Baghdad bureau is housed was hit by

some kind of explosive device overnight. All Fox personnel are ok ... Please offer a prayer of thanks for their safety to whatever God you revere (*and let the ACLU stick it where the sun don't shine*).

April 4, 2004
Into Fallujah: It's called Operation Vigilant Resolve and it began Monday morning with the US and Iraqi military surrounding Fallujah. We will cover this hour by hour today, *explaining repeatedly why it is happening. It won't be long before some people start to decry the use of "excessive force." We won't be among that group.*[20]

Now, the existence of these memos from executive VP John Moody isn't new; they have been written about and discussed for several years. But what has not been revealed until now is the apparent connection between this practice at Fox and the managerial pressure delivered at TVN in the mid '70s— and the common denominator is the presence of Roger Ailes. He was TVN's news director, and in that capacity he appears to have picked up TVN's technique of managerial manipulation and filed it away for future use. He certainly uses some very similar slogans and buzzwords: Fair and Balanced; We Report, You Decide; We're an alternative to the "liberal" media.

Moody was one of Ailes's first hires at Fox News in 1996. Moody is not coy about his political views. "Personally, I'm right of center," he has said.[21] According to journalist Marshall Sella, who has interviewed both men, Ailes and Moody share a worldview, "one that shapes how Fox News operates today ... It's not hard to see why, in their first meeting in 1996, Moody found himself 'finishing Roger's sentences.'"[22]

There's nothing unusual about a news executive's sending memos to news staff; it's a common practice in newsrooms all over America. It's the content of Moody's memos that raises questions. The goals of some of his missives seem to have as much to do with partisan politics as with journalism. The news directors and journalism scholars this author has interviewed believe there is a qualitative difference between these memos at Fox News and how other broadcast news organizations operate. Andy Lack, the former president of NBC News, now with Sony, claims that this kind of overt political management of the news never happened at NBC.

Shortly after the launch of Fox News, Moody told one interviewer, "A lot of the people we have hired have come without the preconceptions of must-do news. There are stories we will forego in order to do stories we think are more significant. The biggest strength that we have is that Roger Ailes has allowed me to do that; to forego stories that would be 'duty' stories in order to focus on other things."[23] Presumably, what Moody calls "duty" stories are what journalist Stanhope Gould would call "covering the news" or actually telling people what happened that day. Instead, Fox News's critics charge, they focus on ways to spin the news and highlight conservative talking points. Moody's memos may be the smoking gun.

There have been numerous published accounts of Fox News employees resigning or being forced out over disagreements about the political reporting of the news. For example, Don Dahler, a former CBS producer, resigned from Fox News after John Moody reportedly "ordered him to change a story to play down statistics showing a lack of social progress among blacks."[24] Moody defended the change as journalistically justified. The *Columbia Journalism Review* reported that "several former Fox employees complained of management sticking their fingers in the writing and editing of stories to cook the facts to make a story more palatable to right-of-center tastes."[25] One of the former Fox employees said, "I've worked at a lot of news organizations and never found that kind of manipulation."[26]

In November 2006, after the Democrats took control of Congress in the midterm elections, Fox News seemed to go into partisan overdrive. Another gem from John Moody:

> November 14, 2006
> The elections and Rumsfeld's resignation were a major event, but not the end of the world. The war on terror goes on without interruption ... and *let's be on the lookout for any statements from the Iraqi insurgents, who must be thrilled at the prospect of a Dem-controlled Congress* ... In the House, newly empowered Dems will shed some fraternal blood before settling in. Murtha will challenge Hoyer for the leadership. A former hawk versus *a political hack*.[27]

Later that day on Fox, news anchor Martha MacCallum asked a terrorism expert from the Christian Broadcasting Network about "reports of cheering in the streets on behalf of the supporters of the insurgency in Iraq, that they're very pleased with the way things are going here and also with the resignation of Donald Rumsfeld."[28] That kind of partisan political direction of the news starts at the top. It actually sounds like what Jack Wilson and Joseph Coors wanted to have at TVN, but they were frustrated that they couldn't get the professional news staff they hired to go along. Until one day Joe Coors hired Roger Ailes.

The original news director of TVN, Dick Graf, was fired in 1974 after Coors and Wilson decided he could not "review and evaluate the work objectively."[29] Graf resisted Wilson's efforts to produce a more politicized version of the news. Wilson told the TVN board that Graf had to go because he was unable to "review and evaluate the work objectively." There's that funny word again—"objectively." After he left TVN, Graf told friends, "The assurances I got from Coors, Gilbert [a TVN official], and Wilson about 'playing it straight' and 'playing it down the middle' were so much bullshit."[30]

With Graf gone, "the floodgates opened," says a TVN staffer. Wilson was now firmly in charge. He would complain to news staffers that "we're not getting the proper message in the news." When challenged, Wilson would change "message" to "balance."[31] (Fair and Balanced?) Now, says Stanhope Gould, instead of writing memos to Joe Coors, Wilson was talking directly to the staff. He was playing the John Moody role.

Wilson also replaced the Washington bureau chief. He hired William Kling, a former *Chicago Tribune* reporter who had gone into politics, working for a Republican congressman and for the American Security Council, a Republican defense policy study group. Wilson now had a bureau chief with whom he could work. Paul Weyrich also became more influential at TVN. Some Washington bureau staffers at TVN knew that Wilson and Weyrich talked frequently, and they believed that Weyrich had considerable influence with news selection. At one Capitol Hill news conference, Weyrich produced a three-by-five index card listing questions he wanted asked and handed them to a TVN reporter, who then dutifully asked the questions.[32]

Wilson told his new news director, Tom Turley, that from now on, all new job applicants had to be cleared by the Heritage Foundation staff.[33] He also told him that now the "middle" wasn't good enough. "I hate Dan Rather," he said. "I hate all those network people. They're destroying the country. We have to unify the country. TVN is the moral cement."[34]

Then, in September 1974, while Turley was away at a broadcast convention, Wilson took the opportunity to clean house. He fired the executive producer of the news feed, the national assignment editor, the national features editor, the Washington assignment editor, the Los Angeles bureau chief, the Los Angeles assignment editor, two reporters, a two-person film crew, two film editors, a bureau business manager, a production assistant, and a secretary. The next month, he fired Tom Turley.

Roger Ailes had been offering public relations advice to TVN management for several months before he was asked by Wilson to become their news director. Since his work for Nixon in 1968, he had formed Ailes Communications, Inc. This company worked for Republican political candidates, provided communications counseling to corporations, and was also involved in a number of entertainment pursuits involving records, stage productions, and television production. Upon becoming news director of TVN, according to the *Columbia Journalism Review*, Ailes turned over responsibility for Ailes Communications' other clients to subordinates.

Ailes was not a journalist. He had never worked in news. So why was he hired as news director of a national news service? "The Coors people trust Ailes because of his affiliation with the Republicans, and because he's not a newsman," said one TVN staffer. "They don't trust newsmen."[35]

But these days, Ailes apparently feels a need to distance himself from his time at TVN. It's been well documented by the *Columbia Journalism Review*, as well as other publications at the time, such as the *Washington Post*, that he was hired by Joseph Coors as its news director in 1974. However, in a 2004 interview with C-SPAN's Brian Lamb, Ailes said he was only a "consultant." His recollection appeared very shaky about the whole experience: "I guess the Coors Company started a network—they wanted to get into the satellite business, as I recall … it was one of my consulting clients. I was never there as a full-fledged job."[36] *Never there as a full-fledged job?* News director was no part-time gig. In light of the evidence from documented sources, his statement to Brian Lamb appears to be inconsistent. And it begs the question: Why would Roger Ailes want to distance himself from TVN?

During the Brian Lamb interview, the whole subject of TVN seemed to make Ailes uncomfortable. It was like he was trying to change the subject or distract Lamb. A sampling:

LAMB: *You got in the business of news in the '70s, something called TVN.*

AILES: *I remember you from those days. Yeah, you were there too.*

LAMB: *I wasn't at TVN.*

AILES: *Dennis Swanson. Well, you came in …*

LAMB: *No, I was in government.*

AILES: *Oh, Okay.*

LAMB: *And that's, I think …*

AILES: *I remember meeting you at that office one day. I don't remember when it was.*

LAMB: *Television News …*

AILES: *You aged better than me, by the way.*

LAMB: *Hardly. Go back to that [TVN], what was it?*

In 1975 Ailes told the *Columbia Journalism Review* that Jack Wilson gave him the freedom to "hire, fire, and program the TVN feed as he sees fit."[37] So the TVN president—overtly political, unyieldingly right-wing, and hostile to professional journalists—gave complete control to Roger Ailes. Rupert Murdoch did the same thing two decades later.

When asked by the *Review* if at TVN he felt a need to "balance" the bias of the networks, Ailes said, "One thing is sure, the networks are not biased to the right." Then later in the interview, he expressed disgust with the press: "[Marlon] Brando gives land to the Indians. If that had been the president of General Motors, the press would have been all over him, talking about tax write-offs and PR stunts. But Brando wasn't asked about that. If you're gonna ask the president of GM, then ask Brando. If that's a right-wing news network, then so be it."

But unfortunately for Ailes and for Wilson, the ultimate problem came down to money—TVN was losing too much of it. The original estimate of $2.5 million for annual operating expenses was far too low. It left out such things as a half-million dollars for studio facilities—the film projectors, videotape machines, and other equipment needed to transmit the film to subscribers. And the necessity of covering news on a worldwide basis meant sky-rocketing expenses and ever-increasing budgets. In 1974 the budget was doubled to over $5 million, but it still wasn't enough.

And the revenue TVN was bringing in wasn't enough to pay the bills. One TVN staffer said management "really expected the industry to break down the doors to get this service ... their financial projections showed they would be in the black in 18 months."[38] But by the middle of 1975, they were nowhere near the black and the service had lost millions of dollars. For one thing, it was very expensive for local TV stations to acquire the service in the first place. The AT&T service that carried the sound and images of television transmission cost about $2,500 a month. The Big Three TV networks paid the cost of that for their affiliates, but TVN clients had to pay it themselves, plus the cost of the TVN news subscription.

TVN's demise also had something to do with the derailing of Joseph Coors's longer-range business and political goals. In August 1974 one of the last acts of President Richard Nixon as he was on his way out the door was to fill several openings on the board of the Corporation for Public Broadcasting (CPB). One of the people he appointed was Joseph Coors. It was seen by most as an odd choice. Coors was no friend to public broadcasting, he was notoriously antiunion, he had very little experience in public service, he was known as a contributor to many far-right political groups, and at the time of his appointment, the federal Equal Employment Opportunity Commission (EEOC) was investigating Coors for workplace violations.[39] But seen in that context, it was probably one of Nixon's last "in your face" gestures to the hated liberal establishment he blamed for hounding him out of office.

With Nixon gone, Coors's appointment to the CPB languished, but he weighed in on CPB issues and policies anyway, writing to CPB staff members about programming and complaining about certain programs on public broadcasting. And he also openly campaigned to get government satellite distribution contracts for the Coors company. Like PBS, TVN relied on AT&T coaxial cables to transmit its programs to affiliated stations. And like PBS, TVN was exploring the possibility of replacing that system with a satellite system. "In the eyes of the senators who eventually voted down Coors's nomination, this represented a conflict of interest ... But to Coors, it was strictly a business arrangement."[40] If Coors could be guaranteed that publicly funded TV signals would piggyback, for a price, on a satellite network that he was going to establish for TVN anyway, everybody would win.

Coors even wrote a letter to Henry Loomis, the CPB president. He pointed out in the letter that the CPB was currently contracting with a commercial group, AT&T, for distribution of their programs. "Would it not be just as feasible to contract for similar services with the additional flexibility and advantages of the earth stations? I can assure you that this can be done at considerable financial savings over what you estimate spending at the present time."

Coors's attempt to steer government satellite business to TVN prompted a number of senators on the Commerce Committee to insist that he divest himself of the TVN directorship before his nomination to the CPB board was acted upon; Coors resisted the efforts to disassociate himself from TVN.

When President Ford put forth Coors's nomination, it generated considerable controversy. Organized labor, public interest, and civil rights groups, supported by several members of Congress, mounted an aggressive campaign against his confirmation. His ownership of TVN, his support for "extremist" groups such as the John Birch Society, his antiunion practices at the Adolph Coors Co., and the investigations into his minority hiring policy assured a nomination fight.

Under questioning from the Senate committee, Coors denied being a member of the John Birch Society but said he had "at times supported them with funds and I support some of their thoughts and ideas."[41] He frequently circulated articles from the John Birch Society's magazine, *American Opinion*, to associates and business contacts, and one of his companies, Coors Porcelain Co., routinely advertised in that publication.

Coors's and Paul Weyrich's more overt political activities also caught up with them, particularly their campaign to "defeat one hundred radicals" in Congress, organized by Weyrich's Committee for the Survival of a Free Congress. Congressman John Moss of California sent a letter to President Ford and to the chair of the Senate Commerce Committee pledging that his state's entire Democratic delegation to Congress would work against the Coors nomination. "I think it interesting to note," wrote Moss, "that Mr. Coors has committed himself to fully supporting efforts to eliminate 100 members of the present Congress as part of his move to remake this nation in an image more pleasing to himself."[42] One of the Republicans on the Commerce Committee—Lowell Weicker, a moderate from Connecticut—voted against the Coors nomination. Weicker said his vote was based on "a general pattern of insensitivity and bad judgment that threads through everything the man does."[43]

Coors's nomination to the CPB went down in flames, along with his plans for a satellite distribution deal that would have carried TVN. By this time TVN was hopelessly in debt, with monthly financial losses growing ever higher. Joe Coors and Jack Wilson announced in October 1975 that TVN would cease its news-gathering operations. In his statement, Wilson said a "continuing lack of revenues" was the major reason for the decision. "Until recently," he said, "we believed that … additional income would be derived from an expanded distribution system using satellite transmission and ground stations at major centers around the country."

Where Coors was unable to successfully build a satellite-based distribution system for his conservative news product, Rupert Murdoch would be phenomenally successful at this some years later.

After the news operation closed its doors, TVN continued a limited number of production projects involving feature documentaries and TV productions. In one project, for example, Roger Ailes accompanied Robert Kennedy Jr., then a Harvard undergrad, to Africa to develop a TV documentary about Kenyan wildlife called *The Last Frontier*. This proved, if nothing else, that Ailes can work with liberals when the situation calls for it, a tendency he once again proved at CNBC in the mid-1990s. Ailes went on to continue his career as a media and communications impresario, working for political candidates and corporate executives.

Paul Weyrich's political activism bore fruit in the 1980s as economic conservatives joined forces with the social and religious conservatives to propel a number of congressional candidates to victories in key districts throughout the country. And many of the Christian-based groups with which Weyrich was affiliated, notably the Moral Majority, were instrumental in building coalitions of voters that helped elect Ronald Reagan. Most interesting, though, is Weyrich's involvement in yet another attempt to create a conservative news operation, National Empowerment Television (NET). Launched in 1993 by the Free Congress Foundation, NET in some ways was a modern, streamlined version of TVN, with a solid conservative Republican focus on national political news and featuring conservative weekly program hosts, such as Newt Gingrich. However, due both to creative differences between Weyrich and NET donors and to financial concerns, the service folded a few years later.

Weyrich said that in his many years of conservative political activism, NET was "the most exciting thing" he had done, stressing the communication benefits that accrue from conservative-controlled media. In words that could have been spoken by Joe Coors or Jack Wilson, Weyrich said that "in any kind of battle, communication is number one. So at last we have a tool that is extraordinary in its ability to interest people, to get them motivated."[44] Unlike TVN or Fox News, NET, however brief its life, did not have to worry about notions such as "journalism" or news reporting. It wasn't Fair and Balanced.

6

Roger the Guru

Okay Ailes, Fix Me!

—One of Roger the Guru's corporate clients in the 1970s[1]

Fired by Nixon's chief of staff Bob Haldeman! Looking back, that must be almost surreal to Roger Ailes. Following Nixon's election victory in 1968, Ailes provided media consulting to the White House. After the success of the Man in the Arena programs, he may even have aspired to follow Nixon into the White House and run his communications operation. But with the publication of Joe McGinniss's *The Selling of the President* in 1969, Ailes came off as the heavy—a gruff, tough-talking operator with sharp elbows, which he is, in fact. Nixon didn't like the publicity generated by the book. And Joe McGinniss said that most of Nixon's staffers, when asked by reporters, denied cooperating with the book efforts—all except for Roger Ailes. That probably didn't win him many fans around the oval office. Also, his need for control very likely was not a smooth fit with the big egos of Nixon's inner circle. But Ailes was brought in to coordinate media events and offer advice as a "consultant." This began a decades-long habit of his sending advice (often unsolicited) to Republican presidents and candidates for president. The release of the rest of Nixon's White House papers in 2007 revealed a look at the Ailes-Nixon-Haldeman relationship.

Ailes's value to the Nixon White House was short-lived, however. For one thing, Richard Nixon wasn't Mike Douglas. And the officials around an American president rarely value the creativity, spontaneity, and risk-taking that defined live television in the 1960s and '70s. Nixon's people craved control— they wanted everything in a can, prepared and ready to go, and they wanted it the way *they* wanted it. Ailes and the Nixon staff crossed swords on several occasions in 1969. For instance, at the ceremony announcing the appointment of

Warren Burger as the new chief justice of the Supreme Court, Bob Haldeman hated the look and feel of the Ailes-staged event. Entries in Haldeman's diary indicate that he didn't think Ailes had a good feel for how to stage White House events—"probably would have done better without him," he wrote.[2] By 1970 the White House was looking for another media consultant—Haldeman informed Ailes that his services would no longer be needed. Of course, it might have been a good thing to have been fired by Bob Haldeman. It might have meant that Ailes had something going for him. This Nixon staff is the group, after all, about whom Bob Woodward's Deep Throat said, "The truth is, these really aren't very bright guys."

In the early 1970s Ailes had become a known commodity. In addition to the Nixon White House, his political consulting clients in 1970 included the Republican nominee for governor of Florida, Jack Eckerd, and Robert Taft Jr., who was running for the U.S. Senate from Ohio. Ailes had helped Nixon win the White House, and the publication of the McGinniss book had given him notoriety as a communications specialist. But aside from politics, how would he channel that notoriety? What could he do with his creative abilities? Like many young Americans at the time, he spent several years in the 1970s trying to "find" himself—a characterization he probably dislikes, since it makes him sound like a hippie or something.

He formed Ailes & Associates Inc., and he did a little bit of everything. He undertook media consulting for Republican political campaigns, did some TV production, and began providing communications advice to corporations. And for several years, in a most interesting and rather odd chapter of his varied career, he was an off-Broadway producer as well. His career has often exhibited this manic, rather restless search for the next big thing—which must be what attracted him to television in the first place. But dabbling in theatrical production does make sense. Ailes has always had a flair for the theatrical, and one could argue that he has brought that style to his television productions.

He had met the famed Broadway producer Kermit Bloomgarden at a party and struck up a conversation. Soon he and Bloomgarden were making plans to produce a play together. Throughout his career, Ailes has apparently bumped into people and then started working with them in unexpected ways—for example, Richard Nixon, Kermit Bloomgarden, Bob Wright (the NBC executive who hired him to run CNBC), and then Rupert Murdoch. He obviously makes a fine first impression.

In 1972, Ailes and Bloomgarden first threw their weight behind a production called *Mother Earth,* an "environmental" musical. It bombed and closed after just twelve performances. Then Ailes and Bloomgarden invested in a show Ailes had heard about called *The Hot L Baltimore,* written by Lanford Wilson. It was about a group of woebegone characters living in the Hotel Baltimore—an old hotel slated for demolition that was so run-down the sign on the building was missing the *e* in the word *hotel.* Opening early in 1973, the production was actually pretty good—it benefited from the talents of some up-and-coming stars, such as a young Judd Hirsch, who went on to star in the NBC sitcom *Taxi.* The show was a hit. It won several awards and ran for more than three years.

In the mid-'70s *Hot L Baltimore* was adapted by TV producer Norman Lear as a half-hour weekly sitcom. It didn't last, but along with Lear's other TV programs, such as *All in the Family,* it broke new ground for prime-time television. True to the Lanford Wilson play, the show featured network television's first gay couple (residents of the hotel), along with two hookers and a sympathetically portrayed illegal alien. Remember, the play was produced before Ailes went to work for the "family values" candidate George H. W. Bush.

Ailes was bitten by the Broadway bug—he later said he was drawn to the excitement of live stage productions, similar in some ways to live TV. He and Bloomgarden, buoyed by the success of *Hot L Baltimore,* looked for other Broadway opportunities. Their next offering, however, fared more like *Mother Earth.* Called *Ionescopade,* a musical based on the writings of the free-thinking Eugene Ionesco, it opened and closed pretty quickly. The elderly Bloomgarden began to have health problems and passed away in 1976. But Ailes continued to dabble in Broadway, partnering up with promoter John Fishback for a 1977 production called *The Present Tense,* another musical comedy. By the late '70s Ailes had grown bored and/or frustrated with New York's theater scene and turned his attention elsewhere.

When he wasn't developing plays, he was toiling in political campaigns, corporate boardrooms, and doing odd TV work here and there. His stint at Television News Inc., first as a PR consultant, then as its news director, came in 1974–1975. He continued to work in television because he loved it and he was good at it. He won an Emmy in 1977 for a TV special about the work of Italian filmmaker Frederico Fellini, called *Fellini: Wizards, Clowns, and Honest Liars.*

Ailes produced a short-lived talk and variety program for CBS called The Stanley Siegel Show. Then in 1981 he was hired by NBC to be the executive producer of *Tomorrow Coast-to-Coast,* with Tom Snyder and Rona Barrett.

(He would later work with Tom Snyder again when Snyder's program was resurrected by CNBC.) Snyder had become well known nationally for his late-night talk show, *Tomorrow*. Rona Barrett was also a well-known presence in television in the late '70s and early '80s, mainly for her entertainment reporting and gossipmongering. Matching Snyder and Barrett together was like mixing oil and water, and probably helped convince Ailes to spend more time working with political candidates. It was reported that Barrett had threatened to leave the show more than once because she felt Snyder was hogging the airtime. Ailes, known for his work in television and with difficult personalities, was brought in to make it work.

Interestingly, Ailes began his 1988 book, *You Are the Message,* with a story from his time with *Tomorrow Coast-to-Coast*. In what is supposed to be a lesson about eye contact, firmness, and taking control of a situation, Ailes lets the reader know how tough he is by recalling the time he stared down the mass murderer Charles Manson. Ailes and Snyder were at the maximum-security prison in Vacaville, California, to interview the notorious nut. While preparing for the interview, Ailes rounded a corner and ran directly into Manson:

> As our eyes locked, I at first said nothing. I realized that a very primitive confrontation and mutual assessment were taking place. Then I said, "Mr. Manson, I'm in charge of this interview. I'd like you to come with me." For a split second more he stared at me. Then he lowered his head, backed away, and suddenly acted very obsequiously. He was happy to meet me, he said, and wanted to know what I would like him to do ... Once he backed away, I knew I had control for the day.[3]

Having tamed Richard Nixon for a time, perhaps Ailes was well prepared to handle Charles Manson.

Ailes was involved with various other television and production projects in the early '80s. He produced the award-winning documentary *Television and the Presidency,* a history of how these two powerful institutions had transformed and influenced each other. Considering his experience, there was probably no one in the country better suited to produce this film than Ailes.

He had done media consulting for a fair number of Republican candidates in the '70s, but not as many as he could have. His interest in television and his corporate consulting divided his time and attention. A scorecard of political consultants and the outcomes of their races reported by *National Journal* in November 1978 shows two clients for Ailes & Associates and a perfect 2–0 record: the winning U.S. Senate campaigns of then representative William Armstrong of Colorado and of Dave Durenberger of Minnesota. Ailes would become more heavily involved in political campaign consulting in the 1980s as it took on a greater percentage of his business and his time.

By the early '80s he was known as a communications guru. He was sought out for his television and communications expertise by politicians, corporate executives, and television producers. He may have been better known for his political and television work, but he was considered a star by the many corporate executives and business entrepreneurs that flocked to his Manhattan office for communications counseling. A partial roster of his corporate clients sounds like a stock market ticker on Wall Street: American Express, AT&T, the Celanese Corporation, General Electric, Polaroid, Consolidated Foods, Union Carbide, and many others that preferred confidentiality.[4]

In the '70s, the growth of television, along with the increased importance of public speaking in the corporate world, had created a demand for better-trained speakers. Ailes & Associates trained business and corporate officials to improve their ability to handle media interviews, press conferences, presentations to stockholders and directors, boardroom presentations, addresses to civic groups, and even testimony before Congress. For a $5,000 fee, the basic twelve-hour course put the executives through their paces—conducting trial-by-fire interviews, staging tough press conferences, and working on public speaking skills, such as eye contact, posture, and body language. Ailes made it clear that he and his company were not "image makers," as some of his colleagues were being called. The term *image*, he said, has a negative connotation, as if one is creating something that isn't there. "What we do is help people learn to project what they already have."[5]

Ailes said he first realized that the corporate world needed better communications training when he was with *The Mike Douglas Show* back in the 1960s. Ralph Nader had come out with his influential book *Unsafe at Any Speed,* about the lack of safety standards in the American automobile industry. "My talent coordinator booked him, and I was basically a political guy, and it seemed inappropriate not to have somebody else here to refute his allegations. So I called General Motors to try to get a spokesperson. I tried to get an executive. They wouldn't even send a press person. They wouldn't even acknowledge that I or the book existed. They went into the ostrich syndrome."[6] Ailes said that can't happen anymore. Communication is too important and the stakes for the business world are too high not to pay attention to public relations and information campaigns.

Ailes said that it's a new world. Whether it is interoffice contact, interpersonal communication, speaking at a convention or after dinner, people in organizations large and small have to be able to communicate orally. At the time, he told one interviewer that he had two types of clients: "Those who want to improve themselves at all costs, because they see themselves on a fast track. They want to move forward, and they recognize communications is going to help them. Those in the second group are sent by their company. They come in here kicking and screaming, and they don't want anybody to mess with them."[7] He believed that part of the problem was that for years, businessmen were trained to be "poker players." That is, they were taught that part of their success is related to keeping their cards close to the vest and not showing emotion. While that may be true, it can lead to wooden and lifeless public speaking. He said they all sound the same. "Each word is spaced and stressed evenly, so a listener has to concentrate heroically to follow the speaker's argument," he said.

He claimed that the typical businessman is not that different from the typical politician, because many, if not most, politicians tend to come from the business world anyway, so there is a good bit of crossover. Both tend to be reserved, often understated, and inexperienced in front of television cameras. According to Ailes, the best speakers are the ones that are comfortable. "Good communication starts with good conversation," he said. He tried to get his clients to think of giving a speech to an audience as not tremendously different from sitting down and having a conversation with someone. "If you can do that and do it well, then you should be able to transfer that comfort level to any format."

Intuitively, these lessons make sense. They are related to what Ailes has referred to as the "likeability" factor for political candidates. If people feel at ease with you, they are much more open to what you are saying and more likely to hear your arguments. Think of it as the difference between a Reagan and a Nixon—the 1960 version of Nixon anyway. Or think of the more popular and successful television journalists, such as Walter Cronkite or Peter Jennings. They had a natural, conversational style. They didn't shout and bang the desk. Ailes would say they communicated with their eyes and their facial expressions as much as with their voices. Of course, most broadcast journalists have either been trained or have taught themselves to speak in a rhythm and cadence that communicates confidence, an all-knowing competence, and naturally, a certain amount of likeability.

Ailes's sessions with his clients invested heavily in what would probably be called "media training" today. He would videotape them in a variety of formats from casual conversation to giving an extemporaneous speech to reading a corporate speech. Then he and his team would review the tapes, picking out what the clients did well and what they needed to work on. Then they sat down with the clients and went over the tape, trying to get the clients to assess their own strengths and weaknesses. "If we try to help them in an area where they think they are terrific, we are not going to get anywhere," he said.[8] Very often the company that sent a client had their own perspective on what the problems were and what areas needed work. So Ailes and company would have to combine their own expert perspective with that of the client and his or her employer to find some common ground. He said that if they had done their job right, the client normally knew where the problems were—"about 80 percent of our people hit their own problem right on the head ... Then we can progress."[9]

Ailes's work with corporate clients actually foreshadowed some of his later political work. For example, he would teach his clients how to deal with "power struggles" during interviews with reporters. He called it "controlling the atmosphere." He believed that a good reporter knows how to use silence well—some speakers often feel they need to fill every moment with sound—the truth is, they don't, and that is a very hard thing to teach. He encouraged clients to be very cautious in dealing with reporters who might be hostile or fishing for bad news, especially if the interview was to be taped rather than aired live. Some people call it the *60 Minutes* trap, which probably makes CBS's Mike Wallace smile.

> I usually tell them that if they are near retirement and have a golden parachute and wish to go out in a blaze of glory, doing taped interviews is probably a good way to do it. But otherwise, I don't advise them to do TV programs that are extensively edited, because there are too many techniques that they are unaware of. The truth is that they will be interviewed for two hours and the network will use 20 seconds.

But if executives do the "Today Show'" or "'Good Morning America'" which are live or live on tape, they have a fair shot at saying what they want to say and being sure that it's intact. If they do an edited show, they are taking their chances.[10]

Ailes put exactly these lessons on display in the famous 1988 television interview of his client George H. W. Bush by Dan Rather of CBS, as discussed in Chapter 4, "Machiavelli's Love Child."

But Ailes did more than just train business executives to be better speakers. From the 1970s to the 1990s, he enjoyed long-term relationships with some of America's largest and most influential corporations. For example, as Chapter 4 documents, he had a very close and very lucrative long-term relationship with the "Big Tobacco" lobby (funded mostly by Phillip Morris), in which he provided public relations advice and advertising services. His company had established a foothold in corporate America that would generate benefits for him and his clients for years to come.

Beginning in 1979, Ailes was once again working for a presidential candidate, his first since Richard Nixon in 1968. The campaigns of various Republican candidates were gearing up for the 1980 election to see which one of them would have the honor of taking on Jimmy Carter. And Ailes was in the thick of it—only not for the candidate most people today would probably guess. He wasn't working for Ronald Reagan; he was working for John Connally.

It's easy to forget that throughout 1979 and into 1980, a good many Republicans thought that former Texas governor John Connally would be the man to beat. Reagan had almost wrested the nomination away from incumbent president Gerald Ford in 1976, and he sailed into the 1980 campaign with star power and high name recognition. But there were still those that doubted he had what it takes. He was too conservative, like Goldwater in '64, said some. He was a lightweight, just an actor turned politician, said others, especially some media commentators.

Connally had become nationally known when, as Texas governor, he was riding in the front seat of President John Kennedy's car when Lee Harvey Oswald opened fire. Connally was wounded but made a full recovery. A former secretary of the navy, he was an advisor to four different presidents, both Republican and Democrat. He had been a Democrat, but in 1973 he switched to the Republican Party. He had a number of disagreements with the liberal wing of the Democratic Party and felt the GOP held priorities that were closer to his own. Many people at the time thought it was a very courageous thing to do, considering that the Republican Party seemed to be in the act of destroying itself during Watergate. A popular political joke at the time was "John Connally reminds one of that rare event of a rat swimming *toward* a sinking ship!"

The Connally for President campaign used his business and political ties to raise a lot of money early—more than any other GOP candidate, including Ronald Reagan. He announced his candidacy early in 1979 to get a jump on the competition; Reagan didn't officially enter the race until November. The Connally campaign's strategy was to advertise nationally and build him up as the alternative to Reagan. He was the first candidate to run an ad for the 1980 campaign. In October 1979 he bought five minutes of airtime on the CBS network, which began a three-week ad blitz. The Connally advertising was designed to soften the image many had of him as a swaggering, wheeler-dealer business lobbyist. Roger Ailes, who, according to *Newsweek*, masterminded the ad campaign, said, "People have gotten the idea that John Connally is a very tough guy … we're trying to show a gentler side."[11] The ad shows Connally as a Texas rancher and doting grandfather who extols the virtues of marriage.

But while Connally was focusing on a national campaign, Reagan and George H. W. Bush were focusing on the early primary states, Iowa and New Hampshire. Connally was never able to overcome Reagan's appeal and his support among rank-and-file GOP voters. He dropped out of the campaign after a disappointing finish in the South Carolina primary early in 1980.

Another political client of Roger Ailes's in 1980 was the young Alphonse D'Amato, who had defeated longtime senator Jacob Javits, a liberal Republican, in the New York GOP primary. The D'Amato campaign against the Democratic Party nominee, Representative Elizabeth Holtzman, bene-fited from an infusion of cash from the Republican Senatorial Campaign Committee, up to $1 million by some estimates. Ailes produced D'Amato's TV ads, which took the "unusual tack" of featuring D'Amato's sixty-six-year-old mother as a representative of middle-class America, complaining about inflation and crime. The *New York Times* reported that it was the first time, according to veteran politicians, that a New York candidate has used his mother as the "star" of a political commercial.[12] Of course, by the end of the 1980s a number of candidates had cast their mothers in their campaign ads. D'Amato himself appears in the ad in the last few seconds, billed as a fighter for "the forgotten middle-class American."

This began a long-term friendship between Ailes and the bombastic D'Amato, who served three terms in the U.S. Senate before being defeated by Charles Schumer in 1998. D'Amato introduced Ailes to many of his future political clients, particularly in New York—George Pataki and Rudy Giuliani, to name two. In 2003 D'Amato began serving as a political analyst on the Fox News Channel.

Ironically, Ailes seemed to solidify his growing reputation as a premier political campaign consultant in a losing campaign, that of the 1982 Republican nominee for governor of New York, Lew Lehrman. Perhaps Ailes received accolades because the Lehrman campaign seemed to have everything going against it (except for money, that is), yet still almost won. New York was a heavily Democratic state, and Lehrman was a newcomer to politics. He was facing a popular, well-funded Democratic candidate, Lieutenant Governor Mario Cuomo, and 1982 was a bad year for Republican candidates nationally—it was the year of the midterm elections in Ronald Reagan's first term, historically a bad year for the party controlling the White House.

Even with these disadvantages, Lehrman came very close to upsetting Cuomo. Part of his success was due to a huge bankroll. Lehrman, a millionare businessman whose fortune was made in his family's Rite Aid discount drugstore chain, spent about $13 million, much more than Cuomo's campaign did. But another reason Lehrman came so close to winning was a successful campaign strategy of introducing him to New York voters as a new face and a different direction. And central to that strategy were the ads designed by Ailes.

Ailes and Lehrman ran a "get tough on crime" campaign, which appealed to many New Yorkers tired of seeing rising crime statistics year after year. One of his campaign slogans was "it's time to take the handcuffs off the police." He also represented a shift to a more conservative economic philosophy, promising a cut in the state income tax of 40 percent over eight years. But most of all, his TV ads created a fresh, appealing image for the red-suspendered, mild-mannered family man, originally from Pennsylvania. He had an attractive family, with young children who often traveled with him on campaign trips.

The best-known Lehrman ad was one referred to as the outtake spot. It began with the candidate sitting on a stool, sleeves rolled up, addressing the camera, talking about taxes. Then he flubs a line and giggles, which is normally an outtake. But he continues, "That one blew me right off the chair.

Holy mackerel! Too much energy." Then the frame freezes and the camera pulls back to show Lehrman sitting and watching himself on a TV monitor— a spot within a spot. He then turns and addresses the camera: "Hey, I make some mistakes, even taping my commercials. I'll make some mistakes as governor ..."[13] It was a popular ad; it showed him as human, a regular guy able to laugh at himself. Ailes had to convince Lehrman's backers to go with the spot—some of them thought it was undignified. But Ailes said the voters wanted their candidate to show a wide range of emotion. "People understand that politicians are human beings," he said.[14] It's like peeking behind the scenes and seeing the real person, and people like that.

The next several years, 1982 to 1986, cemented Ailes's reputation as one of the top Republican ad men and strategists in the country, as he helped a string of candidates win in convincing fashion. In addition to working for a number of U.S. House and Senate campaigns, he was a consultant to the 1984 Reagan reelection campaign's advertising group, called the Tuesday Team. And of course, as profiled in Chapter 2, "The Image Is the Message," he was brought in by President Reagan's campaign advisors to coach him for his second debate against Democratic nominee Walter Mondale.

By the mid-1980s Ailes had in his stable of clients many of the top names in the national Republican Party—U.S. Senators Phil Gramm, Dan Quayle, James Abdnor, Slade Gorton, Robert Kasten, Warren Rudman, and a number of Republican House members as well. In 1985 he handled the media for two of the GOP's premier gubernatorial campaigns, those of Thomas Kean in New Jersey and George Deukmejian in California. By the time of the 1988 presidential campaign and the star turn of Vice President George H. W. Bush, Roger Ailes was the "go-to guy" for Republican candidates who wanted to win.

Hatching Willie Horton

The commissioners wouldn't authorize a full investigation. I always thought there was more there than meets the eye, we just weren't allowed to proceed.[1]

—Lawrence Noble, General Counsel, Federal Election Commission (1987–2000) on the FEC's failure to investigate claims of illegal coordination between Roger Ailes of the 1988 Bush campaign and the creators of the original Willie Horton TV ad

The Willie Horton ad from the 1988 presidential campaign, produced by an independent group called the National Security Political Action Committee (NSPAC), is one of the most famous political ads of all time. It is famous both for its effects—it helped bring down Democratic presidential nominee Michael Dukakis, who led President Bush in preelection polls and for its nastiness—it injected a historic level of racial fear-mongering and inflammatory rhetoric into the '88 campaign.

Ironically, the first person in 1988 to criticize Governor Dukakis's furlough program for Massachusetts state prisoners was Senator Al Gore. Running for the Democratic nomination, Gore was trying to capture the political middle of the party. During the primaries, he went after Dukakis as too liberal to be elected. Exhibit A: the governor's program that furloughed state prisoners, even violent felons, for the weekend. In a debate on the eve of the New York primary in April, Gore pointedly asked Dukakis about his program that gave "weekend passes for convicted criminals." Gore never mentioned Willie Horton but did say that Dukakis's program was beset with problems and represented an unrealistic view of proper American justice.

Roger Ailes and Lee Atwater, Bush's campaign director, knew a golden opportunity when they saw one. And one had just been dropped in their lap. The Bush campaign's research director, Jim Pinkerton, had watched tapes of the New York debate and brought the Willie Horton case to the attention of the campaign. They knew that Governor Dukakis was one of the leading contenders for the Democratic nomination and that if he were the eventual nominee they would have an issue to use against him.

In May the Bush campaign had organized a series of focus groups in Paramus, New Jersey, with moderate Democrats. These small group discussions with swing voters were designed to test possible Bush campaign messages. At the beginning of the conversations, group participants held a generally favorable view of Dukakis, based on his demonstrated leadership and accomplishments in Massachusetts. Slowly, though, voter sentiments turned more negative as key information uncovered by Bush operatives was revealed.[2]

For example, they informed the group that during his term of office, Dukakis's prison administration had released on furlough a convicted black murderer named William Horton. While free, the inmate had brutally raped a white woman and terrorized her husband. The group's response was overwhelmingly negative. They had not known those aspects of the Dukakis record, and the information made them feel much less positive about Dukakis. The Bush team knew they were onto something.

Within weeks the Bush general election strategy was finalized. Republicans would attack Dukakis's record as governor of Massachusetts. They agreed with Al Gore—Dukakis was too liberal, not patriotic, and soft on crime. The Horton furlough was symptomatic of all that was wrong with Dukakis. Lee Atwater later would boast to party officials, "By the time this election is over, Willie Horton will be a household name."[3]

Roger Ailes was in charge of the Bush campaign's communications and media efforts. Convinced that Willie Horton would be the undoing of Michael Dukakis, he remarked, "The only question is whether we show Willie Horton with a knife in his hand or without."[4] To many observers of the 1988 race, the intentions of Roger Ailes and the Bush campaign were clear—they were going to tie Dukakis as closely as they could to Willie Horton and the Massachusetts furlough program.

But they had to find a way to get their anti-Dukakis message out to the general public without risking the backlash of being too negative. In the view of political communications scholar Darrell West, author of *Air Wars*, they decided on a two-track system.[5] Under West's theory, the official Bush for President campaign would attack Dukakis's crime credentials and record as governor of Massachusetts. The public would have to be educated about the deficiencies of the Massachusetts governor. Ads would be broadcast and speeches delivered emphasizing previously unpublicized information designed to drive down his approval ratings.

At the same time, however, taking advantage of a loophole in campaign finance rules, outside groups such as NSPAC would run a second campaign that was much tougher. Such groups are permitted to spend unlimited amounts of money on behalf of a candidate, as long as their activities are not coordinated in any way with the candidate's campaign. The outside track would feature brass knuckles tactics that would appeal to the basest instincts of the American public on the subject of race. This unauthorized and uncoordinated campaign would say things and run advertisements that could not be said by the official Bush organization.[6]

And who was NSPAC? The industrious Floyd Brown, a staple of shadowy right-wing advocacy groups for more than twenty years, was the political director of Americans for Bush, the organizational parent of NSPAC.[7] Longtime GOP consultant Larry McCarthy was hired by the group to provide advertising and public relations. McCarthy is a long-standing associate of Roger Ailes; he was a vice president of Ailes Communications in the '70s and '80s. It was Floyd Brown, Larry McCarthy, and ad man David Carmen, a public relations specialist, who put the ad together.[8] Another longtime Republican PR specialist, Craig Shirley, also worked for NSPAC in developing the ad.[9] The important point to make here is that none of these individuals had official ties to the Bush campaign. But they sure did share Lee Atwater's goal of "scraping the bark off of Michael Dukakis,"[10] and they obviously shared Roger Ailes's musings about whether or not to show Willie Horton with a knife in his hand.

Some of these names should be familiar to those who follow politics. For example, Floyd Brown and Craig Shirley were both heavily involved in anti–Bill Clinton campaigns in the 1990s. Brown, a coauthor of *Slick Willie: Why America Can't Trust Bill Clinton*, labored throughout the '90s churning out anti-Clinton ads, articles, and "independent" research. Shirley, from his Virginia-based PR firm, has worked for clients such as Paula Jones and Gary Aldrich, the former FBI agent who wrote an "exposé" on the Clintons and their marriage, most of which was later discredited. And both Brown and Shirley were involved in efforts against 2004 Democratic presidential nominee John Kerry. Brown's group, Citizens United, produced and aired ads blasting Kerry for expensive haircuts and his wife's wealth, labeling him as "a rich elitist liberal."[11] Shirley worked for a group called Grassfire.org, which also produced anti-Kerry TV spots in 2004.

As a strategy, the two-track program was brilliant. Ailes, Atwater, and company were, in effect, training a generation of campaign operatives (from both parties) in how to run a negative campaign. Some campaign observers believe this two-track approach encouraged people to exploit, albeit permissively, a loophole in the campaign finance laws and use outside groups to deliver hard-hitting messages on behalf of the candidate. Throughout the '90s and into the twenty-first century, this strategy would become commonplace in American elections. Hello, Move-On.Org and Swiftboat Veterans for Truth!

From September 21 to October 4, 1988, NSPAC and its arm, Americans for Bush, broadcast an ad about Horton entitled "Weekend Passes," which criticized Dukakis's record on fighting crime. Their first ad did not use the menacing mug shot of Horton that made him look, in the eyes of the ad's creator, Larry McCarthy, like "every suburban mother's greatest fear."[12] They knew that the photo was an overt appeal to racial fears and worried it might arouse the ire of network censors, who could refuse to run controversial ads by independent groups. However, after the ad cleared media scrutiny, McCarthy quietly substituted a second version that graphically cited the Horton case and used the now controversial mug shot of the African-American felon.[13]

The commercial was a vintage attack spot. It opened with contrasting pictures of Bush (smiling) and Dukakis (looking grim), while the announcer intoned, "Bush and Dukakis on crime." The commercial contrasted Bush's support for the death penalty with Dukakis's opposition and pointed out that the Massachusetts governor "allowed first-degree murderers to have weekend passes from prison."

At that point, the threatening-looking mug shot of Horton appeared on the screen, and the announcer informed viewers that Horton murdered a boy in a robbery and, despite a life sentence, received a weekend pass from prison. While on one of his ten such furloughs, Horton kidnapped a young couple, stabbed the man, and repeatedly raped the man's wife. The ad closed with the punchline: "Weekend prison passes. Dukakis on crime."

After several weeks of NSPAC's blanketing the nation with the Horton story, the Bush campaign's Revolving Door spot began running on October 5. According to author Kathleen Hall Jamieson, viewers could not help associating Willie Horton from the NSPAC ad with the Bush campaign's official spot. Scripted by Roger Ailes, the commercial made no specific mention of Horton, nor did it show a photo of the felon. But it reiterated the point that Dukakis was soft on crime and had a lenient furlough policy. The bleak black-and-white ad opened with prison scenes, then cut to a procession of prisoners circling through a revolving gate and then walking back toward the camera—straight into the nation's living rooms. Jamieson says that by juxtaposing words and pictures, the ad "invited the false inference that 268 first-degree murderers were furloughed by Dukakis to rape and kidnap."[14] The script of the ad reads:

> As Governor, Michael Dukakis vetoed mandatory sentences for drug dealers. He vetoed the death penalty. His revolving door prison policy gave weekend furloughs to first degree murderers not eligible for parole. While out, many committed crimes like kidnapping and rape. And many are still at large. Now Michael Dukakis says he wants to do for America what he did for Massachusetts. America can't afford that risk.

As the announcer talks, the words *268 escaped* appear on the screen. Focus group members, and presumably millions of TV viewers, interpreted this to mean that 268 first-degree murderers had escaped Massachusetts prisons and committed violent crimes. Actually, in a ten-year period, four murderers had escaped, and one of them, Willie Horton, had committed additional crimes after escaping.[15]

Beginning on September 22 and following, news stories began appearing that told the tragic tale of Angie and Clifford Barnes, the couple assaulted by Horton. While on leave from a Massachusetts prison, Horton had broken into their house. According to the victims, for twelve hours Barnes was "beaten, slashed, and terrorized" and his wife raped.[16]

Using visual images of prison inmates slowly moving in and out of a revolving gate, the ad voice-over proclaimed that "Dukakis had vetoed the death penalty and given furloughs to 'first-degree murderers not eligible for parole. While out of prison, many committed other crimes like kidnapping and rape.'"

October news stories about the Revolving Door ad explicitly mentioned that Clifford Barnes and Donna Cuomo, the sister of the youth murdered by Horton, were appearing on a nationwide speaking tour that visited Illinois, Texas, California, and New York, among other states. Most of these articles did not point out that the $2 million tour was funded by a pro-Bush independent group known as the Committee for the Presidency.[17] Barnes also was a guest on a number of television talk shows, such as Oprah Winfrey's and Geraldo Rivera's.

Shortly thereafter, a political action committee broadcast two "victim" ads featuring Barnes and Cuomo, respectively. Speaking into the camera, Barnes told the story of the rape and assault, and complained, "Mike Dukakis and Willie Horton changed our lives forever ... We are worried people don't know enough about Mike Dukakis."

Cuomo meanwhile argued that "Governor Dukakis's liberal furlough experiments failed. We are all victims. First, Dukakis let killers out of prison. He also vetoed the death penalty. Willie Horton stabbed my teenage brother nineteen times. Joey died. Horton was sentenced to life without parole, but Dukakis gave him furlough. He never returned. Horton went on to rape and torture others. I worry that people here don't know enough about Dukakis's record."

Ailes and company had done it again. The advertising strategy was remarkably effective for Bush. Observers hailed it as a textbook example of attack campaigning. According to Harris polling and other national surveys, the percentage of voters agreeing with the statement that "Michael Dukakis is soft on crime" rose to 65 percent between early September and late October.[18] And due to the two-track strategy, Bush got most of the advantages of attack (such as pinning negative impressions on his opponent) without suffering much of a backlash for the attacks. For example, CBS News/*New York Times* surveys revealed that, until the last week of the campaign, as many people blamed Dukakis as Bush for the negative tone of the campaign.

As with the Lyndon Johnson campaign's Daisy Girl commercial in 1964, one of the things that made the ad strategy so successful was the favorable free news coverage it received. An analysis of network news coverage in 1988 found that newscasts ran segments from the Revolving Door ad ten times in October and November, making it the most frequently aired commercial of the campaign. Overall, twenty-two segments about Bush's crime ads were rebroadcast during the news, compared with four for Dukakis's ads.[19]

By amplifying Bush's claims, news reporters gave the ads even greater legitimacy than they otherwise would have garnered. News accounts quoted election experts who noted that Bush's tactics were effective and that Dukakis's failure to respond was disastrous. Because these assessments appeared in the high credibility framework of news broadcasts, they came across as more believable than had they been aired only as paid advertisements.

Not only were these ads successful at dictating news coverage, research also demonstrated their ability to influence voters. People who said they saw the Revolving Door spot were more likely to report an effect on their policy priorities. Those exposed to the commercial were more likely than others to cite crime and law and order as the most important problems facing the nation.[20] This result is reflected also in voter shifts during the course of the campaign. The percentage citing Bush as "tough enough" on crime went from 23 percent in July to 61 percent in late October. During the same period, the percentage of those feeling Dukakis was "not tough enough" rose from 36 to 49 percent.[21]

These ads were effective on the crime issue, but they also gave another advantage for Bush. The spots aroused racial fears as well. Owing to Horton's visage, made clear in the Weekend Passes ad and network news coverage, race was an obvious factor in how voters saw the crime spree. After all, Republicans had picked the perfect racial crime, that of a black felon raping a white woman.

Experimental research drawing on the Horton case demonstrates that viewers saw the story more as a case of race than crime. According to researchers, subjects who were exposed to news broadcasts about the Horton case responded in racial terms. The ad "mobilized whites' racial prejudice, not their worries about crime." Viewers became much more likely to feel negatively about blacks in general after having heard the details of the case. It was an attack strategy that worked well on several different levels for Republicans.[22]

The timing of the commercials from the Bush campaign and the separate ads developed by NSPAC was a one-two punch that helped do in Michael Dukakis. But from the standpoint of campaign finance law, had the two-track Bush strategy broken the rules on independent expenditures? It was at least clear that the Bush campaign and outside political action committees had engaged in ad and news tactics that dovetailed very nicely.

The original Horton ad had been run by NSPAC, not by the official Bush campaign itself. Indeed, when Bush media advisor Ailes put together the official Bush campaign's crime ad, he was careful not to use the name Horton or include any photos of the black felon. After Democrats protested Bush's blatant use of the race card, Ailes replied that outside group ads were using the Horton picture, but the Revolving Door ad was not.[23] This gave the Bush camp plausible deniability that helped its candidate avoid public condemnation for racist campaigning.

Yet soon Democrats would test the proposition that these efforts truly were uncoordinated. For them, the coincidence in campaign tactics appeared far too convenient to have been accidental. Using federal campaign rules as their guide, the Ohio Democratic Party and a group called Black Elected Democrats of Ohio filed a complaint with the Federal Election Commission (FEC) alleging that the National Security Political Action Committee had violated the law on independent expenditures.

The complaint, filed in May 1990, alleged that the Bush campaign violated campaign finance laws by blurring the distinction between spending by NSPAC and by the official Bush campaign. It was legal for NSPAC to expend funds criticizing Dukakis and supporting Bush's election only if the expenditures were independent and uncoordinated between the two organizations. By law, any spending that was made "in cooperation, consultation, or concert, with, or at the request or suggestion of, a candidate, his authorized political committees, or their agents," represented an illegal "in-kind contribution" in excess of federal contribution limits.

This complaint led to a "limited inquiry" by the Federal Election Commission into the relationship between NSPAC and the Bush campaign by the FEC. Initially the three Democratic appointees to the commission pushed for a full FEC investigation into the matter. But the three Republican commissioners would agree to only a "focused inquiry" limited to interviewing the leadership of NSPAC and the Bush campaign.[24] Officials of both organizations were subsequently interviewed by government lawyers and a variety of documents subpoenaed from each group. Several interesting facts were uncovered that seemed to cast doubt on the independence of the NSPAC expenditures.

For example, Larry McCarthy, the NSPAC media consultant who worked for Americans for Bush and helped to create the Weekend Passes ad, was a past senior vice president of Ailes Communications, Inc. (ACI), the main media consultant for the Bush campaign. According to an affidavit filed by McCarthy, he had worked at ACI prior to January 1987. After that time, he continued to handle projects on "a contractual basis with ACI" through December 1987, at which point he became Senator Robert Dole's media consultant.[25]

During 1988, McCarthy confirmed that he had several contacts with Ailes. Some of these were "of a passing social nature," such as "running into one another in restaurants or at airports." In none of these encounters, McCarthy said, did he "discuss anything relative to the Bush presidential campaign, NSPAC or political matters."[26]

But there were two encounters that were more substantive in nature. In June 1988, shortly before McCarthy was hired by NSPAC as a media consultant, Roger Ailes called him. Ailes apparently had heard that McCarthy was being hired to produce political commercials for NSPAC. He told McCarthy that "prior to learning of my [McCarthy's] relationship with NSPAC he was considering subcontracting with me [McCarthy] to produce media spots for the Bush campaign." McCarthy told Ailes that he "could not speak to him relative to any matters pertaining to the campaign, including media or strategy, because [he] was on retainer with NSPAC."

Ailes's version of the conversation was that he had called McCarthy to tell him "he had 'blown it' because the Bush campaign had considered using McCarthy for some comparative advertising. I [Ailes] explained to him that was now absolutely impossible because of his work for an independent expenditure group."[27]

The second encounter came in October. At that point in the fall campaign, McCarthy interviewed Ailes for a feature in the *Gannett Journal*. However, McCarthy testified that "nothing was discussed relative to NSPAC nor any of the media spots which [he] had produced for NSPAC."[28]

The preliminary FEC inquiry furthermore uncovered that Jesse Raiford of Raiford Communications, Inc., a former employee of Ailes Communications who was responsible for postproduction editing of the Weekend Passes spot, "simultaneously received compensation from NSPAC and the Bush campaign, and that he had expended NSPAC funds for the production of the Willie Horton ad."[29]

These were exactly the types of connections that Democratic critics had anticipated when they filed their complaint. The Bush campaign had gotten great mileage out of its claims to have had no role in producing the Weekend Passes ad. Both the content and timing of that spot was the work of an outside group, Bush officials routinely proclaimed. Such a defense helped deflect critics who felt Bush was using unfair and racist appeals. And yet the evidence of contact between Ailes and McCarthy provided a circumstantial case of possible coordination.

However, despite evidence of communication between the two organizations, the FEC commissioners deadlocked 3–3, along party lines, on whether to launch a full investigation and depose key witnesses. According to Commissioner Thomas Josefiak, a Republican appointee, and the key swing vote on the matter, "explanations of [Ailes's and McCarthy's] actions were plausible and reasonably consistent. Their conduct, even as explained, demonstrated some bad judgment that risked the appearance of or provided the opportunity for coordination . . . However foolish or deserving of criticism, the brief, isolated and insubstantial contact between respondents' agents during the campaign did not appear to involve any communications that, by content or timing, could be said to represent coordination."[30]

Similarly, on Raiford's dual employment between the two organizations, the FEC rejected arguments about coordination because Raiford "performed technical tasks—e.g., organizing film crews, bookkeeping, camera operation, post-production and editing work—for NSPAC and the Bush campaign, and played no role in any substantive or strategic decisions made by either organization."[31] The commission found no direct evidence of illegal coordination and the investigation closed with no finding of a violation of campaign finance laws.

Unlike his colleagues who worked on the Horton ad—Floyd Brown, Larry McCarthy, and Craig Shirley—Raiford hasn't been as visible since the 1980s. But he did make the news in 2000 when he donated archived videotapes of Richard Nixon interviews to the University of Georgia library. The tapes, recorded in 1983 and estimated to be worth around $900,000, feature historian Frank Gannon talking to Nixon about his life, his career, and politics.[32]

The three Democratic members of the commission that investigated the ads surrounding the Bush campaign, Scott E. Thomas, John Warren McGarry, and Danny L. Donald, complained that the three Republican members "refused at the outset" to authorize a full and complete investigation. The three Democrats, in a public statement, said there was "much more the Commission could and should have done in this matter. It is regrettable that, in a case of this importance and magnitude, there were not four votes to undertake a full and complete investigation."[33]

The FEC's general counsel, Lawrence M. Noble, also believed that the commission should have authorized a full investigation. In his report to the commissioners, Noble found that some of the statements by Ailes and McCarthy were inconsistent, and he called into question their denials. But given the "limited" nature of the inquiry, he added, he was unable to resolve the discrepancies.[34] But with the commission deadlocked at 3–3, no further action was authorized. Jesse Raiford, the Ailes employee who had worked on the NSPAC production of the Horton TV ad, was never questioned by the FEC in a sworn deposition.

Noble was frustrated and remains so to this day. During a conversation in November 2006, he told this author that he was certain there was more the commission could have done. "Key witnesses were never deposed," he said. "The history between Ailes, McCarthy, and Raiford, and the incidents of contact during the production of the TV ads should have warranted an official investigation. I always thought there was more there than meets the eye, we just weren't allowed to proceed" because of the 3–3 party line vote that effectively ended the matter.

Noble said that one of the key factors that raised his suspicions of illegal coordination was the now famous photo of Willie Horton used in the NSPAC ad. The original version of the ad didn't show the photo; thus it wasn't made patently clear that Horton was black. However, days later, a revised version of the ad aired with the photo—providing the racial backdrop for the spot's emotional appeal to voters.

According to Noble, just days after the FEC deadlocked, his office received an anonymous phone call. The caller claimed he knew how the photo turned up—that it was provided to NSPAC by someone in the Bush campaign. Of course, anonymous phone calls such as this don't prove anything, but they can sometimes provide additional grounds for launching investigations.

The 1988 campaign was a high-water mark of sorts for many of the individuals involved. And it was a crucial turning point for them and for American politics. Roger Ailes had designed a media and communications campaign for George Bush that was simple, direct, and devastatingly effective. Comparisons were made to the Doyle Dane Bernbach agency ad campaign for Lyndon Johnson that helped destroy Barry Goldwater in 1964.

Lee Atwater had taken a promising but very flawed candidate and guided him to the White House. And, of course, George H. W. Bush became the first sitting vice president in 150 years to win the presidency. But these heady times would be followed by sobering ones.

Tragically, Lee Atwater developed an inoperable brain tumor and passed away in 1991. His illness led him to renew his religious faith and, in acts of repentance, apologize to those he had attacked during his political activities, notably Michael Dukakis. In a February 1991 article for *Life* magazine, Atwater wrote:

My illness helped me to see that what was missing in society is what was missing in me: a little heart, a lot of brotherhood. The '80s were about acquiring—acquiring wealth, power, prestige. I know. I acquired more wealth, power, and prestige than most. But you can acquire all you want and still feel empty. What power wouldn't I trade for a little more time with my family? What price wouldn't I pay for an evening with friends? It took a deadly illness to put me eye to eye with that truth, but it is a truth that the country, caught up in its ruthless ambitions and moral decay, can learn on my dime. I don't know who will lead us through the '90s, but they must be made to speak to this spiritual vacuum at the heart of American society, this tumor of the soul.

For President Bush, his fortunes in 1991 and 1992 conspired to end his presidency after one term. The combination of a sputtering economy, an infamous broken tax cut pledge, and a changing global economy was too much for him to overcome. President Bush, during his second presidential campaign, also received some of the most negative press coverage of any political candidate in the modern era. A large part of the reason for that, in the estimation of many observers, was the shallow, intensely hostile campaign he and his organization had run in 1988. The Willie Horton episode, campaign trips Bush made to flag factories, and his overreliance on attack messages hardened the attitudes of the many in the press corps against him.

The 1988 campaign is seen as one of the most negative of all time. Its success helped give credence and credibility to a new generation of attack messages and mudslinging. And it is remembered for fanning racial flames in order to win votes. In the words of Kathleen Hall Jamieson, dean of the Annenberg School for Communication, the Horton ad created "a black face for crime."[35]

And as the next chapter makes clear, 1988 was the climax of Roger Ailes's career in politics. He became a hot potato, and a few years and a few disastrous elections later, he was "redefining" his career once again.

8

Ailes Bails (Out of Politics)

I don't agree with this idea about negative campaigning being so awful. . . the news media last fall [1988] overplayed the "negative ad"' story because reporters are lazy, and instead of talking about issues, they'd rather talk about negative ads.

—Roger Ailes[1]

If you're looking for a turning point in twentieth-century politics, when the nastiness began to get out of control and the politics of personal destruction was cranked into overdrive (where it remains today), many would point to 1988. It was certainly a turning point of sorts for Roger Ailes. It represented his crowning achievement in the trenches of politics, but it was also his last political hurrah.

Ailes's work on behalf of George Bush and Lee Atwater had earned him the ignominious (or inglorious) title Mudslinger-in-Chief for many Americans. To Democrats, he was the evil power behind the White House throne—a kind of Darth Vader. To many journalists and political observers, he became a symbol for what was wrong with American politics, an example of excess and ill will.

He got plenty of political consulting work after 1988; he was a star in Republican campaign circles. But unfortunately for his clients over the next couple of years, *Ailes became the message,* and the message was mostly bad news. He became synonymous with dirty politics. Even today he gets much of the credit or blame for the increasingly negative tone of national politics over the last couple of decades. Commentators from the left and right, as well as other political consultants and candidates, created a buzz that followed Ailes wherever he roamed.

And the media seemed to relish his comeuppance. "Negative Ad Wizard Becomes Part of the Issue" blared one headline in the *Washington Post* in May 1989. When Ailes was hired by a business group in Denver to campaign against building a new airport he became part of the stroy. Within hours after Ailes's first television spot hit the airwaves, the pro-airport forces hit back, making Ailes himself the issue. Airport backers called a news conference to attack him as a "slash and burn New York media manipulator." The group then ran their own ad about Ailes, calling him a "master of the slick and sleazy." And local Denver media also got into the act. Both daily newspapers in the city editorialized against Ailes, each calling him a "liar."[2]

Ailes erupted with his legendary anger. "I am not Attila the Hun," he roared to an interviewer. "What's going on is some very inflammatory personal attacks ... If I smeared somebody like this, the media would go crazy ... What's happening is that the *Denver Post* is about to go under. A bunch of frightened reporters who think they're losing their jobs ... they're trying to smear me. They've become masters of the smear. The power of the press is that they can destroy anybody they want, and they're trying to destroy me to save their ass."[3]

Ailes threatened to sue the political operatives who made the pro-airport TV ad that criticized him personally. And he said he was going to sue the *Denver Post* and *Rocky Mountain News* unless they ran editorials retracting their criticism of him. He suggested that the editorials say, "Roger Ailes has had a distinguished career as a media consultant, and it was unfair and inaccurate for us to criticize him personally."[4] The newspapers refused. Democratic political operative John Frew, creator of the anti-Ailes TV spot, believes the ad worked because Ailes gave them an opening: his first anti-airport ad included factual errors, such as putting the proposed airport in the wrong county. This led credence to charges that the anti-airport campaign was calling in out-of-town attack artists who knew nothing of local issues.

In the end, Ailes's side lost big. To be fair, polls showed that most Denver residents had supported a new airport all along. But there is no doubt that the controversy surrounding Ailes, along with the public relations baggage he carried from his political reputation, sank any chance the anti-airport group had of winning the referendum.

Frew, the Democratic ad man, crowed about taking down Ailes: "We met him in the street and shot him right between the eyes and it worked."[5] Nationally, Democrats took heart from the encounter. In fact, political strategists for the

Democratic National Committee adopted a strategy of using Ailes's reputation against his Republican clients. Mike McCurry, the DNC communications director and later a Clinton White House press secretary, encouraged Democratic state chairmen around the country to call a press conference when Ailes showed up and "remind people of his track record ... The level of outrage about negative ads is great enough that Ailes has become an issue everywhere he goes."[6]

"If I were in a knife fight, I would want Roger on my side, but that doesn't mean I have to like a lot of the stuff he is doing," said one Republican political consultant. "Many of the negative ads, even when factually accurate, raise marginal issues that have little to do with a candidate's fitness for office; and these ads often appeal to people's worst instincts. I'm afraid that Roger has begun to set a standard that other media consultants are quick to imitate."[7]

According to senior White House officials, to counter his image as a ruthless slash-and-burn political consultant, Ailes asked the Bush White House for a more visible role as a presidential advisor.[8] Apparently, the furor had started to take a toll on his political consulting business. By his own admission, he lost the chance to land one U.S. Senate candidate, Colorado Republican Hank Brown, because of the negative publicity surrounding his work in Denver.

Around the same time the anti-airport campaign was falling apart in Denver, Ailes was hired by New York City mayoral candidate Rudy Giuliani. His hiring of Ailes was controversial, not only because of Ailes's growing reputation as an attack artist, but also because Ailes had been working for one of Giuliani's Republican primary opponents, cosmetics millionaire Ronald Lauder.

After working for Lauder for two months, Ailes said he left because Lauder's campaign was planning a series of negative attacks on Giuliani. This, coming from the impresario of attack campaigning, is a bit hard to believe. In all probability there were other reasons for the rift between Ailes and Lauder—perhaps creative differences, a battle for control, or fee structure. It does seem that there may have been too many cooks in the kitchen. Lauder's primary campaign strategist had been legendary New York political operative and attack artist Arthur Finkelstein. Lauder and Finkelstein had been brought together by U.S. Senator Al D'Amato, who was one of Finkelstein's main clients. Ailes may have bailed when he realized he couldn't run the show as he was accustomed to—a pattern he would repeat some years later at NBC. But Lauder and his campaign cried foul when Ailes jumped ship. Lauder called his hiring an "unethical act" by Giuliani and a conflict of interest by Ailes, because he had been a significant part of the Lauder campaign and had seen confidential polling data.[9]

Ailes defended his actions. A Giuliani campaign spokesman said Ailes "was appalled by what he saw in the Lauder campaign … and he wanted to work for us."[10] This incident may remind one of the scene from the movie *Casablanca* in which the prefect of police declares that he is "shocked, shocked to see there is gambling going on in this café!" This, just before the casino manager hands him his winnings from a night at the roulette wheel.

Giuliani ignored the ruckus and rejected any innuendo about Ailes's reputation as a slash- and-burn consultant. He went on to win the nomination, but faced an uphill battle in the fall election against the Democratic Party nominee, the popular Manhattan bureau chief of the party, David Dinkins.

Dinkins, for the most part, sat on his lead and tried to ignore Giuliani. But Ailes wouldn't let him. With the involvement of Ailes, the New York media had anticipated a brawl, and they were not to be disappointed. As detailed in Chapter 3, "Fairness Is for Sissies," this campaign featured Ailes and Giuliani attempting to manufacture another Willie Horton. Ailes told one reporter that the challenge in running against Dinkins was to admit that he was a nice, likeable guy, but that he had an awful public record. "He's not a bad guy," said Ailes, but "his public performance has been disgraceful … David Dinkins was a financial disaster personally and as an administrator—that is what the record shows."[11]

Continuing the get-tough strategy that was so successful for George Bush the year before, Ailes and Giuliani went for the jugular. One ad features a small, tight facial shot of Dinkins, while a heavy, ominous voice warns that "David Dinkins failed to file his income taxes for four straight years." Mr. Dinkins did fail to file his income taxes for four years but insists that he had long ago voluntarily admitted the "oversight" when he was being considered for a job with the city.

Another ad produced by Ailes charges that Dinkins did not report his campaign contributions accurately, hid his links to a failing insurance company, and paid a "convicted kidnapper" through a phony organization with no members, no receipts, and no office. "David Dinkins," says the tagline. "Why does he always wait until he's caught?" The "kidnapper" referred to in the ad is Sonny Carson, an African-American community organizer for the Dinkins campaign, examined in some detail in Chapter 3.

Dinkins admitted he was on the board of an insurance company with financial problems, but he said Giuliani's claims implying that he tried to hide it were patently false and malicious. The Dinkins campaign blamed inaccurate campaign contribution reports on computer errors but took offense with the broadside aimed at Sonny Carson. Mr. Dinkins told reporters he didn't know that Carson, who helped coordinate get-out-the-vote efforts, was convicted of kidnapping, but that he definitely did have an office and his organization did have members.[12]

Now it was open war. Prodded by attacks on his ethics and his character, Dinkins returned fire. His consultants unleashed a negative ad of their own. In a dig at Giuliani's honesty, the ad shows two distorted, unrecognizable photos of two politicians. "Compare two candidates for mayor," says the announcer. "One says he's for banning cop-killer bullets. The other has opposed a ban on cop-killer bullets. One claims he's pro-choice. The other has opposed a woman's right to choose. Funny thing—both of these candidates are Rudolph Giuliani," he says, as the photos, both of Giuliani, come into focus.

A Giuliani campaign spokesman said the Dinkins ad was deceptive. Everyone "knows Giuliani has been pro-choice," he said, "even though he has personal reservations ... and he is generally opposed to cop-killer bullets, but he has had some reservations about the language in the proposed legislation."[13]

In media interviews, Ailes also claimed that there had been a double standard applied to coverage of Dinkins and Giuliani. He argued that because Mr. Dinkins is thought of as a nice guy, and because of his symbolic importance as the first African-American candidate for New York City mayor, he had escaped rigorous scrutiny during the campaign. "There has been a double standard to some degree," he said. "Rudy (Giuliani) was ripped apart and examined. Dinkins was not. I happen to think that the media hasn't been doing its job in examining his record."[14]

But coming so quickly on the heels of 1988 and the year of the Willie Horton saga, Ailes's motives were questioned by many. After Horton, the sensitivity to racial issues was very high. Ailes seemed to be complaining that Dinkins was receiving special treatment because of his race while, at the same time, Ailes was clearly comfortable stoking racial insensitivity with TV ads and campaign statements about Dinkins and his staff—particularly in regard to the attacks on Sonny Carson.

This was the second major campaign in twelve months in which Ailes had been involved where race became a prominent feature throughout. For some, particularly in the New York media, it represented an Ailes/race pattern. Some Democrats accused the Giuliani campaign of agitating the racial climate in New York City. Those perceptions grew when a Yiddish newspaper ran an anti-Dinkins advertisement showing a picture of Dinkins with the Reverend Jesse Jackson, who is a controversial figure among Jews, largely for his inflammatory use of the word *Hymietown* to describe New York City while he was a candidate for president in 1984.

To make matters worse, there were derogatory remarks about Mr. Dinkins by the comedian Jackie Mason after he had signed on to help the Giuliani campaign. Mason apologized and gave up a formal role in the campaign, but it added to the tensions threatening to boil over. Ailes said Mason went too far, but he defended the campaign's advertisement in the Yiddish newspaper. He claimed there was no intention to send racial messages with the ad. "If Mr. Dinkins didn't object to standing on the stage with Jesse Jackson, how could he object to the picture?" he asked. "If Ted Kennedy was up there, we would be talking about Ted Kennedy."[15]

By the final weeks of the race, the Giuliani campaign seemed unable to close the gap with Dinkins—he still had a double-digit lead in most polls. So leading up to Election Day, the Giuliani campaign's attacks on Dinkins grew "increasingly shrill," according to the *Washington Post*'s Howard Kurtz.[16] A last-minute ad produced by Ailes was certainly shrill enough, yet fit Ailes's playbook. It was yet another spot featuring Sonny Carson, this time shown leading a demonstration at city hall and reminding viewers of his criminal past and his relationship to the Dinkins campaign. "A scurrilous attack," said Dinkins's media advisor, Robert Shrum, "and one last roll in the mud ... Some of this will be counterproductive for them ... Maybe I have more faith in human nature than Roger Ailes, who obviously has none."[17]

Dinkins won the election, though it was closer than the polls showed it to be. The Ailes attack machine had worked to some degree, focusing on race and ethical questions. But it also had the effect of driving up the turnout among African-American voters to near an all-time high, complicating Giuliani's efforts to overcome the strong Democratic Party tide in New York City.

Some analysts believed that Ailes had miscalculated by waging a bitterly negative campaign against the mild-mannered, grandfatherly Dinkins. Until the bitter TV ad campaign, many black leaders in NYC had been feuding, eroding the potential base for Dinkins. But African-American leaders, both locally and nationally, rallied to Dinkins's cause in the face of the televised onslaught by the Giuliani campaign.

Next door in New Jersey, Ailes and his reputation for attack campaigning was also one of the prime issues in the race for governor. He represented Rep. Jim Courter in his campaign for governor against Rep. James Florio. His reputation preceded him to the point where Rep. Florio, the Democrat, actually attacked first. Florio took Courter's hiring of Ailes as a sign that he planned to play rough, so Florio decided to take the initiative. A Florio campaign ad called Rep. Courter a "serial polluter" because of his votes in the U.S. House against bills urging environmental controls. Florio justified his preemptive strike on Courter by saying "his attack dog Roger Ailes is going to come after me."[18]

And "go after" Florio is just what Ailes and the Courter campaign did, running ads accusing Florio of being "soft on crime and drugs." Both campaigns called the opponent a "liar," and justified the other side's "lies" with their increasingly negative campaigns. "It is a perfect case study of a negative campaign," said Phillip Friedman, a Democratic political consultant, "where in order not to get hurt by negative ads, the opponent throws out negatives that are even stronger."[19] Ailes said that if the Courter campaign had not retaliated, it would have been like unilateral disarmament and his client's reputation would have been destroyed.

Earlier that year, during the Republican primary, Ailes had produced an ad for Courter reminding voters of the nasty tone of the 1988 elections. The ad said the 1988 U.S. Senate race in New Jersey between Pete Dawkins and Frank Lautenberg had been much too negative and that New Jersey deserved better. Of course, the Courter ad did not mention that his media consultant (Ailes himself) was Dawkins's media consultant in 1988 and was responsible for the worst of those ads.

Throughout the entire campaign Florio maintained a double-digit lead in the polls, and he trounced Courter 62 percent to 38 percent on Election Day. But that didn't stop him from hammering Courter throughout the fall campaign with a barrage of controversial negative ads—using Ailes as his reason for going negative all along. "If you treat it like a tea party when the other side has a machete, you'll get chopped up," said Florio.[20] Unlike the Giuliani/Dinkins race, the Florio/Courter race for governor of New Jersey was never close. It may be that 1989 was a Democratic Party year, but if so, it was partly due to the bad taste left in the mouths of so many voters from the excesses of 1988, including the Bush/Dukakis race and the Dawkins/Lautenberg race in New Jersey.

Ailes was unapologetic and combative, as always. He said he was being targeted by the Democratic Party and by the media because of his success. "I'm not going to change my style," he said. "Has it hurt my reputation? No. I never had a good reputation to begin with. Is it likely to get me angry and make me more effective? Yes."[21]

The next year, when Senator Paul Simon of Illinois was gearing up for his reelection run, he saw Ailes coming, just as Jim Florio did. And he had the same reaction. In fact, Senator Simon used the specter of Roger Ailes to help him raise money. In three separate fund-raising letters, he urged financial contributions to help him fight back against the "Republican attack dog Roger Ailes."

Simon's Republican opponent in that 1990 campaign, Representataive Lynn Martin, was a very popular Illinois congresswoman, who had become something of a national figure. She was expected to be a serious challenger to Simon, who had run for and lost the Democratic nomination for president in 1988. But she knew her consultant had a public relations problem. She knew what she was getting with Ailes—she was getting the premier political media consultant in the country. But she was also getting all the baggage that came with it. So the two of them devised a PR strategy designed to combat the growing "negatives" associated with hiring the renowned political consultant.

Martin accompanied Ailes on an Illinois media tour. They set up private meetings with the editors of major newspapers around the state in an effort to try to preempt some of the negative portrayals of Ailes. She was, in effect, trying to de-fang him. "We said, 'Would you like to meet this awful person? You might be surprised,'" said Martin.[22] Ultimately, the strategy was unsuccessful—partly because the Illinois Senate race was very bitter and very personal, largely because of Ailes's own big mouth.

Initially, some commentators thought that all of the consultant-bashing going on after the 1988 election would result in fewer negative attacks in subsequent campaigns. In Democratic campaign circles, it was common to say that in 1988, Dukakis did not fight back hard enough against the Bush/Ailes attacks. "We're not going to make the mistake that Mike Dukakis made," Simon said at the kickoff rally for his campaign. "If the opposition plays hardball, we're going to play hardball." Other Democratic candidates around the country made similar comments.

Actually, the Dukakis campaign had launched their fair share of negative TV ads against George Bush. The key difference was that Dukakis's ads didn't resonate with the public nearly as well as Bush's. So Democrats like Simon were putting the public, as well as the media, on notice that they were prepared to "go nuclear" if that was what it took. Far from resulting in fewer negative ads, this kind of bravado actually increased the number of such ads in the 1990 elections.

The "nuclear" pace of the 1988 election campaign may have raised the voters' threshold of indignation, paving the way for more cynicism and even rougher political attacks in subsequent campaigns. Kathleen Hall Jamieson of the Annenberg School for Communication at the University of Pennsylvania believes the threshold was raised. "The pattern is that once you get two dirty campaigns in a state, by the third campaign, the voters aren't appalled anymore," she said.[23]

Paul Simon's relatively high profile in the U.S. Senate made him an inviting target for the Republican Party, and his strongly liberal views made him a vulnerable one, at least in the eyes of Republican campaign operatives. In the fall of 1989, Ailes, along with Republican pollster Robert Teeter and Republican Party chair Lee Atwater, convinced Lynn Martin that she could beat Senator Simon. But it would take money. They told her that if she could raise $8 million, she was a shoo-in.

But she couldn't raise $8 million; in the end she raised and spent about $5 million. The Simon campaign had done a good job of inoculating him against the attacks to come from Martin and had had tremendous success raising a ton of money by using Ailes's name as a scare tactic.

And the Martin campaign had its share of missteps. For instance, she opened the campaign talking about what a big and diverse state Illinois is, and referred to downstate voters as "rednecks."[24] She also never found a way to counter the political damage done by President Bush's reversal on the "no new taxes" pledge—something all Republican candidates had to contend with in 1990. Also, Illinois had never before elected a woman to statewide office.

All these problems made it difficult for her to raise the money necessary to beat a U.S. Senate incumbent. Statewide television advertising in Illinois is incredibly expensive, and the Martin campaign was unable to keep up the pace set by Simon. By mid-October, less than three weeks from Election Day, they couldn't afford to stay on TV—"We're off the air, for now," said Ailes.[25] They were conserving their cash for the campaign's final ad push before the election.

The lack of cash and the inability to counter Simon's advertising frustrated the Martin campaign, especially Ailes. So in an effort to shake up the race and respond to some of Simon's charges, Ailes decided to put himself out front. He called a news conference in Chicago to defend Ms. Martin. He must have figured that if he was an issue anyway, he might as well try to use the publicity. But it didn't go so well. He seemed to violate some of his own rules when it comes to communication and politics. He overreached. He called Senator Simon names. He accused him of lying.

"People like Paul Simon are the ones who are hurting America," he said. "Simon is just being Simon, which unfortunately is being slimy … He has ethical problems and he gets away with it because of that bow tie … So far as I can tell, he and the truth have never met … Well, I'm sick and tired of it … He's a complete fraud."[26] Perhaps worst of all, Ailes called the senator a "weenie."

That seemed to do it. Lynn Martin was forced to apologize to Senator Simon for her consultant's "impolitic" remarks. Her campaign against the senator was doomed. As a consolation prize, and perhaps as an apology for having to live with the combative Ailes, the next year she was appointed U.S. secretary of labor by President Bush.

Roger Ailes's twenty-three-year sojourn into political media consulting ended in 1991, after one last car-crash of a campaign. This one was supposed to have been easy. Dick Thornburgh was a dream candidate in many ways. The Pennsylvania native was a former two-term governor, and he had served as George Bush's attorney general as well as holding other government posts. He was experienced in politics, well funded, and a close ally of President Bush's. His Democratic opponent, Harris Wofford, was virtually unknown, having been appointed interim senator the previous May.

Thornburgh started the campaign with a seemingly insurmountable forty-five-point lead in the polls. And his campaign team included Republican heavyweights like Ailes and Robert Teeter. So what happened? The chickens were coming home to roost.

Wofford's come-from-behind victory over Thornburgh stunned the nation, especially the political classes. Thornburgh had the misfortune of running a high-profile political campaign at a time when the standing with the public of his good friend President Bush was in rapid decline, along with the public's confidence in the economy. The recession of '91 was hitting with full force, as unemployment went up, interest rates remained stubbornly high, and the Bush administration seemed not to know what to say or do about any of it.

And Thornburgh ran a self-destructively negative, smash-mouth campaign against Wofford and the Democrats. The most notorious example was a TV ad that showed grainy photos of the billionaire Saudi arms dealer Adnan Khashoggi, who was internationally known for shady financial dealings and arms smuggling. An announcer says, "Adnan Khashoggi. Notorious big arms dealer. Key figure in Iran-Contra. What kind of man would solicit money from him? Harris Wofford!" A grainy photo of Wofford then fades into the picture.[27]

The Thornburgh campaign was implying that Wofford was working with sinister forces. The problem is that the ad is not even close to being true, and it was easy to disprove. In the late '70s, Wofford was president of Bryn Mawr College in Pennsylvania, when Khashoggi offered to finance a Middle East Studies center. Wofford suggested instead that Khashoggi endow a scholarship at the college. Khashoggi declined.[28] That should have been it. But his advisors must have believed they could use the case, as weak as it was, against Wofford. Most observers considered the ad to be a case study in deception and innuendo. The negative fallout from the overaggressive advertising was a body blow to Thornburgh's campaign. Several Pennsylvania newspapers ran editorials highlighting the facts of the case and accusing Thornburgh and Ailes of lying.[29] Wofford's campaign responded with an ad using the controversy to question Mr. Thornburgh's honesty. Game-set-match!

Amazingly, Ailes claimed that Thornburgh lost because he didn't go negative harder and sooner, as Ailes had urged him to. Republicans were in a state of high anxiety. They knew they were in trouble heading into 1992. After all, Dick Thornburgh was a prototypical Bush Republican. If he could lose like he did, then so could the president. And Roger Ailes, the Republicans' superstar consultant, had just taken a drubbing.

It had been only three years since Bush's victory over Dukakis, the Republicans' third presidential term in a row, and the year of the Willie Horton controversy. But Bush, Ailes, and the rest of the Republican brain trust seemed to be at the end of a long road.

One road was certainly coming to an end for Roger Ailes. In December 1991 he announced that he was giving up politics. He had been widely expected to head up President Bush's reelection effort in 1992. But after a string of disappointing campaigns, and a sea change in the country's political tides, it seemed a career change was in the offing. In truth, Ailes had become a political liability, and he knew it. He told one reporter that he feared his involvement in the 1992 Bush campaign would backfire on the president.[30]

That assessment is shared by other observers of American politics. According to David Beiler of *Campaigns & Elections* magazine, Ailes was "a problem because he's become an issue in so many campaigns. In any campaign where he's involved, the editorialists are quick to point out that it's Ailes doing the mudslinging. Lynn Martin definitely got hurt by it. He really became a distraction and a bit of an albatross."[31]

But that isn't how Ailes described it to one interviewer in 2003. "I just got tired of it," he said. "It was a pain in the ass. I was getting older, the candidates were getting younger, I was having to explain too many things... I decided the old role of media consultant was changing. In the old days, you used to be able to win or lose on the candidate's voting record or public statements or strategy or tactics. By the late '80s, everybody was hiring private detectives and doing crazy stuff."[32] If that sounds like a massive rationalization, it probably is.

Perhaps the worst part, as far as the American public is concerned, is that Ailes and others proved how effective negative campaigning can be. Ailes himself may not have stayed in politics, but the style of attack campaigning he nurtured and encouraged sure did. "In a way," said one political consultant, "Roger Ailes has done the whole industry a favor; because from now on, candidates are going to be more convinced than ever that they need to hire a consultant who can really nail the other guy."[33] And the more that campaigns are waged as winner-take-all slugfests, the more cynical and disbelieving the viewing public becomes. And that raises the threshold for grabbing their attention. "Unless you jolt them, you won't get results," said a rival media consultant.[34]

Ailes left political consulting, but he became even more powerful and influential with his next career move. It had been an interesting twenty-five years in politics. But now Roger Ailes was returning full-time to his first love—television.

9

What's the Oprah Winfrey Show Without Oprah?

No one ever accused ol' Roger of being demure . . .
I guess it's just another lowering of the civil limbo
bar . . . the line gets moved everyday, sometimes
perceptibly and sometimes imperceptibly.

—Former Bush speechwriter Christopher Buckley[1]

Roger Ailes had already returned to broadcasting and producing even before he left politics at the end of 1991—well, sort of. Ever the showman, he had always mingled his two career paths, politics and TV. And in the spring of 1991, an opportunity came along for a TV show that he just couldn't resist.

The All-Star Salute to Our Troops was a two-hour broadcast special on CBS to celebrate the troops returning from the Persian Gulf war. Broadcast live from a flag-filled, patriotically decorated hangar at Andrews Air Force Base outside Washington, the TV spectacular featured the likes of Sophia Loren, Glenn Ford, Charlton Heston, Richard Thomas, Alan Alda, Barbara Mandrell, Andy Griffith, Randy Travis, and the original "Tie a Yellow Ribbon Round the Old Oak Tree" man himself, Tony Orlando.[2] And the executive producer of the show? Roger Ailes.

There were other welcome-home shows for the troops on other networks, like the *Welcome Home Heroes with Whitney Houston* on HBO or NBC's *Bob Hope's Yellow Ribbon Party.* But only Ailes's TV show could boast the presence of the president and first lady of the United States.

To hear Ailes tell it, there was never even a thought given to the possibility of the program having any partisan political overtones or playing a role in the reelection campaign of President Bush the following year. He scoffed at the notion that the president would even need any help from a TV special. "I don't know how many more points you could get" in the polls, he said.[3] President Bush's approval rating was in the 80s at the time, a historic high for a sitting president.

Not surprisingly, the Democratic Party had a different take on the whole affair. A spokesperson for the Democratic National Committee said that while doing a TV special celebrating the homecoming of the troops was a "terrific" idea, it was inappropriate for a network to air a special produced by the president's "hired gun" from his 1988 campaign. "I wonder just how comfortable CBS is going to be with this in 17 months when they see this two-hour production sized down to a 60-second spot," the spokesperson said.[4]

"Sour grapes," Ailes retorted. "What can I tell you? The Democrats are very bitter people because they can't get their people elected."[5] He noted that he'd had a long history as a TV producer and that he had included Democrats in the program, such as the actor Alan Alda. Yet, no one who had ever seen or heard about the Man in the Arena programs that Ailes had produced for Richard Nixon could seriously doubt the political nature of the *All-Star* program. It was simply a win-win situation for the president and for Ailes.

Even after he "left" politics in the early '90s, he couldn't stay out of it completely. Ailes was brought in by the White House to help with President Bush's State of the Union address in late January 1992 and, more importantly, that August at the Republican National Convention to assist with the president's acceptance speech for his renomination. His involvement with Bush at the convention led to speculation, and even some reporting, that he was about to take a formal role in the Bush reelection campaign. He quashed this speculation quickly, however. "No way," he said. "I made a commitment to get out of politics, and outside of informal advice to the president on major speeches and debates when called on, I'm not getting back in."[6]

Since leaving the active political stage after 1991, Ailes had been doing television consulting work for clients like 20th Century Fox and Multi-Media Entertainment, and also doing what he termed "corporate crisis" consulting. He was readopting the "Roger the Guru" business model from the '70s and '80s, only focused more on television. By late 1992 he had lost thirty pounds, shaved off his trademark goatee, and completely refocused Ailes Communications, Inc., into a television entertainment production company.

In a way, he was returning to his *Mike Douglas* roots. He was able to put his TV experience to work when he was hired by Paramount Domestic Television to help develop the *Maury Povich Show* for the competitive daytime TV talk wars. And he was also a consultant for some of Paramount's other television shows, such as *Hard Copy*, *John & Leeza*, and *Entertainment Tonight*. And in the move most reminiscent of his *Mike Douglas* years, he struck a syndication agreement to produce and distribute a television program for Multi-Media Entertainment starring radio talk star Rush Limbaugh. Ailes served as the show's executive producer, even after he was hired by NBC in 1993.

Ailes Communications became a whirlwind of activity, much as Ailes had been in the 1970s, when he couldn't quite decide if he wanted to be a political media consultant, a corporate image consultant, or an off-Broadway producer—so he did all three. He said his blood was pumping again and he couldn't wait to show people what he could do in television.

His "sideshow" approach to television production was also evident. His stated goal was to have ten shows on the air within a few years, and he embarked on a nationwide talent search for performers and personalities that could carry a show. Presumably, that's when he encountered ambitious performers such as radio host Sean Hannity, tabloid TV's Bill O'Reilly, the journalistic vagabond Geraldo Rivera, and others whom he would later use at CNBC and Fox.

He told one media industry reporter that he planned to use strategic research from his years in political media consulting to find the right niche for certain television programs and develop a stable of TV personalities. His previous success in creating compelling TV programming and either finding the right performer or tailoring a program around a performer was unquestioned. To Ailes, it was all about personality and performance. "One of the biggest mistakes producers make today," he said, "is that they think they are living in a totally topic-driven world. But what's 'The Oprah Winfrey Show' without Oprah?"[7]

This would be his modus operandi in building successful TV programming, both later at CNBC and especially at Fox News. Content is secondary, almost incidental to what really works on TV—production values, intriguing personalities, news talk, and compelling performances. At CNBC Ailes had the chance to work his magic at the cable network level.

Since its inception, the Consumer News and Business Channel (CNBC) had had what many industry observers called an identity crisis. But that wasn't unusual for cable channels in the early '90s, when the industry was exploding in growth and, at the same time, fragmenting into different markets with different niches and different audiences. By the early '90s there were more than seventy cable networks available on a national level, with more in development and on the way. Amazingly, in just one eighteen-month span, between early 1994 and late 1995, there were fifteen new cable networks launched:[8]

Americana TV Network	(Independent)
Cable Health Club	(Int. Family Entertainment)
Spice 2	(Graff PPV)
Starz!	(Encore)
Turner Classic Movies	(Turner Broadcasting)
Q2	(QVC)
America's Talking	(NBC)
Television Food Network	(Providence Journal Co.)
FX	(Fox)
BET on Jazz	(BET)
Encore Multiplex	(Encore)
Independent Film Channel	(Bravo)
Home & Garden Network	(Scripps Howard)
Romance Classics	(AMC/Rainbow)
The History Channel	(A&E)

Obviously, the cable marketplace was getting crowded. And with the channel capacity on most cable systems (around forty or so channels at the time) filling up, it meant that cable operators had to push their channel capacity to their limits or bump existing cable networks off the system.

In this viciously competitive environment, only the networks that could build an audience quickly would survive. But what kind of programming will keep an audience after business hours, when the stock market is closed and most viewers turn their attention to other issues? Initially, the decision was made to focus evening programming on personal consumer issues and stories related to finance and investments. But after only a few months, the network brass saw the handwriting on the wall—hardly anyone was watching CNBC in the evening—ratings were abysmal. For that matter, its daytime ratings weren't setting the world on fire either.

Then they tried to spice things up. Instead of relying only on financial and consumer issues for its evening programming, CNBC execs added talk shows that included a broader range of issues—politics, social issues, and even popular culture. They had moderate success with live call-in talk shows like *Equal Time,* with the political consultant and analyst Mary Matalin and journalist Jane Wallace. Matalin was a familiar face to many news and politics junkies, and she and Wallace knew how to get the most out of a live call-in show. Ailes would later joke on Don Imus's radio show that Matalin and Wallace were "girls who, if you went into a bar around seven, you wouldn't pay a lot of attention, but they get to be 10s around closing time."[9] TV talk legend Phil Donahue was also given a prime-time slot, along with cohost Vladimir Pozner, an ex-Soviet journalist, who became a familiar face to American TV news viewers in the 1980s.

The network also brought in another familiar face, Tom Snyder. The *Tom Snyder Show* helped pump some life into CNBC's evening lineup, with his bombastic, energetic interviews of key celebrities and personalities. And in a real stretch, another talk show was added called *Real Personal.* Going for a younger age demographic later in the evening, the program featured "on the edge" topics—including, for example, sexual bondage, impotency, and infidelity—complete with live call-in participation.[10]

The change in tone and strategy toward nighttime talk helped the ratings, but not nearly enough. CNBC still had an average of only 0.5 percent of the 48.5 million households watching television in prime time. "CNBC still has a ratings problem," said a senior vice-president for a major advertising agency. "In the viewers' minds, CNBC doesn't mean anything special," compared to say, Nickelodeon or MTV.[11]

General Electric, the corporate owner of NBC, was worried about its investment in cable TV. The president of NBC, Bob Wright, announced the company's plans to create another cable channel which would be called America's Talking. This new channel would focus on talk programming. The plan, according to Wright, was to make CNBC into a pure business and financial network, because "that's the guts of the channel," and to air talk programming on America's Talking.

But they needed something else. For its cable ventures, NBC needed an experienced television programmer who knew how to compete and win. They wanted Roger Ailes. When Ailes took the helm of CNBC in August 1993, Bob Wright was looking for someone who could infuse some life and creativity into its programming. Ailes had gone to see Wright to inquire about purchasing a television station for one of his consulting clients. In an interview, Wright told this author that he and Ailes got into a conversation about the "excitement" of live television, and Wright ended up talking him into coming to NBC.[12]

At the time, no one seemed to know what to do with CNBC. NBC had won a bidding war for the financially strapped Financial News Network (FNN) in 1991 and was focused on building the premier TV channel for business news and analysis. In the same interview, NBC's Wright said that Ailes's programming experience and his success in producing compelling advertising for his political clients had convinced the network that he was the type of "energetic talent" they needed.

Media analysts were dubious. How much talk TV can viewers take, they asked? Ailes and Wright were sure they could make it work. "If you make it entertaining, interesting and relevant, there's always a market out there," said Ailes. "I think I can come up with programming to make people stop on this channel."[13]

As part of his deal with NBC, in addition to running CNBC, Ailes would also be allowed to continue his consulting work for Paramount Television on programs such as the *John & Leeza* show. And he would stay on as executive producer of Rush Limbaugh's television talk show, which was syndicated. How would he juggle all of his responsibilities, while taking over a network and developing America's Talking? "I don't whine about working 70 hours a week," he said. "It's what I like to do. I'm not new-aging myself to death looking at my navel."[14] After all, Ailes was used to juggling a number of balls in the air and keeping them going; he had been doing it for years as a consultant.

Wright and NBC did take some criticism for hiring someone to run one of their networks who was so closely affiliated with partisan politics. Not to mention the controversy and ill will generated by the heat of the 1988 presidential campaign, still fresh in many people's minds. "It's a strange choice because he comes with huge political baggage when you are out trying to sell cable to every political stripe," said media analyst Bishop Cheen.[15] And some people at CNBC expressed concern that Ailes would continue to work with a conservative firebrand like Rush Limbaugh, known for very partisan, very provocative programming both on radio and on TV. Ailes was apparently insistent on retaining his relationship with his good friend Limbaugh.

Wright defended his hiring of Ailes. He said he hired him because he wanted someone who would make people believe "we were serious about CNBC and the talk show genre ... He's one of the most skilled directors and producers of TV talk programming, and he seemed to be the right person to bring us forward with CNBC."[16] He added that "Roger has divorced himself from political advertising, and CNBC is an independent news organization." Andy Lack, then the president of NBC News, saw Ailes's experience in politics as a good thing. "A lot of times, somebody comes in from the outside and gives you a fresh perspective. That can energize what you do," he said.[17]

Ailes described his role as a "corner man, the guy in the ring coaching the boxer to throw his best punches ... Whether it's the president or a performer on television, I think my best skill is getting the best out of people. It's seeing what's good about them, what communicates, and then focusing it for them."[18] Wright agrees. He told this author that it is his belief that Ailes works to make his client a winner, no matter who that client is, conservative or not. Ailes dismissed any suggestions he was too political for TV news. "I think we're all smart enough to understand that there's a difference between what we do in the voting booth and our responsibilities as a network ... What I believe or how I vote will not influence my decisions in hiring or programming at the network."[19]

He had a vision for America's Talking and was excited about its prospects. For one thing, he saw it as an opportunity to develop new on-air talent and try programming concepts that had never been used on television before. He believed cable television provided an opportunity to connect with the American public on a personal level and offer them TV programming that was directly relevant to their everyday lives.

Bob Wright explains that he and Ailes used talk radio as a model for much of America's Talking programming ideas. "Rush Limbaugh was the model ... America's Talking wasn't meant to be a news channel, but focus on individuals, their lives, and the things that mattered to them personally," Wright said. "We brought some people in from radio, some people from TV, some people from news commentary to get a variety of talent and find people that viewers would want to spend time with."[20]

In fact, Wright says they tried to get Rush Limbaugh to do a show on America's Talking, but they couldn't agree on a format and a strategy they could all live with. "It got too complicated, Rush wanted to do his own thing, he wanted to own it and have it syndicated, and we just couldn't get it done."

In building the concept for America's Talking, Ailes posed some questions that typical Americans probably ask themselves "consciously or subconsciously every day."[21] Then he set about to create shows that answer those questions. For example, "What happened overnight while I was sleeping?" The morning program, *Wake Up America*, from 7 to 9 a.m. should answer those questions. Another question Americans ask is, "Am I healthy? How can I take better care of myself?" They could watch *Alive and Wellness* from 11 a.m. to noon. And what about advice on personal relationships? *Ask E. Jean*, hosted by writer E. Jean Carroll, would focus on those issues. In sum, said Ailes, America's Talking is a boxed set of shows that comes in the different flavors of one's life. If people find a network that is about them and their lives, they'll watch it, he insisted.

Other programs included *What's New*, a show on hot consumer gadgets and technology; *Pork*, a political talk show focusing on government waste; and *Politics with Chris Matthews*, a political talk show that later moved to MSNBC and was renamed *Hardball with Chris Matthews*. *Hardball* is the only Ailes creation from America's Talking that is still on the air in some version today. Ailes himself hosted an hour-long celebrity talk show on the network called *Straight Forward*.

And even though Ailes criticized many of the programs on rival cable stations for what he called their "dysfunctional programming"[22] and their high-lighting of "freaks" and "bozos,"[23] he created his own shows at America's Talking that seemed cut from the same bit of "dysfunctional" cloth. For example, *Am I Nuts?* was supposed to be a psychological self-help program hosted by two psychologists, but seemed to offer mostly emotional voyeurism for TV viewers. *Bugged!* was a comedic look at what bugs people. And *Break a Leg with Bill McCuddy* was a mid-afternoon talk show hosted by the winner of a CNBC-sponsored talent contest.

What did indeed seem to be missing from the CNBC lineup or from America's Talking under Ailes's tenure was any overt conservative political programming. This was due to the insistence of NBC management and President Bob Wright. Particularly after the criticism NBC took over its hiring of Ailes, the "peacock network" wanted to avoid any taint of partisan politics and drove this point home to Ailes. But according to Wright, Ailes never tried to push conservative views on the air at CNBC. "Roger was interested in coming back to live TV, that's what really excited him ... he understood that what he was going to be doing at CNBC had to be non-political and he was OK with that."[24]

In his conversation with this author, Wright deemphasized Ailes's political partisanship. "Roger likes to play with a winning hand," he said. "I think he's a true political consultant—he does the best for the people that hire him. The candidate he works for today is the candidate he is for. And the candidate he works for tomorrow is the candidate he is for then. I don't know that Roger is a conservative at all. He often works for conservative candidates or organizations and he does his best to help them win."

In fact, Ailes worked with quite a few liberals at CNBC—Chris Matthews, Charles Grodin, and Geraldo Rivera, to name a few. Consistent with the ground rules he had been given by his NBC bosses, he was trying to find smart, entertaining people he could build a show around. Of course, later at Fox, working for Rupert Murdoch, he was working with a different set of ground rules, with an entirely different business plan.

But he still had Rush Limbaugh. When Ailes went to run CNBC, he did so with the understanding that he would still produce Limbaugh's syndicated TV show. This must have been some kind of spiritual tonic for Ailes—between dealing with news programming for CNBC and the "tabloidlike" material at America's Talking, he still got to skewer liberals and Democrats over at the Rush Limbaugh program.

At first, CNBC didn't seem too concerned about Ailes's activities outside his main job with them; they just wanted better ratings. The NBC brass surely understood what they were getting in Ailes—a TV producer who is also a Republican political consultant—but they obviously thought that if he could help them become more profitable, then it was worth any potential downside.

But events may have changed that impression and affected Ailes's position at NBC. Case in point: the controversy surrounding accusations of a cover-up by the Clinton White House during the Whitewater investigation, including the supposed "murder" of Clinton aide Vince Foster. Bill and Hillary Clinton's role in the Whitewater Development Corporation, a failed Arkansas real estate venture in the 1970s and '80s, gave rise to allegations of political pressure from then governor Clinton to provide illegal loans to his partners in the company.[25] Foster, who had been a partner in the same Arkansas law firm as Hillary Clinton, was deputy White House counsel and handled some of the Whitewater-related tax returns for the Clintons. Foster's transition to the Washington political scene was difficult, and he suffered from depression and anxiety.[26] The allegations against the Clintons were never proved, but Foster's apparent suicide spurred rumors, innuendo, and conspiracy theories about his death. During the media's feeding frenzy over the Whitewater controversy and Foster's death, some right-wing journalists and political operatives were pushing "scandal" talk. The Clintons and their cronies were supposedly involved in a huge conspiracy to hide their crimes in the Whitewater case and were going to extreme lengths to cover their tracks.

On his March 10, 1994, radio program, Rush Limbaugh excitedly told his listeners about a tip he had received:

> Okay, folks, I think I got enough information here to tell you about the contents of this fax that I got. Brace yourselves. This fax contains information that I have just been told will appear in a newsletter to Morgan Stanley sales personnel this after-noon ... What it is, is a bit of news which says ... there's a Washington consulting firm that has scheduled the release of a report that will appear, it will be published, that claims that Vince Foster was murdered in an apartment owned by Hillary Clinton, and the body was taken to Fort Marcy Park.[27]

The information Limbaugh broadcast to an audience of millions was obtained from a small insider's newsletter, which ultimately had nothing to offer but rumor and speculation. And the tip Limbaugh received about the newsletter's report was inaccurate—the report did not claim that Foster was murdered or that the apartment was owned by Hillary Clinton. During the broadcast, Limbaugh referred to the information as a rumor but used it to claim that there were stories circulating that Foster was murdered to cover up Whitewater crimes.

Responding to the criticism that followed, Limbaugh defended his handling of the issue, saying that he never suggested Foster was murdered, only that there were rumors to that effect. But in his public comments about the case, Roger Ailes was much more upbeat. Appearing on the Don Imus radio program, he was proud of Limbaugh's work. He boasted that Limbaugh's reporting about a "suicide cover-up, possibly even murder" was a scoop.[28] He said to Don Imus, "The guy who's been doing an excellent job for the *New York Post* ... for the first time on the Rush Limbaugh show said that he did not believe it was suicide ... Now, I don't have any evidence ... These people [the Clintons] are very good at hiding or destroying evidence."[29]

The *New York Post* reporter to whom Ailes referred is Christopher Ruddy, who now runs the right-wing Web site Newsmax and was implicated in numerous efforts to push the idea of a Whitewater conspiracy into the mainstream press in the 1990s.

But that wasn't the end of Ailes's interview on the *Don Imus Show*. After the Vince Foster murder talk, Ailes joked about Bill Clinton's reputation for womanizing, saying Clinton went to New York "because he heard [Olympic skater] Nancy Kerrigan is on Saturday Night Live—She's the only one he hasn't hit on."[30] Then he took aim at Hillary Clinton: of the three lawyers she had brought to Washington—Webster Hubbell, Bernard Nussbaum, and Vince Foster—one was being investigated by the Justice Department, one was forced to resign, and one was dead. "I wouldn't stand too close to her," Ailes joked.

This is typical Roger Ailes, according to people who know him and have worked closely with him. He has a very sharp, sarcastic sense of humor, and he uses it like a sword. He's very frank, whether in conversations, in business meetings, or in front of a microphone. And he's not shy about roughing up his opponents, whether in politics or in the television business.

President Clinton's chief of staff called NBC president Bob Wright to complain that Ailes's comments on the Don Imus program "were simply inappropriate."[31] A CNBC spokesman defended Ailes, pointing out that the CNBC president was merely "joking."[32] But a senior Clinton administration official said, "He is not a political consultant anymore, and he can't hide behind this crap that it was a joke ... Roger Ailes is a network executive, and he ought to be held accountable. Is this the view of NBC News? Of General Electric? It's outrageous."[33]

Ailes was also giving advice to the Steve Forbes presidential campaign in 1995, while he was CNBC president.[34] Ailes has claimed that his advice was of a purely personal, not political, nature. He saw no conflict: "We are friends, and I'm under no obligation to give up all of my relationships just because I work in television." Others didn't see it that way. "That caused a lot of problems even before the news broke," a CNBC producer told *MediaWeek*. "We all knew about it. And we knew that it could hurt him at NBC." In the past, of course, Ailes himself has been the first to throw stones at what he considers most journalists' "cozy" relationship with Democrats.

Ailes's activities and comments raised the question of whether someone should be held to a different standard of conduct if they have moved from partisan politics to television news. Public relations executive Paul Gleason, a veteran of corporate crisis management issues, said Ailes's behavior had "cast a subjective pall over his organization."[35]

In their quest for higher ratings, NBC was willing to take a gamble on Ailes and his political baggage when they hired him. And Ailes is credited with increasing CNBC's ratings and profitability. Revenue went from approximately $43 million to more than $80 million under his stewardship. But his tenure there seems to have been one balancing act after another. They clearly wanted him to be nonpolitical while running CNBC, and they couldn't have been happy about his extracurricular activities with the Rush Limbaugh program and off-the-cuff comments like those he made on the *Don Imus Show*.

But the coming storm was only just beginning to brew.

Ailes (middle) with members of an Ohio University honor society, 1962.
Courtesy Ohio University.

Roger Ailes's senior picture from the Ohio University yearbook, 1962.
Courtesy Ohio University.

John Kennedy and Richard Nixon with CBS Producer Don Hewitt just before their first debate, September 25, 1960, in Chicago. Nixon wore a gray suit and had a pale face, while Kennedy wore a dark suit and had a deep tan. CBS Photo Archive/Getty Images.

Roger Ailes helped TV host Mike Douglas (far left) connect with 1960s pop culture by booking guests such as soul singer Wayne Cochran (middle, next to Douglas). Also pictured are ventriloquist Shari Lewis and singer Paul Anka. Philadelphia, 1965.

Two Ailes clients. Ronald Reagan (right) campaigns with Richard Nixon, 1972. Ailes had helped create a new Richard Nixon. In 1984 he would come to the rescue of the Reagan reelection campaign. Dirck Halstead/Time Life Pictures/Getty Images.

A January 1977 *Time* magazine cover depicting Rupert Murdoch as King Kong. He had just begun his move into American media with the launch of *Star* magazine and his purchase of *The New York Post*. Ted Thai/Time Inc./Time Life Pictures/Getty Images.

George H. W. Bush campaign manager Lee Atwater works the phones in March 1988. Atwater and Ailes ran one of the most notoriously negative political campaigns in American history. Cynthia Johnson/Time Life Pictures/Getty Images.

Microsoft founder Bill Gates looms larger than life at the launch of MSNBC in 1996. Seated, left to right, are NBC CEO Bob Wright, NBC journalist Jane Pauley, NBC News President Andy Lack, Microsoft VP Peter Neupert, and NBC News Anchor Brian Williams.
Jon Levy/AFP/Getty Images.

The wizard behind the curtain? Ailes sits in the control booth at Fox Studios in New York, May 1, 2001. Catrina Genovese/Getty Images.

Roger Ailes addressing a television industry gathering in Pasadena, California, 2006. Frederick M. Brown/Getty Images.

10

The Ohio Project

It was clear to me that Roger didn't want to work for the news division and report to Andy Lack.

—Bob Wright, former president of NBC[1]

David Letterman took a dark joy in skewering his corporate bosses at NBC in the 1990s on his late-night talk show. Howard Stern had notorious running battles with NBC Radio when he was with the network. Roger Ailes's tenure at NBC was almost as stormy, but his disagreements with his bosses just weren't broadcast. Like many consultants who go to work full-time for a corporation, there were control issues and turf battles.

For one thing, Ailes liked to be his own boss, and part of his agreement in coming to NBC was that he would report directly to NBC president Bob Wright or to the chairman of GE, Jack Welch. This probably irked Tom Rogers, who was the president of the NBC cable division and technically oversaw Ailes's shop at CNBC. The two men sparred often over programming, distribution, and marketing. Ailes let it be known how little he thought of Rogers. At one meeting to discuss programming for CNBC, Ailes dismissively said, "You're a lawyer!" (Rogers came to NBC from a career in regulatory law.) "What do you know about programming?"[2]

But the peacock network's feathers really got ruffled when Ailes took his feud with Rogers public in the print media. In a 1994 interview with Multichannel News, an industry trade publication, the old, combative Roger Ailes surfaced. When asked about Rogers, he said, "Tom's had a little trouble letting go because he used to basically run CNBC ... I think he likes to see his name in the paper ... Every once in a while, we send a disinformation press release to Tom's office just to keep him on his toes."[3] No one outside of Ailes's people at CNBC thought it was funny. Trying to keep egos and personalities in check is always a challenge for management, but especially in a high-profile environment like a television network. Bob Wright tried. Rogers was livid. Wright went to Ailes and asked him to apologize to Rogers for the good of the company, but Ailes refused.[4]

More consequential in the long run, however, was Ailes's deteriorating relationship with David Zaslav, the head of cable distribution and business development for NBC. Zaslav, also a lawyer, went to NBC in 1989 and was heavily involved in NBC's dive into the cable television business. Zaslav, by 2007 the president of Discovery Communications, which owns and operates the Discovery Network, among other ventures, wouldn't talk to this author about his relationship with Ailes. But their battles are pretty well known.

Most of the trouble centered around Roger Ailes's baby, America's Talking. As Andy Lack, the NBC News president, had said, "NBC wanted to get into the cable news business." The desire for NBC to expand its presence in cable television and look for new markets was very consistent with GE chairman Jack Welch's overall philosophy, which was basically Grow or Die. A 1993 *New Yorker* article by Ken Auletta discusses the goal of Welch to make NBC the worldwide brand name in global communications. Auletta reports that

> many NBC executives say Welch is eager to eclipse [Rupert] Murdoch, who has already created the first global entertainment-and-news network. Now that GE has owned NBC for eight years, Welch believes that Bob Wright and his team can make NBC the world's foremost network. He wants NBC to become as important in its field as GE is in most of its eleven other businesses ... Since Welch became GE's chairman and CEO in 1981, he has followed one rule assiduously: If a division can't be No. 1 or No. 2 in its business worldwide, sell it. Welch feels that in Bob Wright he has a kindred spirit.[5]

This is where Microsoft and Bill Gates come in. Microsoft wanted to invest in interactive media. They were looking for a broadcast partner to operate a joint news venture using their on-line capabilities. Microsoft had been negotiating with Turner Broadcasting to form an association with CNN. But Bob Wright and David Zaslav came along and offered Microsoft a better deal. Instead of the $1 billion it would cost Bill Gates to form a partnership with Turner, he could buy a half stake in NBC cable for only $220 million, then pay $20 million a year for content and $50 million over five years for operating costs. That's about half what it would have cost with Turner Broadcasting.[6]

And it was a good deal for NBC too. For not much more than it was already costing them to produce and carry CNBC and America's Talking, NBC was going to be partnering with the world's biggest name in on-line communication. It would get a jump on its competitors as far as distribution of its content and the branding of worldwide news. And it was going to be doing it for less than what it cost CNN.

Here's the catch. America's Talking would have to be sacrificed. In one important sense, there would be no room for it. NBC cable simply would not be able to manage CNBC, a new cable news network with Microsoft (MSNBC), and America's Talking all at the same time. And the priority for NBC was cable news, not a talk channel, which is what America's Talking was. Equally important, there would be no room with cable carriers like Comcast and Time Warner for an additional cable TV channel—it made more financial sense to replace America's Talking with MSNBC. By taking over that channel, MSNBC was able to debut in over 20 million homes, with the prospects of growing rapidly over the next several years. So that was the deal NBC struck with Microsoft—Bill Gates was essentially buying a half stake in the America's Talking channel, then converting it to MSNBC.

Most of this came as news to Roger Ailes. Aware of the talks by NBC to form an interactive channel with Microsoft, he at first thought it was an interesting idea, particularly because the new cable channel would benefit from the talents of NBC heavyweights such as Tom Brokaw and Brian Williams. But, according to Andy Lack, Ailes was skeptical of the ability to build an audience and draw advertising dollars.[7] But when Ailes learned that the new cable channel would replace America's Talking and that it would be managed by the NBC News division and not by him, it was like Moses parting the Red Sea.

Ailes thought it was a mistake. And more important, it represented a huge demotion for him on the NBC corporate food chain. He fought for America's Talking, and he fought for his place at the NBC table. He and David Zaslav had butted heads on a number of issues, but this caused an irreparable rift between the two. Zaslav, backed by Tom Rogers, Ailes's old foil, insisted that the Microsoft deal would work only if MSNBC took the America's Talking slot and that it would have to be managed by the NBC News division. It would have to be a "hard news" operation, and that meant it would be run by Andy Lack, not by Roger Ailes. Ailes thought he had lost a "power struggle" to bureaucrats who "probably doubted my ability to run a business."[8]

There was bad blood. For one thing, the secret negotiations with Microsoft to form MSNBC came to be called by a code name: The Ohio Project. Now, Roger Ailes is from Ohio. He is convinced that this code name was a sly dig at him and his native state by his rivals at NBC.[9] In this author's conversation with Bob Wright, he said he had never heard the term Ohio Project before. Andy Lack had only a vague recollection of ever hearing that phrase before. So, obviously, it was not an official name that appeared on documents or in official conversations, but was an unofficial code name adopted by some in on the deal, below the pay grade of Wright and Lack. One can imagine the water-cooler conversations: "Pssst. Hey, how's the Ohio Project going?"

Ailes accused David Zaslav and Tom Rogers of working behind his back on the MSNBC deal. Things became awkward after that. According to author Scott Collins, in November 1995, when Ailes and Zaslav accompanied other CNBC executives to California for a cable industry show, "It was very, very uncomfortable." One former NBC staffer said that "Roger was not speaking to David. David was not speaking to Roger. And here they were, being the face of CNBC."[10]

And it also strained the relationship between Ailes and Wright, the man who had brought him to NBC in the first place. Wright told this author that

> Roger felt that America's Talking had been hijacked from him. I told Roger that we really wanted to be in the cable news business, and the best way to do it was with the America's Talking channel slot, which had 30 million subscribers, and we had good relationships with the cable operators. He felt that Lack had out-maneuvered him and that he was losing his baby ... He didn't want to accept the fact that he was going to lose America's Talking to the news division. That just really irked him.[11]

Andy Lack, who became an executive with Sony in 2001, was president of NBC News from 1993 to 2001. In that time, he was credited with turning the news division around from an organization in a fair amount of disarray, with staff cutbacks and production issues, to the number one news division among the Big Three networks. In Lack's conversation with this author, he said that he and Roger Ailes "never crossed swords ... Those kinds of decisions [about MSNBC]) were made above my rank and pay grade." NBC was trying to look to the future, and profitability was concern number one. He said that he knew losing America's Talking was very hard on Roger. "I didn't really understand the stakes for him at the time," Lack said, "but Roger felt really disappointed and very angry at what he saw as shabby treatment from NBC."

When NBC and Microsoft launched MSNBC at a splashy news conference in December 1995, Roger Ailes was conspicuous by his absence. Bob Wright was there, Andy Lack was there, and even GE chairman Jack Welch was there. Tom Brokaw and Bill Gates appeared via satellite. But no Roger Ailes. It did not go unnoticed. In fact, for a couple of days it was the talk of the town. "Where was the president of CNBC and the father of America's Talking?" asked *MediaWeek*. "He wasn't in sight," cackled a *Newsweek* correspondent.[12] "Did you hear?" asked the *New Yorker*'s Sidney Blumenthal. "Ailes wasn't even there." "Gone, he's gone," said an NBC reporter. None of them looked sad, reported the *MediaWeek* correspondent.[13]

Only a handful of people knew it at the time, but Ailes had pretty much already made the jump to Rupert Murdoch's loving embrace. He had produced his last program for NBC, and he formally resigned from the peacock network only a couple of weeks later.

His stated reasons for resigning, though, only skimmed the surface of what had gone on the previous several months. The *New York Times* reported that Ailes was opposed to the Microsoft deal, "but [Ailes] said yesterday that it was not the primary reason he decided to leave CNBC. 'I thought that America's Talking was a very valuable asset, but I understood the corporate imperative about wanting the deal with Microsoft,' Mr. Ailes said."[14] He told the *Times* that a more significant reason for his resignation was the network's decision to move CNBC under a company-wide sales department instead of allowing it to run its own sales operation. He said that meant CNBC would be unlikely to reach the same level of success it had achieved the year before. "I just didn't think I could hit my revenue figures under this structure," he told the *Times*.[15]

The Associated Press and the *Wall Street Journal* reported similar rationales. "NBC decided to take away his control over relations with cable systems," reported the *Journal*. "Under the restructuring, NBC's cable operations will have a single division responsible for getting cable systems to carry its different networks ... Mr. Ailes said he wasn't comfortable with losing control of a major revenue stream."[16] Of course, at the time, no one outside of NBC knew anything about the internal chess game that had been going on the last year and a half.

The industry was buzzing with rumors, and everyone had their own perspective. Why would Roger Ailes leave? "Are you serious?" said an editor of the *Weekly Standard*. "Roger likes to be in charge. This is the man who ran the Bush media campaign in '88. Do you think Roger would just take his check and let his network be taken away from him?"[17] The *MediaWeek* correspondent said, "Ailes likes to program autonomously and corporate prefers team-thinking. Or, as a CNBC executive explains it: 'Roger is a gunslinger, and NBC wants a posse.'"[18]

"Roger did a good job for us," said Bob Wright. "In fact I said to him when he was on his way out the door, 'You know you're crazy for doing this, because you're about to get enormous recognition for what you're doing here at NBC. In a fit of anger you're just going to go across the street.' Of course he was perfectly willing to go and talk to Rupert Murdoch."[19]

Indeed, within only a couple of weeks after Ailes left, he and Rupert Murdoch had their own major announcement to make. At the news conference announcing the launch of the Fox News Channel, Murdoch beamed as he turned the microphone over to his new hire. It would be a totally different environment at News Corp. There Roger Ailes found a home. Rupert Murdoch was as committed to a conservative political agenda as Ailes was. And he was liberated from the corporate culture he had been trapped in at CNBC.

Let Ailes be Ailes!

11

Talk Is Cheap . . . Talk Radio Is Priceless!

GET OFF THE LINE, YOU CREEP!

—Joe Pyne, famed radio talk show host

As discussed earlier, it's an accepted theory by now that Barry Goldwater's presidential candidacy in 1964, though doomed to failure, laid the foundation for what became the modern conservative movement in America. Politically, this movement crested with the presidency of Ronald Reagan in the 1980s, but apparently has been coughing and sputtering since then.

Not true with the conservative media, though. The '70s and '80s were a watershed time for the conservative movement in the mass media—new conservative publications were founded, right-wing think tanks and foundations provided research and funding, the strong conservative presence among the talking heads of TV news programs began, and most importantly, conservative talk radio emerged as a major force in American media and politics.

The development and the success of conservative talk radio programs helped lay the foundation (in a Barry Goldwater sense) for the Fox News Channel. Roger Ailes's programming experiments at CNBC and America's Talking were basically the first attempt to take what was successful on talk radio and transfer it to television. Then when Ailes went to work for Rupert Murdoch, he largely replicated much of this formula in the development of Fox News and built much of its viewership on the fan base of talk radio. Let's not forget that Ailes's first job was at a radio station, where he developed an appreciation for what grabs a listening audience's attention.

Much of this story line centers around one of the most polarizing media figures in the world today, Rush Limbaugh—truly, either you love him or you hate him, there isn't much middle ground. Limbaugh is an interesting character. He clearly doesn't have a self-esteem problem ("Talent on loan from God," he often says about himself). There is little doubt that he is extremely intelligent, is mostly self-educated (he dropped out of Southeast Missouri State University, where, according to his mother, he "flunked everything"),[1] and through experience and observation, taught himself the basics of effective communication and broadcasting.

He is a traditional, midwestern, patriotic kid from a small town, having inherited his rock-ribbed conservatism from his parents, Rush and Mildred (Rush is a family name). His strongly anticommunist father was a WWII fighter pilot. He also comes from a family of lawyers—his father, grandfather, uncle, and brother—which may partially explain his argumentative broadcast style and his penchant for making a case and rendering a verdict.

Limbaugh grew up to remake the radio industry and to create the juggernaut that conservative talk radio has become in the last twenty years. He bounced around various radio jobs—taking a break from radio in the early '80s as director of promotions with the Kansas City Royals. He's a huge sports fan, often interjecting sports analogies in his programs and interviewing athletes. But his big radio break came in 1988 when he was brought to New York and WABC Radio by Ed McLaughlin. Limbaugh had built an audience at KFBK in Sacramento, where he had begun refining his hectoring, lecturing, in-your-face conservative monologues.

From WABC in New York, the Limbaugh radio program was syndicated nationally to, at first, a couple hundred radio stations. But his listening audience grew, and his high Arbitron ratings induced more stations around the country to carry his show. By the early '90s he was being heard on more than 400 radio stations, and eventually that grew to just under 700 stations. Clearly, he was onto something. His cocky, acerbic, witty diatribes against liberalism, big government, taxes, and most of all, Bill Clinton, struck a chord with moderate to conservative listeners nationwide, who dubbed themselves ditto-heads. (Listeners who called in would often say "ditto" in agreement with his views.)

Limbaugh's influence is undeniable. His legion of ditto-heads stand ready to e-mail, telephone, and otherwise cajole elected officials in the direction Limbaugh wants them to go. And regular listeners to radio news are likely to be regular voters. Republicans certainly think he has made a big difference in their electoral fortunes. Top conservatives, such as former House Speaker Newt Gingrich and Tony Blankley, once Gingrich's staff director and then editorial page editor of the *Washington Times,* are willing to give him a significant amount of the credit for their past success. Blankley believes that "starting in 1994, with the Republican election of Congress, I think Limbaugh made the difference in electing the Republican majority. In the following three elections he made the difference in holding the majority. And in 2000, in the presidential race in Florida, he was the difference between Gore and Bush winning Florida and thus the Presidency."[2] While some of that (especially the last part) is debatable, it's an assessment with which Limbaugh himself would agree.

Limbaugh has always had his share of critics, but sometimes his worst enemy is his own big mouth, as he would likely admit. In 2003, he was almost suspended from the air by some of the stations that carry his program because of comments he made about the African-American quarterback of the Philadelphia Eagles, Donovan McNabb. While working as a commentator for ESPN's *Sunday NFL Countdown* (a weekend gig), he offered the opinion that McNabb was getting built up by the media because he was black. "I think what we've had here is a little social concern in the NFL … The media has been very desirous that a black quarterback do well," he said.[3] This created a firestorm, as it should have, which led to his resignation from ESPN. Then in the election season of 2006, he accused the actor Michael J. Fox, who suffers from Parkinson's disease and who appeared in several campaign ads for Democratic candidates who back federal funding for stem cell research, of "exaggerating the effects of the disease" in the ads in order to generate sympathy. Limbaugh later apologized.

Talk radio is a strange animal. It is unlike any other medium. It basically relies on conversation. No music. No pictures. Just people talking. That puts a premium on radio hosts who are interesting enough to listen to for long periods of time and who can carry a conversation. Not a lot of people can do that, and it's not really something that can be taught. The successful radio talk hosts are the ones who create a buzz—by being edgy, funny, insulting, or controversial, sometimes all of the above. After all, it is a media business and it survives on ratings and advertising, as most media do.

Most of the time, the credit for "discovering" the talk radio format goes to Barry Gray, who, as a disk jockey for WMCA in New York, grew bored with spinning music one evening in 1945 and put a telephone up to his microphone so that his audience could listen in to his conversation with popular bandleader Woody Herman. It was spontaneous and it was brilliant. And it was a huge hit with the listening audience. He convinced station management to let him make it a regular feature of his show, and he began doing listener call-ins. Gray went on to have an up-and-down, but mostly successful broadcast career and is considered by most to be the founder of talk radio.

The other talk radio stalwart worth mentioning, because of his influence on the medium and on future radio stars, is Joe Pyne. An emotional, opinionated, confrontational on-air talker, Pyne is credited with developing the bombastic style so many successful hosts use today. A WWII vet who earned three service stars and lost a leg in battle, he began his talk radio career at WILM in Wilmington, Delaware. It was there that he began developing his freewheeling, opinionated style—often arguing heatedly with guests and with callers. "Go gargle with razor blades!" he would shout into the microphone when he had had enough.

In the 1950s Pyne moved to California and built a successful broadcast career, doing radio and some television. In the mid-'60s his radio program went national, syndicated to more than 200 radio stations, and his "infamy" grew. Pyne was a conservative, which is undoubtedly one reason he is so lionized by the successful radio talkers of today, who are almost all conservative. He supported the Vietnam War and railed against hippies and feminists—he would love one of Limbaugh's favorite terms, "Femi-Nazis." Yet he was an outspoken critic of racial discrimination and was generally supportive of organized labor, characteristics he shared with Barry Gray, interestingly enough.

His syndicated radio program is remembered for the insults and the confrontations for which he was famous. On-air arguments and insult contests with celebrities like musician Frank Zappa were welcomed by his loyal listeners. He would often hang up on callers and throw guests out of his studio—"Take your false teeth out, put 'em in backwards and bite yourself in the neck!" was another trademark invective. His most famous line, "Get off the line, you creep!" is still used today, as a sort of tribute, by talk radio hosts such as Mark Levin who alters it somewhat to "Get off the phone, ya big dope!" *Fox News's* Sean Hannity, who has a popular radio show on WABC, has been known to play a tape of Levin's "Get off the phone." put-down when frustrated with a caller. A darker side of the confrontational, insult-driven talk radio style is represented by another New York–based radio host, Bob Grant. As with Limbaugh, conservatives love him and liberals hate him—not many gray areas here. At his retirement party in 2006, he was lauded by New York governor George Pataki, Ann Coulter, William F. Buckley Jr., and Newt

Gingrich. He began his broadcast career in Los Angeles in the 1960s, moving east in 1970. From New York's star-studded WABC radio in the 1980s, Grant dominated afternoon radio, where he railed about politics, media, and modern society in general. As with Joe Pyne and other trail-blazers of talk, Grant was known for hurling insults and confronting guests.

Some of Grant's favorite targets were New York and New Jersey politicians, as well as nationally known Democrats. He is widely credited with assisting in the reelection defeats of New York governor Mario Cuomo and New Jersey governor Jim Florio, whom he called "Flim-Flam Florio." He once referred to New York City's mayor David Dinkins as "the men's room attendant at the 21 Club,"[4] an apparent stab at racially disparaging humor.

Most of Grant's controversies centered around his frequent racially inflammatory characterizations, though his defenders insist he is not racist. According to Fairness and Accuracy in Reporting (FAIR), a left-wing media watchdog group, Grant on a number of occasions referred to African-Americans as "savages."[5] The *New York Times* reported in 1995 that Grant used the term "savages" when referring to South African blacks.[6] He once said that if Martin Luther King Day were not observed in America, there would be trouble from the savages. He later apologized for this remark. His most infamous remark, for which he was fired by WABC, came in 1996 when the airplane carrying U.S. Secretary of Commerce Ron Brown crashed. He told a caller, "My hunch is Brown is the one survivor ... maybe it's because at heart I'm a pessimist."[7] He made those remarks before the extent of the crash was known, but when Brown was found dead with the rest of the passengers, Grant's comments were seen as tasteless and cruel, and his contract was terminated.

His career survived, though, as he moved over to New York's WOR radio and built a solid audience, even going into national syndication in the late 1990s. For all of his controversy, he is lionized by many broadcasters today. Howard Stern credits Grant as a major influence on his style. *Talkers* magazine, the radio talk show industry's trade publication, ranks him as the sixteenth greatest talk radio host of all time. But in January 2008 a radio industry magazine, *Radio & Records,* withdrew a lifetime achievement award they had planned to give to Grant. The Los Angeles publication said it "is sensitive to the diversity of our community and does not want the presentation of an award to Mr. Grant to imply our endorsement of past comments by him that contradict our values and the respect we have for all members of our community." [8]

If Rush Limbaugh is the star of conservative talk radio, many believe his costar is the Fairness Doctrine—or more accurately, the demise of the Fairness Doctrine. Want to start an argument in a roomful of Republicans and Democrats? Just mention the six-decade-old federal policy. The Fairness Doctrine, which emerged in 1949, has always been controversial and has been applied unevenly through the years by the federal courts—probably because they couldn't really decide if it was a good or a bad thing for a democratic society. The idea of the doctrine is to ensure that a diversity of viewpoints is communicated through publicly broadcasted, government-owned and regulated frequencies, such as radio and television stations.

In the 1969 Supreme Court case of *Red Lion Broadcasting Co.* v. *FCC*, this was interpreted to mean that if an individual or his/her ideas were criticized on a broadcast frequency, then the franchise holder of that frequency (the TV or radio station responsible for the broadcast) must allow free airtime for that individual to respond. However, just five years later, the Court seemed to be cautious of such controls, for First Amendment reasons. The 1974 case of *Miami Herald Publishing Co.* v. *Tornillo* resulted in the Court's ruling that a government-enforced right of access to broadcast time "inescapably dampens the vigor and limits the variety of public debate."[9]

By the 1980s the doctrine had largely fallen into disuse, as the courts were uncertain of its constitutionality, and pressure from broadcasters and corporate franchise holders against government mandates led the FCC to shy away from it. Then came its demise. The *Wall Street Journal*'s Daniel Henninger says that Ronald Reagan may not make it to Mount Rushmore for winning the cold war, but he "secured his place in the conservative pantheon for tearing down another wall: the Fairness Doctrine."[10] For vast right-wing conspiracy theorists, this is a whopper: A Republican president, under pressure from corporate broadcast interests, works to end a restriction that encourages the broadcast of multiple viewpoints, thereby ushering in the domination of radio by conservative commentators.

Hold on, though. The 1984 Court decision that helped bring down the doctrine was written by one of the bench's foremost liberals, William Brennan—again for First Amendment reasons. In *FCC* v. *League of Women Voters*, Brennan noted the Court's concern that the doctrine was "chilling speech," and said the Court would have to revisit the constitutionality of the doctrine if it was reducing rather than enhancing speech. And an increasingly conservative federal judiciary in the mid-'80s, wary of government interference in the first place, further weakened enforcement of the doctrine, notably appeals court decisions by Robert Bork and Antonin Scalia in 1986.

But it was Reagan's FCC that administered the *coup de grâce*. Emboldened by the Court, the FCC voted to abolish the Fairness Doctrine. Its decision read in part: "the intrusion by government into the content of programming occasioned by the enforcement of the Fairness Doctrine restricts the journalistic freedom of broadcasters ... and inhibits the presentation of controversial issues of public importance to the detriment of the public ..." The FCC, not the Supreme Court, found the doctrine to be "unconstitutional." That same year, Congress passed legislation to codify the Fairness Doctrine and mandate its consideration by the FCC, but the bill was vetoed by President Reagan.

With the Fairness Doctrine gone, the need for broadcasters to balance viewpoints from the left and right was no longer a concern. And with the Rush Limbaugh program bringing in listeners and advertising revenue in the early '90s, an increasing number of radio stations began carrying the Limbaugh show and more conservative radio hosts were given shows in local radio markets around the country. So did the abolition of the doctrine lead to conservative dominance of talk radio? It played a role, but there are other factors equally important.

Why such conservative dominance? Limbaugh says it's a reaction to the domination of the mainstream media, or what he calls the "drive-by media," of left-wing viewpoints and liberal reporting. He says the essence of the political left is that "the people can't be trusted and don't have any judgment, which fits into traditional journalism."[11] But talk radio, he says, reaches out to people; it lets them in, it's interactive.

Others in the industry, including Michael Harrison, the editor of *Talkers* magazine, say it is primarily talent-driven. And because Rush Limbaugh is a very talented and entertaining broadcaster, he has pushed radio in a conservative direction and has influenced other broadcasters to follow a similar path. "Why is there suddenly so much interest in golf since Tiger Woods came on the scene," Harrison asks. "Well, maybe because guys like that don't come along every day. Guys like Rush Limbaugh don't come around every day."[12] In other words, Limbaugh has provided broadcasters with a successful business model. Jon Sinton, founder of the liberal radio network Air America, agrees. It's all due to Limbaugh's talent, he says: "Rush could just as easily have been a flaming liberal, and the other side would be complaining ... It became very easy to replicate the success of a Rush Limbaugh and come up with a G. Gordon Liddy, and come up with a Sean Hannity, and a Michael Savage."[13]

Left-leaning radio host and author Thom Hartmann says it is mostly about quality programming, a good business strategy, and lots of cash. "Particularly the cash," he says. He believes the conservative forces in radio have simply been better funded. "Well-funded syndicates get together and buy block time, put a conservative host on the air, and then find sponsors to pay for it," he claims. "If the income from the sponsors exceeds the cost of buying the block time, they make a healthy profit."[14]

It also has largely to do with who's listening. According to Arbitron's annual reports and studies by the Project for Excellence in Journalism, the audience for radio news and talk "skews Republican."[15] In its 2006 annual report, Arbitron noted that of those who tune in to radio news/talk/information programs, 36 percent were Republicans, 27 percent were Democrats, and 26 percent were Independents. The Arbitron report stated that as a general tendency, commercial talk radio appeals to a Republican audience.[16]

Two other factors help skew the listening audience for talk radio toward the conservative side. One is gender. According to the same Arbitron studies, the audience for commercial news and talk radio is primarily male—57 percent male versus 43 percent female. That's a sizeable difference and is significant when one considers that demographic reports and electoral data consistently indicate that males are more likely than females to hold conservative views and to vote Republican.

The other factor affecting the results is the availability of public radio. A partisan and ideological breakdown of the listening audience for public radio programs, such as National Public Radio, is pretty much the reverse of what you find for the commercial talk radio audience. According to the Pew Research Center for the People and the Press, the audience for public radio talk programs skews Democratic. Of those who tune in regularly, 40 percent identify themselves as Democrats, 30 percent as Republicans, and 39 percent as Independents.[17] Not surprisingly, studies by the National Association of Broadcasters show that the Fox News Channel is the top primary news source among all commercial talk radio listeners. In the universe of talk radio, there is a considerable amount of self-selection occurring.

Rush Limbaugh, as he admits, is first and foremost an entertainer. He doesn't claim to be a journalist, and he believes this means, as he has stated, that he is under "no obligation to be factual."[18] Well, that must be very liberating. According to *Talkers* magazine, through 2007, he dominated the medium, reaching an average of 13.5 million listeners on a weekly basis. The next closest is Sean Hannity, who in addition to his TV gig on Fox also hosts a radio show for WABC. And even though they are not really journalists and they adhere to a strictly "tabloid" style of broadcasting, they sound like Plato and Aristotle compared to the insane blathering of the number-three-rated host on *Talkers'* list, Michael Savage.

The audience for liberal, or progressive, talk radio is much smaller. A perusal of *Talkers* in 2007 indicates that the highest-rated radio program on the progressive side is the *Ed Schultz Show*, syndicated nationally by the Jones Radio Network. Schultz averages around three million listeners a week. The best-known and most talked-about liberal alternatives to talk radio are the programs of the Air America radio network, which became mired in financial problems and was sold in 2007 to new investors. In late 2006 its most popular program hosts, Al Franken and Randi Rhodes, were each pulling in about one and a half million listeners weekly. Ditto for Sean Hannity's nightly adversary on Fox News, Alan Colmes, who also has a syndicated radio program. Franken has since left the Air America network to go into, of all things, elective politics.

There are approximately 100 radio stations in the United States carrying some kind of liberal talk radio program, compared to over 600 for the Rush Limbaugh program alone. This kind of radical imbalance has led some to call for either reestablishing the Fairness Doctrine or mandating local licensing requirements to try to attain a more even presentation of viewpoints on public airwaves.

The left-of-center think tank Center for American Progress issued a report in June 2007 called "The Structural Imbalance of Political Talk Radio." According to the report, out of 257 news/talk radio stations owned by the top five commercial station owners, 91 percent of the total weekday talk radio programming is conservative and 9 percent is progressive. The center suggested three steps for increasing the presence of liberal talk in radio: restoring local and national caps on the ownership of commercial radio stations, ensuring greater local accountability over radio licensing, and requiring commercial broadcast owners to abide by public interest obligations to pay a fee to support public broadcasting.

The report came out around the same time as efforts by congressional Democrats to consider legislation that would codify certain sections of the Fairness Doctrine into federal law. Support for such a measure was voiced by senators Diane Feinstein, Dick Durbin, and John Kerry, among others. "It's time to reinstitute the Fairness Doctrine," said Durbin. "I have this old-fashioned attitude that when Americans hear both sides of the story, they're in a better position to make a decision."[19] Republicans declared open war, believing it to be a coordinated plan by the political left to reimplement the Fairness Doctrine wholesale.

However, the report by the Center for American Progress never actually called for reimplementing the Fairness Doctrine. In fact, many feel the doctrine is too tainted with controversy to be politically viable. Instead, future action by Democrats, and by those interested in requiring more ideological diversity in radio, may rely on efforts by Congress and the FCC (particularly if there is a Democratic administration in Washington after 2008) to use already existing federal guidelines to compel broadcast companies and local license holders to provide more diversity in radio programming. Most broadcasters, and virtually all Republicans, argue that if broadcasters are forced to provide this kind of alternative programming, the advertising support won't be there and they will lose money.

In this author's view, it seems unlikely that whatever pressure is brought to bear on broadcasters and local station owners will be enough to significantly alter the radio landscape. The ratings and revenues for the conservative-dominated programming have simply been too good. It would take a lot of convincing to get station managers, not to mention advertisers, to take a chance on doing something different. In fact, it would probably take a fairly heavy-handed approach, something from which a new administration, even a Democratic one, would likely shy away.

What happened in the commercial talk radio market in the 1980s and 1990s is similar to what has occurred with the Fox News Channel in the last decade. Namely, conservative listeners/viewers gravitated to the news/talk program that validated their political values and worldview. The audience for Fox News is built largely on the middle-aged, conservative, mostly male audience that tunes in to talk radio. From this perspective, Rush Limbaugh and other conservative radio talkers provided a base of listeners/viewers that Roger Ailes and Fox News were able to tap in to in their campaign to make Fox a cable TV ratings winner.

The rise of talk radio is key to understanding the media culture that Ailes has helped to create and define on cable television. His approach to programming at CNBC, and especially at America's Talking, was very heavily influenced by talk radio. In fact, one could argue, as many do, that America's

Talking was basically an attempt to bring talk radio to television. Ailes was brought to CNBC to spice up their programming and to make America's Talking an "innovative talk" channel that would create a buzz. Most of the programs Ailes developed while there, such as *Am I Nuts?* were designed with the radio talk format in mind.

There's no better example of Ailes's belief in the talk radio/television connection than Rush Limbaugh himself. After all, before there was a Bill O'Reilly or a Sean Hannity, Ailes tried to make Limbaugh a TV star. When he left the political consulting business and went back to working in television, one of the first things he did was to negotiate a syndication agreement for a Rush Limbaugh television program. It was his first attempt at taking what works on talk radio and adapting it to TV. Ailes himself produced the half-hour show, in which Limbaugh brought his talk radio persona into the TV studio. The Limbaugh TV show had mixed reviews and never built strong ratings—let's face it, Limbaugh has a face for radio—but it was an important experiment in Ailes's development of the formula he would later use at Fox.

Slate's Jack Shafer makes a good case for this radio/TV nexus in a commentary about David Foster Wallace's analysis of talk radio. Wallace wrote a feature-length article in the April 2005 *Atlantic Monthly* called "Host," which follows the trials and tribulations of John Ziegler, host of a radio talk program at KFI-AM in Los Angeles. Shafer says that Wallace never makes the link directly, but that "it's obvious that Fox News Channel and its imitators have incorporated many of talk radio's basic lessons into their architecture."[20]

In his article, Wallace says that Ziegler is "not a journalist—he is an entertainer—or maybe it's better to say that he is part of a peculiar, modern, and very popular type of news industry, one that manages to enjoy the authority and influence of journalism without the stodgy constraints of fairness, objectivity, and responsibility . . . "[21] Shafer suggests that Wallace could just as easily be talking about Bill O'Reilly or Sean Hannity: "These radio and cable entertainers do precisely what they damn mainstream media reporters for doing—they interpret, analyze, and explain news inside their narrow political context."[22]

In his *Atlantic* piece, Wallace insists that it is a "fallacy" that political talk radio is motivated by ideology. "Political talk radio is a business," he says, "and it is motivated by revenue ... the conservatism that dominates today's AM airwaves does so because it generates high Arbitron ratings, high ad rates, and maximum profits." No doubt Shafer and Wallace are correct that no matter how one defines "quality journalism," no type of journalism can survive very long if it lacks a commercial component to attract audiences and advertisers— and this is what Ailes has found so attractive about the talk radio style.

In developing television programming for America's Talking and then for Fox, Ailes found the talk radio format beneficial in two ways. First, it has high entertainment value—it has proved to be a ratings-grabbing mix of news and talk that works on cable TV in a way that wouldn't work as well on broadcast network TV. And second, particularly important for Fox News, the mostly conservative, male orientation of the average talk radio listener finds a comfortable fit in the edgy, right-of-center opinion-driven programming offered by Fox News. Unlike during his tenure at CNBC, Ailes was freed by Rupert Murdoch to orchestrate the Fox News programs to appeal directly to the conservative side of the aisle.

Fox, says Shafer, excels at adapting the talk radio format to television, "right down to the talk radiolike cut-ins for news briefs at the half-hour; many segments running 10 or less; and the ever-present 'sweepers,' the broadcasting term of art for the tag line the show or the station wants its audience to associate with it – think it 'Fair and Balanced,' and 'No Spin Zone.'" As with talk radio, Fox News personalities are good at providing a sense of urgency and "danger" to rope in audiences and keep them hooked—a look at Bill O'Reilly's headlines from his "Talking Points" segment reveals tabloid-style headlines such as "More Danger from the ACLU," "Undermining the War on Terror, Part 97," and "Using Doctors to Hide Sex Crimes in Illegal Abortions."[23]

And with the *Hannity & Colmes* program on Fox News, Ailes completed the talk radio–style television program he started with Rush Limbaugh in the early '90s. Sean Hannity is just as bombastic, confrontational, and conservative as Limbaugh, but with a made-for-TV smile and a friendlier demeanor.

12

Ailes and the Dirty Digger

We'll rue the day we let Roger and Rupert team up.

—Jack Welch, chairman and CEO of General Electric,
parent company of NBC and CNBC[1]

Roger Ailes and Rupert Murdoch had met on several occasions, and the two men knew they shared a philosophical approach to government, politics, and as it turns out, also to business. But in the mid-'90s, circumstances brought them together in ways neither could have imagined just a few years earlier. When Ailes left NBC, actually before he left, one of the first phone calls he made was to Rupert Murdoch. He had done some media consulting work for several Fox television shows in the early '90s, so Murdoch was very familiar with his work, and he was quite impressed with what Ailes had accomplished at CNBC in so short a time.

Ailes's unique gifts for talent development, television programming, and political maneuvering were just what Murdoch was looking for. He needed someone to take charge of his plans for a new cable news network to go head-to-head with CNN and Ted Turner, and Ailes's résumé was perfect. From Ailes's perspective, it was a dream come true. He was being hired by arguably the biggest media mogul in the world to start a new television network. His new boss had deep pockets, big goals, a broad definition of what constitutes journalism, and a long-standing dedication to conservative/libertarian political views.

Murdoch. Few names today are so immediately recognizable, so laden with emotion that they bring an immediate reaction from their mere mention. The very name has become so recognizable, in such a way that it is almost synonymous with the popular media culture of the early twenty-first century. In some ways the name Murdoch is like a national Rorschach test. Liberals probably think of sleazy tabloids and right-wing political posturing.

Conservatives think of HarperCollins Publishing, Newt Gingrich, and Fox News. Many New Yorkers almost certainly think of the *New York Post*. But when anyone thinks of Rupert Murdoch, the very first word that should come to mind is *profits*. It is an incredible understatement to say that the man knows how to make money in the media business. Such a worldwide media magnate the world has never seen. By some estimates,[2] based on the amount of money it would take to acquire all of a company's stock, his company, News Corporation, is the number one media company in the world. He makes John Foster Kane, the lead character in Orson Welles's classic movie *Citizen Kane*, look like a Bible salesman.

What do we know about Rupert Murdoch? A lot, actually.

1. He has built a worldwide multimedia empire from a family-owned newspaper publishing business in Australia;

2. According to some critics, his specialty is "tabloid" journalism, producing mass-market publications featuring sensational headlines, gossip, and color photography;

3. He has skillfully used his media properties to advance political agendas, and conversely, has used those political assets to advance his media properties;

4. His empire, the News Corporation, includes newspapers, magazines, book publishing, cable television, broadcast television, satellite television, the Internet, radio, film studios, recording studios, sports franchises, advertising, and real estate (see Appendix for a full list of News Corp. holdings);

5. He has perfected the art of "predatory pricing," offering cable carriers money to include Fox News, for example, or obtaining the *Wall Street Journal* by offering a per-share price well above its market value; and

6. He is willing to lose money to make money—the *New York Post,* for example, loses millions, yet provides Murdoch a platform to influence the national political dialogue.

One of the biggest criticisms of Murdoch is that he has consistently used his media organizations to advance the economic interests of his other holdings, raising ethical issues and judgment questions. He has also blurred the lines between editorial policy and news reporting, often in support of his corporate holdings and political interests.

The following sentiment, from Russ Baker in the *Columbia Journalism Review*, is typical:

> Murdoch uses his diverse holdings, which include newspapers, magazines, sports teams, a movie studio, and book publisher, to promote his own financial interests at the expense of real news gathering, legal and regulatory rules, and journalistic ethics. He wields his media as instruments of influence with politicians who can aid him, and savages his competitors in his news columns. If ever someone demonstrated the dangers of mass power being concentrated in few hands, it would be Murdoch.[3]

During his quest for the *Wall Street Journal* in 2007, the *Journal* itself recognized the ethical questions and image issues that Murdoch brings to the table. "In Murdoch's Career, A Hand on the News" is the title of an article about the mogul's career that looked at some of the controversies from Murdoch's career in journalism. The article recognized that

> a detailed examination of Mr. Murdoch's half-century career as a journalist and businessman shows that his newspapers and other media outlets have made coverage decisions that advanced the interests of his sprawling media conglomerate, News Corp. In the process, Mr. Murdoch has blurred a line that exists at many other U.S. media companies between business and news sides—a line intended to keep the business and political interests of owners from influencing the presentation of news.[4]

The question everyone began asking after Murdoch's purchase of the *Journal* was, Will this kind of independence and integrity from the news division continue? Analysts who have studied Murdoch's career and the patterns that emerged from his other newspapers would suggest the answer is no.

Over the last half century Murdoch has parlayed his father's stake in a small Australian newspaper company into one of the largest and most successful multinational media conglomerates in world history. His father,

Keith Arthur Murdoch, a lifelong newspaperman, had acquired a controlling interest in the News Limited, an Adelaide, Australia, company publishing an afternoon newspaper called the *News*.

As a student at Oxford University, young Rupert studied philosophy and economics, but after his father died suddenly in 1952, he went into the family journalism business full-time. According to published sources, while in college Rupert had developed a taste for gambling and making money even before he went into the news business, and this tendency has shown itself throughout his business career.

He seemed to develop an appetite for the media business, and for expansion, after he became managing director of the *News*. His first new acquisition was a small Sunday newspaper in Perth, Western Australia, which he built into a successful and popular publication. His drive for increased newspaper sales, combined with a flair for tabloid-style stories, made his newspaper holdings a success. In 1956 he began publishing Australia's first weekly television magazine, *TV Week*. Around the same time, he also acquired an interest in the country's oldest women's magazine, *New Idea*. His newspapers and magazines were profitable and financed further expansion, with the help of the Commonwealth Bank of Australia, a government-owned institution dedicated to supporting Australian business development.

Murdoch's first brush with politics came when he had to defend himself and the *News* from charges of treason, stemming from a series of articles the paper ran criticizing the South Australian government's prosecution of a young aborigine for murder. It is the only time this author, or anyone this author has talked to for this book, can remember Murdoch taking the side of the weak and defenseless against the resources of the powerful. A Royal Commission investigated the case, confirmed the guilt of the accused, and recommended criminal charges against the publisher of the *News*. To avoid a criminal trial, Murdoch met with government officials; he was forced to admit his paper was in error and also agreed to pay the administrative costs of the Royal Commission's investigation. The experience humbled the young Murdoch, but it seems to have taught him some valuable lessons about political power and the influence that individual politicians have over their environment. It apparently also taught him that he should play on the side of the privileged and powerful in the future. He began to pay more attention to political issues and electoral politics, and began spending time with political party and government officials in Australia. He found politics to be an indispensable tool in shaping the business environment.

Throughout the late 1950s and early 1960s, he expanded his media holdings to include suburban and provincial newspapers in New South Wales, Queensland, Victoria, and the Northern Territory, including the Sydney tabloid the *Daily Mirror*. And for the first time, Murdoch's interests ventured into multimedia, obtaining the Sydney-based recording company Festival Records. Then in 1964 he launched the country's first national daily newspaper, the *Australian*. The national daily was intended to be a quality national news source, but it was also meant to boost Murdoch's ability to influence the national political agenda.

In the late 1960s and '70s, Murdoch used his media holdings to become more involved in national politics in Australia and also began expanding his media empire internationally for the first time. He moved into the British market with the acquisitions of the *News of the World,* the *Sun,* and the *Times,* and became a major force in British media and politics. His move into Britain solidified his image as an aggressive collector of multiple media outlets and an expert at turning a profit from mass-marketed tabloid publications. He was dubbed the Dirty Digger by his critics in England—"digger" being a colloquial term for an Australian soldier. He has been adept at building readership for his glossy, entertainment-oriented publications that critics say are light on journalism and high on sensationalism and gossip. Profits have been good— for example, the *Sun,* one of his major British holdings, is a major revenue producer for News Corporation.

In 1973 he acquired his first American publication, the *San Antonio Express-News.* Soon the paper looked like many of Murdoch's other newspapers, with headlines like "Midget Robs Undertaker at Midnight," "Aliens Fought Over Urine in Desert Battle," and "Vampire Killer Stalks City."[5] He then launched *Star,* a supermarket tabloid, and in 1976 bought one of his flagship operations in the United States, the *New York Post.* His ownership and management of the Post is how most Americans became acquainted with Murdoch. He took what had been a solid, if underperforming, newspaper and took it "down-market," as those in the news business say. It became a tabloid, not that different in many respects from *Star.* Murdoch biographer William Shawcross typifies the view of many critics, saying Murdoch's publications tend to be "grey broadsheets or racy tabloids," neither of which attracts excellent journalists.[6]

Once in the American market, he continued expanding. News Corporation was founded by Murdoch in 1980 as a holding company. It was headquartered in Australia until 2004, when it was reincorporated as an American corporation in Delaware. In 1985 News Corporation bought the 20th Century Fox movie studio and announced the purchase of the Metromedia group of television stations. These acquisitions laid the foundation for the Fox Broadcasting Company. In order to get approval for the purchase of the TV stations, Murdoch became an American citizen, which like everything else he has done, was a business decision.

His transition from print media to electronic and broadcast media in the 1980s has become one of the defining events in the history of modern media. It has changed broadcast news, and will continue to do so. He has built his empire by acquiring and producing vast quantities of multimedia content, and then acquiring and controlling the means to distribute that content. The critical event in this transition was the founding of America's fourth broadcast network, Fox Television, in 1986. There had not been a new American television network in several decades, but Murdoch knew he could transform the American media landscape if he could influence television the way he had influenced print media.

If Murdoch and News Corporation are largely defined in print by the *New York Post* and by its British counterpart, the *Sun,* then Murdoch's television image is closely associated with such Fox programs as the tabloid TV show *A Current Affair.* A television version of Murdoch's newspaper tabloids, the show went straight for the bottom line: sex, scandal, celebrity gossip, crime stories, and other outrageous features and over-the-top guests gave the show a sleazy feel. It was hosted by Maury Povich, a feature reporter at one of the Metromedia TV stations that Murdoch had acquired, WTTG in Washington, D.C. Another notable feature of *A Current Affair* is that several of its on-air reporters and producers went on to work for Murdoch and Roger Ailes at the Fox News Channel some years later, and in the early '90s Ailes's media consulting company, Ailes Inc., counted *A Current Affair* and Fox Television among its clients.

Murdoch has a long history of using his media properties as political tools. What separates News Corporation media outlets from other sources of news media, in the estimation of most media observers, is the willful and intentional use of news reporting for political purposes. While most news media editorialize about political issues and personalities, the news reporting adheres to a set of professional standards about objectivity, and fairness. Those standards might vary somewhat from journalist to journalist and from newsroom to newsroom, but they are at least a goal and a source of professional identity for an organization's employees.

However, at Murdoch's media companies his operations are often used for expressly political purposes. The *New York Post* is not profitable in a financial sense for Murdoch, but it has been invaluable to him as a battering ram for political causes and vendettas. Another Murdoch biographer, Neal Chenoweth, writes that Murdoch has

> used the *Post* ruthlessly to promote his favored politicians and to savage their opponents . . . The long list of victims and beneficiaries goes from former New York Mayor Ed Koch, whom the *Post* backed; to one-time vice presidential nominee Geraldine Ferraro, whom the *Post* crucified; to Rudy Giuliani, whom the *Post* ferociously supported; to Hillary Rodham Clinton, whom the *Post* described as a 'rejected wife,' a perpetrator of a 'veritable crime wave in the White House,' who 'couldn't find the Bronx unless she had a chauffeur, and couldn't find Yankee Stadium without a seeing eye dog.'[7]

Murdoch has long been associated with conservative or right-wing politics. In the United States he has been a longtime supporter of the Republican Party and a booster of a whole slew of Republican officeholders, such as Ronald Reagan, Bob Dole, Newt Gingrich, Al D'Amato, George Pataki, as well as the previously mentioned Rudy Giuliani—more on that later. His newspapers on all continents routinely advocate for pro-American foreign policy positions, pro-Israeli and anti-Palestinian sentiments, anti-European Union positions, and so on. And along the way, he and his media properties have earned a less-than-stellar record on civil rights.

HarperCollins Publishing, owned by News Corp., has repeatedly paid stunning book advances to public figures who can be helpful on the political front. Former British Conservative Party leader and influential member of the House of Lords Jeffrey Archer was paid several million dollars for novels many found to be of dubious quality. "Since such books rarely earn back their advances, they appear to be outright gifts—or worse."[8] The $4.5 million advance HarperCollins paid to newly installed U.S. House Speaker Newt Gingrich is a prime example. It seemed like bribery to many, and the fact that the meeting between Gingrich and Murdoch to discuss the deal was arranged by Murdoch's lobbyist, Peter Padden, didn't help appearances—major telecommunications legislation was before Congress at the time.[9] And then there were the regulatory concerns about the foreign ownership of Fox TV. Of course, there was a firestorm of controversy, followed by congressional ethics committee meetings and a commitment by Gingrich to give back the advance.

But Murdoch got what he wanted out of the Federal Communications Commission (FCC). It seems he has always gotten what he wanted out of the FCC, which is one reason he builds all of this political capital in the first place. In 1993 the FCC waived its cross-ownership rule—barring a company from owning a newspaper and/or a radio or TV station in the same market— allowing Murdoch to buy back the *New York Post,* which was in bankruptcy at the time. Through intense political pressure, the FCC went against its own staff recommendation in 1995 and endorsed Murdoch's position that News Corp.'s ownership of American television stations was not a violation of the law barring foreign ownership greater than 25 percent of a TV station, but was in fact in the public's interests. This allowed him to continue his quest to build the Fox network and to launch Fox News. In 2003 he successfully lobbied the Bush administration to block, on antitrust grounds, the merger of the two largest satellite operators. This maneuver allowed Murdoch to reenter negotiations to buy Direct TV, America's largest satellite company. Then he convinced the administration to push the FCC to lift the cap on the percentage of American households that one company's TV stations can reach, which is exactly what FCC staff proposed.[10]

Murdoch has used his newspapers as political weapons going all the way back to Australia in the 1960s and '70s. In Great Britain his newspapers, most famously the *Sun,* strongly supported Margaret Thatcher and her policies throughout the 1980s and were credited with helping her Conservative successor, John Major, retain power with a come-from-behind election victory over the Labor Party in 1992. The *Sun* and the *Times* became known as Tory attack dogs, viciously attacking Thatcher's and then Major's detractors. During the Thatcher and Major administrations, Murdoch's businesses, particularly his newspaper ventures and his British Sky satellite service, were repeatedly favored with easing of regulations and with the government's choosing not to invoke monopoly oversight. And not coincidentally, HarperCollins Publishing paid Thatcher $3 million for her memoirs.

In the late '90s his British newspapers did support Tony Blair, but only after Blair and the Labor Party had abandoned their left-of-center political views and it became clear that the British Conservative Party was a "spent" force. So the evidence shows that Murdoch is not a rigid ideologue; he's willing to switch horses when necessary for business and profit reasons. For example, he created a tempest in 2006 when he hosted a fund-raiser for Hillary Clinton. The arch-conservative Rupert Murdoch helping conservatives' "public enemy number one" raise money? Was he merely being pragmatic once again, as he was in the '90s with Tony Blair? Was he making the calculation—as many, including his friend Newt Gingrich, have done—that in 2008 the Republicans won't stand a chance of winning the election, and so was hedging his bets (and protecting his investments) by playing nice with the enemy? It's particularly intriguing considering the vitriol with which Murdoch's paper has gone after Senator Clinton in the past.

And more broadly, he has consistently put his media companies to work on behalf of his other holdings. According to journalist Eric Alterman, Murdoch's magazines and newspapers support his television programs and movies and vice versa. "His reporters make up news that other companies would have to pay public relations firms millions to try to place," writes Alterman. "No newspaper in America is less shy about slanting its coverage to serve its master's agenda—be it commercial or political—than the *New York Post.* Judging by the *Post,* every Fox program is either 'jaw-dropping,' 'mega-successful,' 'highly anticipated,' or all three."[11]

In 1996, the *New York Post* ran a two-page spread about Fox News's opening of its Manhattan studio, with photos of Murdoch, Rudy Giuliani, and Roger Ailes mingling with celebrities. The *Post* waxed eloquently that "politicians, celebrities, and journalists gathered under one festive tent last night to toast Sixth Avenue's newest—and newsiest—showcase: the Fox News Channel."[12] That same year, the *Post* savaged Murdoch's millionaire rival Ted Turner and Time Warner Inc. over a major dispute involving Time Warner's decision not to carry the Fox News Channel on its New York cable system. "Is Ted Turner Nuts?" the *Post* headline asked. Under Murdoch, the *Post* has also gone to war against his crosstown rival, the *New York Daily News* and its editor Mortimer Zuckerman. "Suck-Up Zuck," screamed one headline.

According to many of his critics, one need look no further than his relationship with the Communist government of China to peer into Rupert Murdoch's soul. The soul of a business tycoon, that is. When you look at the record, Mr. Murdoch has had some pretty disgusting things to say in regard to China. In defense of his relationship with a government that has one of the worst human rights record in world history, Murdoch is noted for having made the ridiculous comment, "The truth is—and we Americans don't like to admit it—that authoritarian societies can work."[13] He has spoke, disparagingly of one of the Chinese government's worst enemies, the Dalai Lama, referring to him as "a very old political monk shuffling around in Gucci shoes."[14] His son James lashed out at the Falun Gong, a religious movement persecuted by the Chinese government, calling them "dangerous and apocalyptic."[15]

Murdoch-owned HarperCollins Publishing gave a $1 million advance to the daughter of former Chinese leader Deng Xiaoping to write a fawning, historically dishonest biography of her father at the same time News Corp. was seeking approval to extend its broadcast ventures in China. This is the same publisher that canceled a book contract with the last British governor of Hong Kong, Chris Patten. The book, *East and West*, was a frank and unflattering assessment of Chinese policy and leadership. At first, News Corp. said the reason for dumping the book was that it just wasn't very good. Murdoch called Patten, whom the Chinese leadership absolutely loathed, a "terrible governor."[16]

However, the Patten book had been critically praised by virtually all who had seen it. The HarperCollins editor who worked on the book, Stuart Proffitt, told Patten that he had never read a book "by any modern politician which is so lucid or engrossing or which has quickened my blood so frequently."[17] Not good enough, eh? When an internal HarperCollins memo surfaced detailing Murdoch's concerns about the "negative aspects of publication" of the Patten book, the publisher was forced to apologize. Proffitt, who was suspended over his objections to Murdoch's decision to cancel the book, sued. Patten found another publisher and now ironically credits the Murdoch-inspired controversy with boosting sales of *East and West*. Of Murdoch, Patten said, "I don't see how you can be in favor of free speech in one part of the world, and less keen on it in another."[18]

Only a few years earlier, Murdoch had removed the BBC from his STAR satellite system's offerings to China, reportedly because the Chinese government was upset by a BBC documentary about Mao Tse-tung and other programs about China that the political leadership didn't like. For example, during programming breaks, BBC would often show photos and videos of world events—one of them included the lone man standing in front of a tank during the Tiananmen Square crackdown on pro-democracy protestors. Murdoch told author William Shawcross in a 1994 interview that "they say it's a cowardly way, but we said that in order to get in there and get accepted, we'll cut the BBC out . . . it might have occurred to me, this might not hurt relations with Beijing."[19]

Chinese officials dislike Western-style media. They vehemently dislike how China is portrayed by Western media organizations, and they desperately want to present China in a more flattering light. Rupert Murdoch has helped them. In 1996 he entered a joint venture with a onetime radio host for the Chinese People's Liberation Army to broadcast a news and entertainment channel called Phoenix. The channel steers clear of anything embarrassing or uncomfortable to official Chinese policy and thus operates much like a propaganda network for Chinese leaders.

News Corp. also helped China Central Television to develop a new Web site, in fact sending a team from Fox News to help them set it up. Furthermore, News Corp. brought delegations of Chinese officials to its facilities at the Murdoch-owned British Sky satellite television headquarters in London to show them how to encrypt satellite transmissions. The initial intention was for News Corp. to contract with the Chinese, but they ended up simply adopting the technology back in China on their own, so News Corp. essentially gave away the technology.[20]

This next sentence may have to be read twice to be believed. Amazingly, Murdoch and News Corp. launched a multimillion-dollar joint venture with the *People's Daily,* the mouthpiece of the Chinese Communist Party, to produce an on-line news service. That's right—Rupert Murdoch and the Communist Chinese government jointly bring to the Chinese people its daily helping of party propaganda and anti-Western news! Take that, Karl Marx!

Mr. Murdoch has been honored by the leadership of China for all of his service to its government and to the Chinese Communist Party. In 1998 President Jiang invited him to a private meeting where, through the official Chinese news agency, Xinhua, President Jiang expressed his appreciation for "the efforts made by world media mogul Rupert Murdoch in presenting China so objectively and cooperating with the Chinese press over the last two years."[21]

The prime minister at the time, Zhu Rongji, noted that Mr. Murdoch had become an American citizen to comply with television station ownership requirements in the United States. He joked that if Mr. Murdoch wanted to do more business in China, then he should consider becoming Chinese.[22]

So is Rupert Murdoch a right-wing ideologue or not? The answer appears to be, "Yes, unless it interferes with making money." He is not an ideologue in the same sense as some of his political friends, like Newt Gingrich. He'll support whatever party or movement best serves his business model at the time. He supports Republicans in the United States for the same reason he supported the Conservative Party in Britain in the '80s and early '90s—because Republicans are the party of deregulation and smaller government. Even if he hadn't given Republicans all that money over the years and used his newspapers to shill for them, they still would have given him practically everything he wanted, because that's their nature—less government regulation, less oversight and monitoring, less of a tax burden, and maximum protection for private sector enterprises. Maybe he could have saved his money.

Actually, he thinks of himself as a libertarian, not a Republican, and he belongs to libertarian policy organizations and gives money to libertarian causes. But that doesn't help explain the apparent hypocrisy of supporting conservative causes and right-wing politicians on the one hand, while serving the interests of perhaps the leading example of big government and centralized power held by the Chinese Communist leadership. Libertarians are for minimal government interference in the lives of citizens and express a strong preference for liberty—everything mainland China is against!

In his 1996 book *Full Disclosure,* Andrew Neil, fired by Murdoch as editor of the *Times* over what many thought to be aggressive reporting that angered the British government, said of Murdoch, "Where political principle and business expediency clash, you can be pretty sure expediency will win. When his business interests force him into an expedient solution, which goes against his political grain, a convoluted thought process takes place to justify his position."[23]

It's a business model he has used repeatedly in his extremely successful career and is one of the things that led him to hire Roger Ailes to run Fox News. Ailes is more of a conservative ideologue than Murdoch, but his goals and Murdoch's goals seem to converge on most points. Both of them knew that there was a market niche for a conservative cable news organization and that it could be successful financially. Fox News serves Murdoch's political and business goals within News Corp., and it gave Ailes an opportunity to achieve what is apparently a lifelong goal: domination of the news by conservatives.

Another characteristic of Murdoch's business strategy might be called predatory pricing. As discussed, he is willing to lose money on a venture if it serves another need, as for example the *New York Post,* which allows him to influence politics and policy, or the *Weekly Standard,* another money loser. But he is also very willing to spend vast quantities of money to get a business established and has shown a willingness to pay significantly above the market value of a business in order to acquire it. You need two things to make this work: tons of operating cash and a long-term business strategy. His many holdings in

News Corp. give him the financial strength and flexibility to finance numerous business ventures, some at a loss; and like the good businessman that he is, he understands long-term planning.

A great example is the Fox News Channel. In fact, Murdoch turned the normal business models of the cable television world on its head. To get Fox News off the ground and in the homes of as many cable households as possible, he was dangling huge sums of cash in front of cable operators across the country. As Scott Collins points out in *Crazy Like a Fox,* this was a reversal of the usual financial arrangement between programmers and cable television systems. Traditionally, local cable companies "pay a per-subscriber fee to programmers in exchange for a license to carry channels" on their system.[24]

Distributors usually pay for programming content, or at least share revenues, not the other way around. Movie studios and production companies arrange for distribution deals that make money for both sides. What Murdoch did is a little bit like a recording artist paying a record company to distribute his music.

In the 1980s and '90s, cable networks developed business models that paid healthy dividends. For example, a CNN or an MTV basically sold their program content to cable companies based on how many subscribers the local system had. If CNN charged an average of 35 cents per month per subscriber, a cable carrier that had one hundred thousand subscribers would pay CNN $35,000 every month. That's just one carrier. A network has multiple arrangements with carriers all over the country, generating tons of monthly income. And that doesn't include advertising revenue. Life was good. It especially helped a network like CNN when it had a virtual monopoly on cable news.

But in 1996 Murdoch entered the game and changed the rules. A start-up network is a risky proposition, especially in the case of Fox News, which, with no organization, no track record, and no big names, was going up against an industry giant. Murdoch knew that cable carriers would have little or no incentive to pay for his product, at least right away. So what did he do? Offer it for free? No—he offered to pay them! In a move that stunned industry insiders, Murdoch agreed to pay cable carriers that would carry the Fox News Channel a huge sum up front—at least $10 per subscriber. The carriers would have to pay subscriber fees to Fox once the network was established, but it represented a huge advance, and a huge investment in the viability and the future of Fox News by Rupert Murdoch. As Roger Ailes said at the time, "Rupert is a man who can make a billion-dollar decision without blinking."[25]

No question, from the time he became attracted to gambling, in his twenties,[26] Murdoch has shown a great poker face, steely determination, and a talent for the "long" game. Some of his companies ran up considerable losses for years, which was okay because the other branches of his media empire were cranking out profits. The *Australian,* the national daily he founded in 1964, took more than twenty years to make a profit. The *Times of London,* which he acquired in 1982, will show its first operating profit in 2008, according to News Corp. execs.[27] As long as the bottom line is profitable at News Corp., he can keep up this shell game for years.

13

Fox News: *A Current Affair* Meets CNN

They always laugh in the beginning. That never bothers me.

—Rupert Murdoch's response to Ailes's comment,
"You know, they're laughing at us," after the
press conference launching Fox News in 1996

Roger Ailes's communication strategy—for him, a philosophy of interpersonal communication—is to build rapport and credibility with the audience through warmth, humor, and understanding. Where John F. Kennedy had this naturally, Nixon had to be trained and managed. As one journalist wag noted, Ailes and the other consultants around Nixon were ultimately successful at teaching him how to "imitate a human being on television."[1] Ronald Reagan had to be reminded of what his innate strengths were, and George Bush Sr. had to be more or less built from the ground up for his run for the gold.

Ailes brought the same standards and philosophy to television news. Straight news reporting is mundane, vanilla, and passionless—he once compared watching CNN to visiting a funeral parlor. What really gets people's attention and stirs them up is conversation, the clash of opinions, and interaction with the audience. This is the approach Ailes brought to CNBC and then to Fox. This kind of programming also makes it easier to arouse people's passions, influence their opinions, and motivate them to act—much more suitable for framing conservative political thought and waging war on the "mainstream media."

America's Talking was built on Ailes's premise that viewers would respond to an entertaining mix of talk, news, and opinion—and he was right.

That programming at CNBC became, in essence, the prototype for Fox News. Ailes himself has admitted this in interviews, and the man who hired him to run CNBC and America's Talking, Bob Wright, believes that Fox News is in large part the offspring of AT. But when Ailes went to work for News Corp. and Fox, he had an entire network to play with, a much more receptive owner-ship in Murdoch, and a symbiotic ideological approach to the news between the two of them. This is what Ailes had desired the most, and at long last, he had it. Now he would have to make it work.

When Fox News was launched in 1996, Ailes, with Murdoch at his side, echoing Joseph Coors and Jack Wilson more than twenty years earlier, proclaimed a new day: "We'd like to restore objectivity where we find it lacking."[2] There is no question that the "framing," or market positioning, of this new venture was brilliant. The whole rationale for starting Fox News was to serve as a corrective for the "biased," pro-liberal slant of the other news networks—CNN, ABC, NBC, and CBS. Unlike those other guys, said Ailes and Murdoch, Fox would be Fair and Balanced. They set out to brand Fox News as the objective news operation—the one that would be open to all sides.

Ailes was using the same playbook he had used in politics. Find a way to make Nixon seem like a reasonable guy—warm him up, make him smile, put him in an arena with friendly faces, and brand him as the statesman with experience. Thus he becomes credible and trusted. Same with Bush, and same with Fox.

In positioning Fox as the fair, objective news network, Ailes and company were taking advantage of years of survey findings and public opinion analyses that suggested the major media outlets in America were "liberal." As Ailes told *Brill's Content* magazine in 1998, "The fact is that Rupert Murdoch and I and, by the way, the vast majority of the American people, believe that most of the news tilts to the left."[3] Statements like this are based largely on some highly publicized research findings over the years. The best known is a 1986 book called *The Media Elite,* which surveyed journalists at national media outlets such as the *New York Times* and the *Washington Post,* and the broadcast networks. The study found that most of these journalists were Democratic voters whose attitudes were well to the left of the general public on a variety of topics, including such hot-button social issues as abortion, affirmative action, and gay rights. The authors concluded that journalists' coverage of controversial issues reflected their own attitudes, and the predominance of political liberals in newsrooms therefore pushed news coverage in a liberal direction. This book has been used as a cause célèbre by conservatives to prove their accusations of media bias.

But theories are difficult things to prove, and statistics can be a double-edged sword. Subsequent studies have verified that more journalists are Democrats than Republicans, but none have proved a link between the personal political affiliation of reporters and biased news coverage. Even the authors of *The Media Elite* conceded that journalists "whose news judgments stem blatantly from their politics are unlikely to survive long in mainstream news organizations . . . Those who remain in the mainstream usually accept the necessity to overcome one's biases as the hallmark of the journalistic profession."[4] Efforts to conclusively "prove" a liberal media bias may have fallen short, but the public perception of a liberal media is strong nonetheless. And that is what mattered to Roger Ailes and Rupert Murdoch. Most Americans did believe that the media were liberal, and therefore Fox News was tapping into a receptive nationwide audience. When friends confided to Ailes that they feared he would be accused of blatantly promoting right-wing viewpoints, he said, "Good! That'll drive my ratings up!"[5]

The Fox marketing strategy also dovetailed nicely with a twenty-five-year decline in the public's confidence in journalists. Most reporters and broadcasters were no longer seen as trustworthy and responsible. In fact, occupational surveys showed that by the 1990s, the public ranked journalists alongside lawyers and used-car salesmen in terms of ethics and values.

This is not some fiction created by Roger Ailes or anyone else. This is reality. Why had journalists become so unpopular? Because, whether or not one agrees with Ailes, in the public mind, journalism has become a broken instrument. In his book *Feeding Frenzy,* political scientist Larry Sabato documents the progression of reporters and editors from a "Watchdog" mentality in the '60s and '70s to a "Junkyard Dog" approach in the '80s and '90s. By Junkyard Dog, he means an overly aggressive and overly negative style of news reporting, a presumption of guilt when reporting on political figures, and a constant search for any hint of scandal, gaffe, or even minor mistakes that would put a politician in a bad light.

Sabato's political science colleague Thomas Patterson says much the same thing in his book *Out of Order.* Patterson claims that journalists are guilty of the "Bad News Syndrome," in which they prefer to report bad news and look for negative angles first. They do this because, according to Patterson, the "default" position of most reporters is that politicians are corrupt and unethical, or they wouldn't be politicians in the first place. To Patterson, this is dangerous for any democracy because it perpetuates the notion that political figures cannot be, and should never be, trusted. Patterson asserts that the public also resents the tendency of journalists to "interpret" the meaning of news, instead of "reporting" the news.

In Ailes's mind, these two factors in the public consciousness—the liberalness of reporters and their declining credibility—went hand in hand and made him confident that Fox News would succeed.

The thing is, the slogan of Fair and Balanced is just that—a slogan, not a statement of principle. It has more in common with the curtain used by the Wizard of Oz, a barrier to prevent the public from understanding what is really going on and an inside joke for those in the know, who repeat it with a wink and a nod to one another. And what is really going on? The step-by-step creation of a news network, the first in history that favors conservative views.

The Richard Nixon that America saw on TV in 1968 was artificial; the George Bush that America saw go after Michael Dukakis and Dan Rather in 1988 was a pale imitation of Ronald Reagan. These "Ailes Specials" weren't what they appeared to be. But as with everything on television, it is the perception that matters. Fox News purports to be impartial, but can an organization staffed largely by conservatives be any more impartial than organizations staffed largely by liberals? Isn't that Ailes's argument—that most news organizations are run by liberals and are therefore too liberal? Have Roger Ailes and Rupert Murdoch cornered the market on objectivity and fairness? If one believes his rhetoric, it would make Ailes the only news executive in America, or the world, capable of running an impartial news service. Well, his pedigree simply doesn't back that up.

And is Fox News staffed and run by conservatives? Let's take a look at personnel. It starts at the top. News Corp. chairman Rupert Murdoch, along with Ailes, is a long-marcher in the conservative movement. Murdoch has funded and supported numerous right-wing causes and candidates around the world (except for China). Ailes himself is one of the most ruthless and effective Republican Party operatives of the last forty years. Enough said. And then there is John Moody, the head of Fox's news division—a veteran conservative journalist, formerly with *Time* magazine. It is Moody that many former Fox employees seem to complain about the most with regard to being overly political with the news.

As Chapter 5, "Coors to You," makes clear, Moody has become known to many people as the "memo" guy. He writes a daily memo to his news staff about the day's stories and the approach the organization should take. There have been numerous articles in magazines, blog posts, and other outlets about the right-wing political slant these memos from Moody demonstrate. The Web site of FAIR lists thirty-three of these memos that they say betray a Republican bias.

An examination of the memos does show that Moody seems to have an overt political agenda, especially for a newsman. For example, in one of the better-known and more controversial memos, written in the days following the November 2006 election, in which the Democratic Party took majorities in the House and the Senate, Moody encouraged his news staff to "be on the lookout for any statements from the Iraqi insurgents . . . Thrilled at the prospect of a Dem controlled Congress."[6] In looking at Ailes's history with Joseph Coors and Television News, Inc., and Rupert Murdoch's cavalier approach to journalism, Moody's apparent newsroom behavior very well could be by design.

It often seems as if Fox News personnel aren't really trying to hide a conservative bias, but that they revel in it. Consider this pretty surprising admission from Bill O'Reilly in a conversation with journalist and author Ken Auletta: "These people, not only in the print press but other network people, and some powerful people in boardrooms, are basically frightened of the Fox News channel . . . They understand that the power has shifted into an organization that is right center."[7] And O'Reilly gave the credit to Ailes, of course. "Roger Ailes is the general, and the general sets the tone for the army." When asked if a more accurate tag line for Fox News might be "*We* report, *We* decide," he said, "Well, you're probably right."[8]

And in another stunning quotation, Fox's London bureau chief told the *Wall Street Journal* in 2005:

> Even we at Fox News manage to get some lefties on the air occasionally, and often let them finish their sentences before we club them to death and feed the scraps to Karl Rove and Bill O'Reilly . . . Fox News is, after all, a private channel and our presenters are quite open about where they stand on particular stories. That's our appeal. People watch us because they know what they are getting.[9]

Actually, as far as this author can determine, Fox seems to have just one host of a major program who is not openly conservative. That would be Greta Van Sustern, host of *On the Record.* The rest—Sean Hannity, Bill O'Reilly, Brit Hume, Shepard Smith, John Gibson, Neil Cavuto, and most of the on-air hosts—are conservatives or, at least, openly sympathetic to conservative views. Republican journalist Tony Snow, a speechwriter for the first president Bush, was a senior editor and correspondent at Fox News for several years before returning to the White House to become George W. Bush's press secretary. So the right-wing tilt is there, in the political leanings of most Fox executives and staff.

So how does that get translated into news with a conservative bias? First of all, remember, Fox isn't so much about reporting breaking news as it is about providing commentary and discussion with regard to the news. And it is in these discussions and analyses that the fight is won.

Judging from appearances, Roger Ailes likes a rigged fight. Just as he did with Richard Nixon and the Man in the Arena TV programs in 1968, and the brilliantly crafted attacks on Michael Dukakis in 1988, Ailes and his producers stack the deck. On most Fox News programs, conservative guests and commentators simply outnumber their liberal counterparts. It's common to see, for example, John Gibson or Neil Cavuto discuss an issue with three conservatives and one liberal. Or even four conservatives and no liberals. Cavuto once gushed to the scandal-tarnished former House Republican leader Tom DeLay, "You know, a lot of your loyal fans, Mr. Majority Leader, say, 'That has nice ring to it, but they like 'President DeLay.' You interested?"[10]

When Ailes hired Brit Hume from ABC News, Hume was known among his journalism colleagues as a staunch conservative. Apparently, being a staunch conservative did not prevent him from rising to the top of his "liberal-dominated" profession—he was ABC's chief White House correspondent for eight years and won an Emmy Award in 1991 for his coverage of the Gulf war. But when he was hired to anchor Fox News's main evening news broadcast, he felt the need to say that he was very excited to be doing a broadcast that "people can trust."[11] As if what he had been doing for twenty-three years as a reporter for ABC was some kind of a sham.

Hume is the cream of the crop at Fox News—a solid journalist with a nose for news and a sophisticated understanding of American politics. And yet, as the anchor of Fox's main news program, his political ideology seeps into his reporting and his news analysis just as much, or even more so, than it does for most of the broadcast journalists that he and Roger Ailes dismiss with such disdain. Fox's main evening newscast, "Special Report with Brit Hume," like Ailes's other programs, seems to go out of its way to stack its political analyses to the right. Hume himself has a conservative outlook on politics and policy that comes through subtly, but then he turns to Bill Kristol, editor of the conservative *Weekly Standard* (a Rupert Murdoch publication), who has no need of subtlety. The panel also includes Mort Kondracke, who is moderate to conservative on most issues and is editor of the widely respected *Roll Call*, and the conservative journalist Fred Barnes (also of the *Weekly Standard*). And just to make things Fair and Balanced, a moderate-to-liberal token female—often Mara Liasson of National Public Radio—gets to sit in. Several reviews of Hume's evening news program by media watchdog groups found that guests tend to be "overwhelmingly" conservative and Republican.

Hume is accused by some critics of identifying guests on his program in a way that masks their conservative agenda. One of the examples put forth by Media Matters, a left-of-center advocacy group, is a 2005 interview of John Yoo, a former deputy assistant attorney general, about a federal court challenge to the Bush administration's handling of "enemy combatants" being held at Guantánamo Bay, Cuba. According to Media Matters, Hume presented Yoo as an impartial legal expert (a law professor at the University of California, Berkeley), without informing his audience that Yoo is in fact one of the primary architects of the Bush policy he was being asked to comment on. Hume made his feelings on the Guantánamo Bay situation known on the June 13, 2005, edition of his program when he said, "I think that these kinds of problems and accusations and so forth grow out of a community that stretches from the American left through much of Europe to enemies across the world from which terrorism springs, who want the world to believe that America is what's wrong with the world." Roger Ailes couldn't have said it better himself.

Another interview conducted on Hume's program that same year included comments from Barbara Comstock, a former Justice Department official, on President Bush's nomination of John Roberts to be chief justice of the Supreme Court. The Fox correspondent, and Hume, failed to identify Ms. Comstock as a strategic advisor to Progress for America, a conservative advocacy group actively campaigning for Roberts's confirmation.

Other Fox critics accuse the network of incorporating talking points and press announcements from the Republican National Committee and other Republican advocacy groups into its reporting and news analysis. One example is a claim that a "significant segment" of liberals opposed military action after

9/11, when, according to Media Matters, public opinion polls showed otherwise. Advocacy groups also point to the use of quotations from the RNC in defense of President Bush's Social Security reform proposals. And perhaps most embarrassingly, Hume once defended Fox's coverage of "conspiracy" theories, claiming that the plane crash killing former Clinton-era Commerce secretary Ron Brown was actually an assassination by Clinton confidantes.[12]

Even when the ratio of conservatives to liberals is one to one, Ailes still tilts the scales. Take, for example, Sean Hannity and Alan Colmes. Is one supposed to believe these two are equal partners or that they are evenly matched? Poor Alan Colmes, he seems earnest enough. But Ailes and Hannity seem to have him on a very short leash. Not surprisingly, when the Hannity show was first created, Ailes had temporarily labeled the show *Hannity and a Liberal to be Determined*.[13] Reportedly, Ailes tried out several other liberal commentators to face off against Hannity, but thought they were too aggressive. The show is really a platform for conservative radio star Sean Hannity. Colmes is an afterthought. The *Hannity & Colmes* program routinely performs well in its time slot and is very popular with Republicans, who consider the Hannity program "red meat" for the conservative diet. Hannity is a talented, compelling, and relentless spokesperson for the right, which is why Roger Ailes brought him to New York and gave him a prime-time show in the first place. Rush Limbaugh wasn't available.

There have also been questions raised about the objectivity of Fox News's chief political correspondent, Carl Cameron, or Campaign Carl, as Fox anchors like to call him. In the 2000 presidential election, Cameron was covering the Bush campaign for Fox at the same time his wife was active in the Bush for President organization. In the Robert Greenwald film *Outfoxed,* Cameron is shown preparing to interview candidate Bush, telling him before the filming started how much his wife was enjoying working for his campaign and how it was a pleasure for her to campaign alongside Mr. Bush's sister. Cameron has accused the producers of *Outfoxed* of taking his comments out of context. His banter with candidate Bush might be defended as "small talk," but if one watches the video, it does raise questions about Cameron's objectivity.

Cameron got into more hot water in the 2004 presidential election season with what Fox officials called "a poor attempt at humor." Apparently, Cameron posted several quotations on the Fox News Web site attributed to Democratic presidential nominee John Kerry. The quotations, which were an attempt to ridicule Kerry—something about receiving a manicure—were fabricated by

Cameron, who insists that it was all just a joke. An official with Fox News said in a statement that "Carl Cameron made a stupid mistake which he regrets. And he has been reprimanded for his lapse in judgment." An editor placed a note on the Fox News Web site stating, "Earlier Friday, FoxNews.com posted an item purporting to contain quotations from Kerry. The item was based on a reporter's partial script that had been written in jest and should not have been posted or broadcast. We regret the error, which occurred because of fatigue and bad judgment, not malice."[14]

But when they're really stumped for news commentary or analysis, Fox often turns to one of America's elder statesmen, that famous political figure world-renowned for objective, middle-of-the-road, nonpartisan thinking: Newt Gingrich!

Many readers might be thinking, Well, what about Susan Estrich? Isn't she an example of a liberal commentator at Fox News? Isn't that an example of Fair and Balanced? Well, Susan Estrich wouldn't talk to this author, so she is unable to defend herself here against charges some on the political left have made against her that she is "Roger Ailes's pet Democrat." According to the liberal Web log the *Daily Kos,* Estrich "creates and perpetuates false issues and false fights to weaken Democrats." For example, the blog accuses Estrich of trying to "silence" Elizabeth Edwards, the wife of Democratic presidential candidate John Edwards, after Ms. Edwards criticized Democratic front-runner Hillary Clinton. Estrich, according to the *Daily Kos,*[15] "pretends that Elizabeth is shrilly insulting other candidates . . . and to top it off, Estrich manages to fire off personal insults" while accusing Edwards of being too mean. A number of liberals accuse Estrich of "providing cover" for Roger Ailes. Is Susan Estrich a female version of Alan Colmes?

What's really interesting about the Estrich situation, of course, is that she was the campaign manager for the man Roger Ailes and Lee Atwater mugged in 1988, Michael Dukakis. After the kind of media campaign Ailes ran that year against Estrich's old boss, it's a wonder she would even speak to Ailes, much less work for him at a news organization accused of favoring conservative political causes. But as she has said, Fox News pays her well.[16]

The Fox News Channel is really an entertainment channel interspersed with news. If CNN and the tabloid show *A Current Affair* were people, and they got married to each other, their offspring would be the Fox News Channel. That's not to say that Fox News isn't fun to watch, and it's definitely a ratings winner; it just is what it is.

But that is what Roger Ailes does; this is what he has been doing for more than forty years. He produces compelling, winning television, whether it is for Nixon, George Bush Sr., or Rupert Murdoch. He helps a client get to the bottom line (winning) first by creating an environment that plays to the client's strengths, then by building a highly marketable product.

Ailes understands something that, it seems, few others do: cable television is mostly about entertainment—yes, even the news. If a viewer wants straight news, he or she can pick up a newspaper, go on-line, or even flip on the Jim Lehrer program on PBS, for God's sake. Even the network news operations cover breaking news if it's a big enough story. But for that constant coverage, that insight into the meaning and significance of the news, and the commentary that accompanies the news, cable is king.

When Roger Ailes was building the Fox News organization in 1996, he brought in his old mentor from *The Mike Douglas Show*, Chet Collier, to be senior vice president of programming. The two had kept in touch over the years and had worked together on occasion. Most importantly, though, they shared a philosophy about what made good television—it's about *people* and *performance*. Find the right people and get them to perform. As Ailes told one reporter, great television means great performances, whether from a politician, an executive, or a talk show host. People are the essence of the medium, the reason that viewers watch in the first place. "If I have any ability," said Ailes, "it's probably to find talented people and set up a structure they can work in."[17]

Collier wasn't brought to Fox to worry about the quality of the journalism, he was there to help Ailes make great TV. In fact, he viewed journalists with an amused detachment, referring to them as "newsies." Like Ailes, he is first and foremost an entertainer. "My job was to see that the news was presented with the most excitement," said Collier.[18]

Ailes and Collier believe that the excitement of news is derived from good writing and casting. Collier says that to have good TV news, you have to use the "best elements of the entertainment world." That's true of any television show, he claimed, documentary, situation comedy, whatever. "Take the best material you can get . . . and cast it with the best possible people because people watch television because of the individuals that they see on the screen."[19]

This was the approach that ultimately helped Fox achieve and maintain a ratings edge over CNN and MSNBC. It made some at Fox News uncomfortable, and the focus on entertainment and style continues to be one of the main criticisms of FNC. But Collier made no apologies, and Ailes continues to laugh all the way to the bank. Said Collier, "It was always a balance between what is the news and what is entertaining . . . Of course the newsies all go crazy when you say that 'cause essentially you're corrupting a great institution or some bullshit . . . but you have to get people's attention if you're gonna get any ratings, 'cause you don't want to end up like MSNBC."[20] Currently, MSNBC trails Fox and CNN in the cable ratings war, but shows signs of beginning a rebound.

It's no accident that a good bit of the Fox News talent has a background in what some call Tabloid TV. Take the 800-pound gorilla of Fox News, Bill O'Reilly. Before coming to Fox News, O'Reilly was best known for hosting *Inside Edition,* an entertainment, tabloid-style knockoff of *A Current Affair.* He had a career in local TV and network stints at CBS and ABC, in which he frequently butted heads with management, before agreeing to host *Inside Edition* from 1989 to 1995. In the early '90s, O'Reilly had appeared as a guest on CNBC's *America's Talking A.M.* and struck Ailes as "appealing in a kind of likable Irishman way."[21] When O'Reilly pitched Ailes his idea for an aggressive, opinionated news program at Fox, Ailes pounced.

From a pure ratings standpoint, it's hard to argue with success. As Roger Ailes has said, his biggest asset is his ability to spot talent, and with O'Reilly he found the perfect person to develop a show that is a combination of news discussion and professional wrestling. Together they have built cable TV news's highest-rated show. It is a show that would never work on network TV, but is perfect for cable. It's edgy, opinionated, and built on confrontation. It's this author's theory that O'Reilly's audience is composed equally of those that like him and agree with him and those that hate him and would like to see him roasted over an open flame. In this, O'Reilly resembles radio disc jockey Howard Stern—viewers/listeners tune in just to see what he will say next.

Another example of Ailes's penchant for glitz and tabloid-style "infotainment" is Shepard Smith, host of *The Fox Report with Shepard Smith,* an hourlong, fast-paced rundown of the day's news at 7 p.m. In 1996, Smith came directly to Fox from the hit tabloid show *A Current Affair.* Sandwiched in between *Special Report with Brit Hume* at 6 p.m. and O'Reilly at 8, the impeccably dressed, gel-haired Smith provides a sassy, fun-with-facts look at the news—as John Kerry might say, "in a fashion reminiscent of John Tesh at *Entertainment Tonight.*" The Fox News Web site actually brags that Smith's program covers "more than 70 stories in an hour." Now that's entertainment.

"Shep" Smith is probably the best example of how Fox News is different from CNN or any of the network news organizations. He doesn't pretend to be Peter Jennings. He doesn't want to be Peter Jennings. After all, Peter Jennings would never have said something like "it won't kill us to give 20 seconds of cute dogs!" Smith's show is apparently not meant to be journalism at all, but an entertainment program. It is pure *A Current Affair,* and is very likely something that Ailes would have produced for America's Talking back in the '90s. Fox is criticized for its "tabloid" approach, but NBC's Bob Wright says America's Talking had a lot of that. "Production values were important, you know at America's Talking we had the luxury of not having to be judged by journalistic standards . . . it was a TV show, we were doing entertainment."[22] If Roger Ailes and Rupert Murdoch were intellectually honest, they would admit that they are doing the same thing with much of the programming at Fox News.

There are news segments on Shepard Smith's program, but only in a bulleted, headline style. Its style is much closer to *A Current Affair* or *Entertainment Tonight* than an evening news program. It's sort of like turning on the TV and hearing your local weatherman talk about Yassir Arafat and the Palestine Liberation Organization. But you know what? Smith is killing the competition in his time slot, proving once again that Roger Ailes knows how to program TV and he knows what his audience wants. Just don't call it journalism.

Another Fox News correspondent, David Lee Miller, spent ten years as a reporter and producer at *A Current Affair* before coming to Fox. It seems that when building his staff in 1996, Roger Ailes raided all the tabloid shows. It might be a strategy he and Chet Collier came up with to capture the "excitement" of the news. But according to journalist Ken Auletta, Ailes has in the past acknowledged that America's Talking had been the model for much of what they do at Fox News.[23]

Which brings us to the morning program at Fox, which is called *Fox & Friends.* Now, morning news is supposed to be softer and more fun— remember Katie Couric? And Ailes doesn't disappoint. *Fox & Friends* is a downright hoot! And its ratings reflect this. Steve Doocy, with a background in local news and weather reporting, teams with Gretchen Carlson (the straight man of the act) and Brian Kilmeade, also with a background in local news and sports reporting.

Again, if the goal is ratings, it's hard to argue with success. Ailes and Collier likely put their heads together and came up with the idea of teaming a weatherman, an attractive blond news reporter, and a sports guy as the perfect morning team.

And speaking of attractive blonds . . . wow. Fox News may have the highest proportion of attractive blond female journalists of any news organization in history. But it shouldn't be too surprising, when you consider that Fox's audience is mostly male and that Roger Ailes always understands who his audience is. Actually, they're not all blonds, but who's counting? They're all there, from A to Z—from Alicia Acuna to Maya Zumwalt. No one is saying that these women aren't fine journalists. Yet Roger Ailes has put together, as they say in boxing, inch for inch and pound for pound, the best-looking news division in the history of the world.

So do Roger Ailes and Rupert Murdoch simply prefer young, attractive (usually blond) female anchors and correspondents? Well, rest assured that they believe their audience does. There is a strategy at work here. Pure and simple, it's about entertainment. Apparently, the calculation was made that Fox's mostly male audience would enjoy the news more when hearing it from attractive women. There's really nothing new about that. TV news organizations, especially local TV news, have favored young, attractive-looking female journalists for decades now. TV ratings studies indicate that it does work, at least in some markets. But Fox News may have taken it to the extreme.

The Fox News Channel has highly rated programs because Roger Ailes knows his audience. And unlike during his days at CNBC, he has a free hand at Fox. From the beginning, he has positioned Fox as an alternative to the mainstream liberal media, appealing to moderates and conservatives. And he and Chet Collier piled on the glitz—building an entertaining, provocative stable of programs that engages the audience and keeps them tuning in.

In one sense, Fox News has benefited from a certain amount of "brand loyalty" from conservatives, because basically they have nowhere else to turn except to talk radio. In reaching out to these alienated conservatives, Roger Ailes gave them a home, a sort of safe house that they could come to trust with the news. He gave them a friendly face in Brit Hume, a guard dog in Bill O'Reilly, and a relentless battle drone in Sean Hannity.

NBC's Bob Wright (Ailes's former boss) looks at it as a business and marketing success story:

> What he and Murdoch did at Fox has a lot to do with branding, it's a marketing strategy, and they've tried to be very faithful to that. Fox is much more male-oriented than we were. But it's a lot of the stuff we tried to do on America's

Talking—you know "they're getting you down again—the big guy's beating you up, stand up and be counted," you know, that kind of thing. Part of it is trying to make people feel good about themselves, and feel they are part of something. It's a little bit like the Peter Finch character in the movie *Network:* "I'm mad as hell, and I'm not going to take it anymore!" That's the mindset they're operating in.[24]

A series of events from 1998 to 2005 helped to galvanize the Fox audience's moderate to conservative core in a way that did not happen for CNN, MSNBC, or any other news outlet. The 2000 Bush election campaign, followed by the Electoral College controversy, was one such event. Then came September 11, the war in Afghanistan, the war in Iraq, and the hard-fought 2004 presidential election.

Nothing galvanized this core audience group more than Fox's coverage after the September 11 attacks and reporting on the war on terror. Fox news anchors wore American flags on their lapels and spoke of the American military as "our troops." Fox News's Shepard Smith had a very eloquent response to those who criticized Fox's pro-American coverage. "Fuck them!"[25] Charming.

Most important, though, Fox put a small American flag in the upper left corner of the TV screen. This was a hit with many of the folks at home, but looked to some like taking advantage of the tragedy and wrapping itself in the flag. But Roger Ailes and John Moody were unapologetic. Fox News had become the place for "American" coverage of the news, because that's what their viewers wanted and expected. But it's also true that it is what Fox management wanted. It was unabashedly a pro-American news operation.

In building their audience and staying true to their marketing strategy, they were undoubtedly onto something. Contrast the environment at Fox News with the fictional "North Kosan" incident. In his book *Breaking the News,* journalist James Fallows relates what happened when journalists tried to answer hypothetical questions about reporting on Americans in combat during a war in the fictional country of North Kosan. In a PBS program called *Under Orders, Under Fire,* Peter Jennings of ABC News and Mike Wallace of CBS News were among a number of citizens on a panel asked what they would do if they learned American troops were about to be ambushed in the field. What would they do? Try to warn the Americans somehow or simply roll tape and cover the incident?

At first Jennings said he would try to warn the Americans. But Mike Wallace sternly disagreed, saying it was simply "a story he was there to cover." Then Wallace turned to Jennings and lectured him on the sanctity of journalism. "You're a reporter," said Wallace to Jennings. "I'm a little bit at a loss to understand why, because you're an American, you would not have covered that story. You have no higher duty. You're a reporter." Jennings, feeling the heat, caved. "You're right," he said to Wallace. "I lost sight of the journalistic duty to remain detached." According to Fallows, "As Jennings said he agreed with Wallace, everyone else in the room seemed to regard the two of them with horror."[26]

There, in a nutshell, is the attitude that many Americans have about journalists. Roger Ailes and Rupert Murdoch instinctively know this—it is one of the things that make the Fox News "brand" stand out as different and distinctive. And Fox's core audience loves them for it. But relying on a partisan ideological base can have its drawbacks for a news network. Fox News's ratings were down in 2007, no doubt partly due to the decline of the Republican Party's prospects for holding on to the White House in 2008 and the "depressed" nature of the Republican electorate, according to public opinion surveys. CNN's ratings were up slightly over the same period and MSNBC also saw ratings gains in 2007. But if Ailes's formula for ratings success sputters, then he'll find a new formula—he always does.

14

Roger, Rudy, and Rupe

The city's action violates long-standing First Amendment principles that are the foundation of our democracy.

—U.S. district court judge Denise Cote in the case of
Time Warner v. *New York*[1]

These three amigos go way back. As previous chapters show, Rupert Murdoch has always traded off of his political ties. He spends a good deal of time, and a great deal of money, cultivating these political connections. In fact, one of the things that made Roger Ailes the perfect person to head up Fox News was the many contacts he had made in his long and fruitful political career.

Rudy Giuliani is Exhibit A. The longtime ties between Ailes and Giuliani are well documented and known to everyone. The two met at social get-togethers in the 1980s and discovered they both had a mutual admiration for Ronald Reagan. In his book *Leadership,* Giuliani explains, "I had found myself at several dinners with Roger, including at his house, and each time we would wind up talking about how much we liked Ronald Reagan, and how much we agreed with his policies."[2] But this in itself is a rather bizarre explanation. One has to assume that at the social occasions the two of them attended in the 1980s, at least half of the people in the room were big fans of Ronald Reagan.

In any case, the two became friends and kept in touch with each other. Then, of course, came the 1989 New York City mayoral campaign, in which Giuliani brought Ailes in to shake up his team and provide a fresh start in his campaign against David Dinkins. Giuliani lost, but he did not lose his respect and admiration for Ailes, even though his mayoral campaign was the beginning of a long string of very difficult campaigns for Ailes, in which he became a campaign issue himself, ultimately leading him to leave politics.

But Ailes's media consulting career kept him primarily in New York City, so he and Giuliani, who became mayor in 1993, saw quite a bit of each other. When Ailes was named president of CNBC in 1993, Mayor Giuliani spoke at a glitzy reception thrown by NBC in the Rainbow Room. "I'm personally gratified to see that Roger has reached a new pinnacle in his remarkable career, because Roger has played an important role in my own career," said the mayor.[3]

But it is Mr. Giuliani's role in running interference for the Fox News Channel on behalf of Ailes and Rupert Murdoch in 1996 that so many people remember. It was a media battle of the titans. Murdoch and News Corp. were trying to get Fox News added to the cable mix in New York, and they ran into a brick wall when Time Warner refused. The fight was all about money and ego—mostly money.

When Time Warner acquired Turner Broadcasting (a deal that Ted Turner has said was the worst mistake of his life, by the way), the Federal Trade Commission required Time Warner to make a second twenty-four-hour news channel available to at least 50 percent of its cable subscribers. The FTC wanted to avoid a monopoly situation and to encourage market competition in the cable television industry. The problem for Fox and for Murdoch was that General Electric and NBC had just launched MSNBC, and they wanted a piece of the same action.

According to journalist and author Scott Collins, Fox seemed to have the upper hand in the beginning. "We had a deal in place," he quotes Ailes saying.[4] But NBC was offering financial incentives almost as good as what Murdoch was offering, and Time Warner had already reserved a space in its cable lineup for NBC's America's Talking, and they figured they could just slip MSNBC into that slot. For a while, Gerald Levin, the Time Warner CEO, considered carrying both MSNBC and Fox News on its cable systems.

Of course, Turner would have preferred that Time Warner carry neither. He hated the idea of other cable news operations cutting into the market of his baby, CNN. But with the Federal Trade Commission decree staring them in the face, that really wasn't an option. Time Warner execs ended up choosing MSNBC because it seemed to make the most financial sense. But Murdoch and Ailes smelled a rat.

Ted Turner and Rupert Murdoch were sworn enemies. Turner Broadcasting and News Corp. were two of the biggest media companies in the world, and Turner and Murdoch seemed to be in a personal competition to become the world's biggest media mogul. Turner had long harbored the dream of owning a news network, playing with the idea numerous times of either purchasing one of the broadcast networks or merging. And now Murdoch seemed to be stealing his thunder.

Or at least that's how it seemed to News Corp. and Fox. In the past, Turner had called Murdoch a "disgrace to journalism"[5] and compared him unfavorably to Adolf Hitler,[6] and when Murdoch launched Fox News, Turner had famously promised to squish Murdoch "like a bug."[7] But Murdoch and Ailes know how to play hardball. Murdoch and some of his media outlets had suggested that Turner had a screw loose. The *New York Post* once said that Turner was "veering dangerously toward insanity,"[8] and reminded its readers that he had taken lithium for depression.

Now, anyone who knows anything about Turner's family history knows this is a low blow. His father, owner of a successful billboard company, suffered from depression, ultimately committing suicide. Sure, Ted Turner is eccentric. When his yacht won the America's Cup, he apparently had one celebratory drink too many and fell out of his chair at the press conference. He once fired the manager of the Atlanta Braves and went down to the field to manage a game himself. He frequently says things that sound goofy. But so do a lot of other people. Crazy? No, not even close.

In any case, Murdoch and Fox News thought Turner and Time Warner were shutting them out for personal reasons. Ailes said that New York City now had a cable system czar—Ted Turner—and that he was keeping Murdoch out of New York City as part of a "personal vendetta."[9] Personal or not, News Corp. wasn't about to quit. So they got busy. Ailes called his old friend Rudy Giuliani, who was now mayor, and asked him to get personally involved. At the party celebrating the launch of Fox News, Murdoch was seen chatting with Mayor Giuliani's top aide, Fran Reiter. Murdoch's attorney, Arthur Siskind, was seen in "intense conversation" with the attorney general of New York, Dennis Vacco.[10] And Ailes himself was working the room hard—"It was pretty clear we wanted any assistance that we could get," he said.[11] Calls were also made to Governor George Pataki and U.S. Senator Al D'Amato. What came next was an apparently coordinated pressure campaign on behalf of Rupert Murdoch and Roger Ailes.

The potential conflicts of interest are almost too numerous to count. Murdoch had contributed heavily to the New York Republican Party for years. Roger Ailes had not only been Giuliani's consultant in the past, but he had also worked for Governor Pataki and numerous other government officials who went to bat for Fox News in this standoff. Murdoch's *New York Post* had been an indispensable ally in Giuliani's successful 1993 campaign for mayor. And Giuliani's wife, Donna Hanover, was a reporter for Fox television's New York affiliate.

Court records show that News Corp. employees had more than twenty-five conversations and at least two private meetings with senior Giuliani administration officials, in what reporter Clifford Levy called an "unusual alliance between government and a major corporation."[12] City attorneys threatened to effectively revoke Time Warner's Manhattan cable franchise, by refusing to approve the transfer to the newly merged company (Time Warner and Turner Broadcasting) after having indicated that there would be no further obstacles to the merger assurances. In a strategy designed by the mayor's office, the city held the merger approval hostage to Time Warner's agreeing to carry Fox News on a cable channel. The city denied this, arguing that it was deferring its decision out of a legitimate concern that Time Warner had engaged in anticompetitive behavior. Feathers were ruffled. Eyebrows were raised when the normally mild-mannered and ultrapolite corporate president of Time Warner, Richard Parsons, who had been a previous supporter of Mr. Giuliani's, said the mayor is "either a bully or a vigilante."[13]

The mayor's office was full of creative solutions to the dispute. For example, Giuliani's office suggested that Time Warner could simply bounce the History Channel or the Discovery Channel over to one of the city's public interest channels. Time Warner refused. Then the mayor's office asked them for a waiver to allow the city of New York to put Fox News on one of the public channels themselves. When Time Warner refused this too, the mayor's office decided that under the First Amendment it could do whatever it liked with the city's public channels, and then announced, without holding any hearings or getting a legal opinion from the state attorney general, that it would forthwith give one of its public interest channels to Fox News. The deputy mayor, Fran Reiter, said, "I really believe that the mayor believed what Time Warner was doing was wrong."[14]

Time Warner cried foul, claiming the city was depriving it of its First Amendment rights to program its cable channels without government interference. And of course, Fox News claimed that its First Amendment rights were being denied by Time Warner by excluding it from Manhattan. It seemed the First Amendment was getting its head beat in. Michael Bloomberg, founder of Bloomberg Information Television and Rudy Giuliani's successor as New York

City's mayor, claimed his First Amendment rights were being violated too, because if Fox News was getting a public channel, then his business news service deserved one as well. That probably seemed like an opportunity to make it appear fair and appropriate, so Mayor Giuliani quickly agreed, and Bloomberg got a channel.

It was inevitable that this whole thing would end up in court, and so it did. The case of *Time Warner* v. *New York* was a cause célèbre in the media and political world of the Big Apple. The court's decision wasn't good news for Fox. U.S. district court judge Denise Cote found that Mayor Giuliani and the city of New York had acted improperly. "This case concerns the power of a city to influence, control, and even coerce the programming decisions of an operator of a cable television system. . . The city's action violates long-standing First Amendment principles that are the foundation of our democracy," said the judge. Judge Cote rebuked the mayor's office for its brazen efforts to "reward a friend and further a particular viewpoint" and for abusing its power.[15]

The city appealed, but Judge Cote's ruling was upheld by the U.S. Court of Appeals for the Second Circuit. So Murdoch went to work on another solution. At a media industry conference in Sun Valley, Idaho, he approached Time Warner's Levin and discussed ways to resolve the impasse.[16] Murdoch linked the dispute with another difficult issue involving the two companies—News Corp. was selling its U.S. satellite operation, American Sky Broadcasting, to a rival satellite company controlled partially by Time Warner.

He proposed that in exchange for Time Warner's guaranteeing Fox News eight million subscribers on its New York City cable systems in the next five years, News Corp. would drop its antitrust suit against them. Time Warner would collect fees of $10 per subscriber, and in exchange Murdoch would be given a nonvoting minority stake in the newly combined satellite operation. Mayor Giuliani's office agreed to forfeit one of its public channels (in order to make space on the cable system) in exchange for Time Warner's dropping its suit against the city. Levin probably saw the offer as his best opportunity to resolve the mess and move on—undoubtedly, he was concerned about declining revenues and shareholder reports. Ironically, the combined satellite operation was later sold to Direct TV, owned at the time by Hughes Electronics, which was later acquired by News Corp.! Talk about having your cake and eating it too—Murdoch is a genius at long-term planning.

But the dispute was settled, and in News Corp. offices and Fox News headquarters, there was a lot of high-fiving going on—they knew they had gotten the better part of the deal. Fox News was now in the crucial New York market, and they were confident that their marketing strategy and programming plans would make it a success there and elsewhere. New York is important, Ailes told reporters. "Opinion leaders live here, advertisers live here, the press thinks it's the only place in the world," he said.[17] Privately, some Time Warner execs and media industry analysts were scratching their heads over why Levin gave in so easily after winning in federal court.[18] Once again, Rupert Murdoch, with his eyes on the long-term prize, had emerged victorious.

So Ailes, Murdoch, and Giuliani had now been through battle together, and these brothers-in-arms would watch each other's backs from now on. Ailes and Giuliani have remained close and, as the *New York Times* reported, attended each other's weddings, and when Ailes was briefly hospitalized in 1998, the mayor showed up at his bedside with gifts: a book about New York landmarks and an issue of *Wine Spectator*. And of course, Ailes watched approvingly as the mayor went on to become something of a national hero for his efforts during and after the 9/11 attacks, earning the title America's Mayor.

So naturally, as Rudy Giuliani became a leading Republican contender for president in 2008, his friendship with Ailes and Murdoch became an issue. For example, the political journal *Hotline* noted that in the first half of 2007, Rudy Giuliani logged more than 115 minutes of airtime on Fox News, which was 25 percent greater than that of his next closest Republican competitor for the nomination, and double that of the next closest candidate, Senator John McCain. All of this begs the question, Was Fox News showing favoritism to Mr. Giuliani because of his friendship with Roger Ailes and his past support of Rupert Murdoch and News Corp.?

As expected, all the official sources denied there was any kind of special treatment or manipulation of the news going on. Fox News personnel said flatly that Giuliani's appearances on Fox were driven by his news value as a leading presidential candidate and had nothing to do with his personal relationship with Roger Ailes. Brit Hume, anchor and news director of Fox's evening newscast *Special Report with Brit Hume,* issued a strong denial: "I can't remember his [Ailes] ever saying anything, one way or the other, about our coverage of the Giuliani campaign . . . and I am under no injunctions, restrictions, encouragements or directions of any kind as to how that campaign should be covered."[19] And Giuliani aides as well as Fox News staffers said simply that the two men were friends, had been for more than twenty years, and there was nothing more to it than that.

The problem is, as documented here, that Fox News has a reputation with many for not exactly playing it straight with the news. And as we have seen, Rupert Murdoch's media organizations are notorious for using the news for personal, political, and business purposes.

It has also been pointed out that most of Mr. Giuliani's time on Fox, 78 of the 115 minutes from January to July 2007, were spent on one Fox News program, *Hannity & Colmes.* Hannity is a big admirer of Mr. Giuliani, according to *Hotline,* and a Fox News spokesperson made it clear that Mr. Hannity makes his own decisions about bookings without any interference from Roger Ailes or anyone else.

The thing is, the editors and reporters at Rupert Murdoch's other news organizations, such as the *New York Post* and his British papers, the *Sun* or the *Times,* say much the same thing. All together now: "Rupert Murdoch is not in the news room telling us what to do . . . we make our own decisions about what to cover and how to cover it." *Post* personnel know where their bread's buttered; they don't have to be reminded on a daily basis of what they were hired to do.

Certainly Sean Hannity *does* admire Rudy Giuliani. In fact, since 2001 Mr. Giuliani has appeared on *Hannity & Colmes* a number of times, not just since he became a presidential candidate. But there can also be no question that Hannity, Colmes, Brit Hume, the cleaning lady, and everyone in their building are crystal clear on the fact that Giuliani has a special tie to their bosses.

Interestingly, the Ailes–Giuliani axis has drawn a lot of comparisons to the friendly relationship between Bill Clinton when he was president and newsman Rick Kaplan when he was president of CNN in the '90s. Defenders of Murdoch, Giuliani, and Ailes point to the Clinton–Kaplan friendship as being no different. And the critics of Roger Ailes say it's an example of his hypocrisy because he used to complain loud and long about CNN's chief executive's being a friend of a sitting president of the United States. In the '90s, Ailes accused CNN of slanting its coverage to favor President Clinton, calling CNN the Clinton News Network.[20]

No question about it, Kaplan and Clinton were friendly. In their defense of Ailes, the right-wing Media Research Center dug up a 1998 *Vanity Fair* article that spelled out some details of the relationship. Scott Collins, author of *Crazy Like a Fox,* reports that Kaplan raised eyebrows within news circles for his "remarkably close relationship with President Clinton and his wife."[21] Apparently, Kaplan had come to know the Clintons when he was a producer on the *CBS*

Evening News with Walter Cronkite and Bill Clinton was the attorney general of Arkansas. The *Vanity Fair* piece noted that as a network news producer during the 1980 presidential campaign, Kaplan had hired Hillary Clinton to help prepare coverage. He advised Bill Clinton on how to recover from the Gennifer Flowers accusations; he called to console Hillary Clinton after Vince Foster's suicide; while a producer at ABC News, he spent a night in the Lincoln bedroom in the White House; and he urged his network colleagues to be "careful" in pursuing stories about the Whitewater investigation into the Clintons.[22]

The truth is, a lot of reporters liked and admired Bill Clinton when he was president, and agreed with many of his policy goals. But that does not mean that they didn't do their jobs as journalists. As political scientist Larry Sabato points out in his popular book *Feeding Frenzy,* when reporters smell blood, they pounce. Getting the scoop over the competition and making a splash with a story trumps ideology for most professional journalists. By the end of the Clinton administration, through the Whitewater investigations, the universal health care debacle, Monica Lewinsky, and impeachment, few would say that the media "took it easy" on the Clintons. They couldn't afford to. They'd be out of business if they did.

During some of the most intense coverage of Clinton's problems, he often lashed out at the media. The Clinton White House for a time took to calling NBC the Nail Bill Clinton network. And CNN was there, Rick Kaplan or no Rick Kaplan.

Fox is a little different, though. Most of Rupert Murdoch's media holdings operate by a different set of rules. The producers of Fox News have set themselves up from day one as being "different" from other news organizations, and they are, though probably not in the way they mean.

A *New York Times* story in August 2007 focused on the cozy relationship between Ailes, Giuliani, and Murdoch and asked questions about Fox News's coverage of the 2008 candidates in light of the friendship between Ailes and Giuliani. The *Times* coverage resonated with many, but it was also dismissed and criticized by others, especially from Fox News, News Corp., and numerous pundits and Web sites. The conservative Media Research Center, for example, said the *New York Times* was using a double standard because it had never "exposed" the close ties between Rick Kaplan and Bill Clinton. A review of *New York Times* articles from the 1990s reveals that the *Times* had in fact reported that Kaplan and Clinton were friends, but the relationship had never been featured as a stand-alone story.

But it was the timing of the *Times* story on Ailes and Giuliani that bothered most of the journalists who found fault with it. It came in the midst of Rupert Murdoch's negotiations with the Bancroft family to purchase Dow Jones & Company, Inc., and the *Wall Street Journal*. Some saw it as an attempt to throw some mud at the Murdoch empire in preparation for a showdown between a Murdoch-owned *Wall Street Journal* and the *New York Times*.

Panelists on the TV show *Inside Washington* on the local Washington, D.C., PBS station WETA were critical of the Times piece. Evan Thomas of *Newsweek* said it was an example of "the *New York Times* thinking that Ailes is Darth Vader, because they made him out to be this monster who's given all this time to Giuliani—but the story itself and the graphics supporting it don't support the story. I don't think there really is any evidence that, yes Giuliani goes on the Hannity show a lot, but aside from that I don't think there's much there."[23]

The show's host, local D.C. anchor Gordon Peterson, pointed out that Giuliani got 115 minutes on Fox, and only 7 minutes on ABC, 19 on CBS, 6 on NBC, and 13 on MSNBC. Syndicated conservative columnist Charles Krauthammer insisted, "There's nothing in this story. Of all these minutes on Fox, about two-thirds is on Hannity, and Hannity books his own. So Roger Ailes isn't in the loop. If you compare the minutes that Giuliani has on Fox, he gets less than Biden has on CNBC." The *Washington Post*'s Colby King added that "this is exactly why newspapers are in trouble. To devote that kind of space to that kind of an issue now is what people don't want. Who read it?" Evan Thomas offered his view: "It says more about the paranoia of the *New York Times* than anything else."[24]

Maybe. But it could also be that a lot of people are missing the overall point. And what's the point? Simply this: with the acquisition of the *Wall Street Journal* being the latest example, Rupert Murdoch and Roger Ailes may be well on their way to dominating American mass media, and based on their records, that is not a good thing for the country or for the world.

The Ailes–Giuliani–Murdoch nexus made the news again late in 2007, only this time with the additional names of Judith Regan and Bernard Kerik thrown into the mix. As the head of Regan Books, an imprint of the Rupert Murdoch–owned HarperCollins Publishing, Regan was near the apex of her field. She became somewhat of a celebrity, even getting her own show for a while on Fox News, courtesy of Roger Ailes.[25] She also had a secret: She was having an affair with the New York City police commissioner, Bernard Kerik, who was married.[26] She had met Kerik in 2001 while her company was publishing his memoir, *The Lost Son.*

The trouble seemed to begin in 2004 when, at Rudy Giuliani's urging, Kerik was nominated by President Bush to become the new secretary of the Department of Homeland Security. Kerik's nomination eventually fell apart—there were questions about his background and his qualifications, as well as a well-documented "nanny problem."[27] In the media scrutiny of Kerik, his affair with Regan came to light. According to a lawsuit filed by Regan in 2007, an "unnamed" News Corp. executive became concerned that "what Regan knew about Kerik would derail the nomination and thus damage Giuliani's political prospects." Her complaint states, "In December 2004, this News Corp. senior executive told Regan that he believed she had information about Kerik that, if disclosed, would harm Kerik's Homeland Security nomination, and more importantly Giuliani's planned presidential campaign. This senior executive was concerned about this information being made public, and counseled Regan to lie and withhold information from investigators concerning Kerik."[28]

According to Regan, News Corp. executives have remained wary about what she knew about Kerik and Giuliani and have sought to discredit her. Their opportunity, she says, came with the planned publication of the O. J. Simpson book *If I Did It,* in which Simpson would all but confess to the murders of his ex-wife Nicole Simpson and her friend Ron Goldman. Regan and News Corp. had planned a splashy TV interview with Simpson on Fox News around the scheduled publication of the book in November 2006. But when the details of the book and the publicity campaign came out, the public reaction was mostly one of revulsion.[29] News Corp. backed off from publishing the book and went into damage-control mode. Regan was fired a month later, ostensibly for anti-Semitic remarks she made during an interview about the book. She has denied making any such comments, saying her words were taken out of context.[30]

Her lawsuit against News Corp. alleged that the company and its executives had conspired to protect the political career of Giuliani. When her complaint was filed, of course, tongues began wagging. But specifically, who is the "unnamed" News Corp. executive who wanted to cover up the whole thing and tried to get her to lie to investigators? More than one source suspect that it is none other than Roger Ailes himself. A longtime observer of Ailes and Giuliani, the *Village Voice's* Wayne Barrett, author of *Grand Illusion: The Untold Story of Rudy Giuliani and 9/11*, said flat out that it was Ailes: "Roger

Ailes is clearly the person she is referring to as this senior executive who made all these suggestions to her."[31]

It may very well be Ailes. He would have had plenty of motivation to protect his old friend. After all, the doomed 2004 nomination of Kerik to head Homeland Security and his subsequent legal problems—Kerik was indicted in November 2007 on federal tax fraud and other charges—helped to derail Rudy Giuliani's 2008 presidential campaign. After Mayor Giuliani left office, he brought Kerik into one of his business ventures, Giuliani Partners. Around the same time, it came to light that another company with which Kerik was associated was suspected of ties to organized crime.[32] *New York Times* columnist Frank Rich speculates that Regan may know plenty more about Kerik and Giuliani's relationship, and is clearly sending that message with her lawsuit.[33] In January 2008 Ms. Regan and News Corp. settled her lawsuit. A News Corp. statement on the settlement said, "The parties are pleased that they have reached an equitable, confidential settlement, with no admission of liability by any party . . . After carefully considering the matter, we accept Ms. Regan's position that she did not say anything anti-Semitic in nature, and further believe that Ms. Regan is not anti-Semitic. . . News Corp. thanks Ms. Regan for her outstanding contributions and wishes her continued success."[34] The dollar amount of the settlement is not known, but according to the *Wall Street Journal,* Ms. Regan had previously turned down a settlement offer of over $6 million. [35]

The merits of Regan's lawsuit notwithstanding, this whole sordid episode may be yet another example of the ties that bind Ailes, Giuliani, and Murdoch. The Ailes/Giuliani connection, the Regan/Kerik mess, and the outcome of the Time Warner/Fox News battle in New York in 1996 all seem to be part of a long pattern of Rupert Murdoch's building and using political connections for business reasons. Roger Ailes and Rudy Giuliani had a preexisting relationship, and when Ailes went to work for Murdoch, that connection became Murdoch's property. Based on Murdoch's background and his financial and regulatory interests, there's little doubt in this author's mind that Rupert Murdoch, Roger Ailes, and Fox News were doing what they could to help Giuliani get elected president. Now that it didn't work, let's see if Murdoch tries once again to cozy up to a new president.

Nixon's Revenge: Murdoch and Ailes Take Over Journalism

The New York Times *used to be the paper with all the news fit to put into the bottom of your dog kennel . . . Now, when their owners leave, the dogs are calling up and canceling their subscriptions . . . It's a dying asset.*

—Roger Ailes[1]

Jim Cramer, the hyperactive multimillionaire host of CNBC's *Mad Money,* says Rupert Murdoch came to him more than a decade ago to talk about buying Dow Jones and its crown jewel, the *Wall Street Journal.* Cramer operated his well-known hedge fund at the time and was a minority shareholder in Dow Jones. He was an agitator. He calls himself a "shareholder activist." He tried to cajole Dow Jones managers into thinking more about profits and taking advantage of emerging business opportunities in digital information. Dow Jones was never run like a business, according to Cramer. "It was run more like a vast college newspaper, bent on maintaining journalistic integrity regardless of the business implications. The idea of turning a profit, even as a side benefit, was too sinful for the ultra-righteous management or clueless-but-revered Bancroft family, which controlled the company."[2]

Well, Bancroft family, meet Rupert Murdoch, Prince of Profits. At their 1996 meeting, Murdoch asked Cramer what he thought Dow Jones was really worth. At the time, the market value of the stock was about $35. He told Murdoch he thought the company was worth around $74 a share— more than twice what it was trading for! But Murdoch didn't blink. "I'll pay that," he said. Fast-forward to the summer of 2007. Amid much hoopla on

Wall Street and the gnashing of teeth in the media, Murdoch offered the Bancroft family $60 per share, or roughly $5 billion—still considerably higher than its market value, but quite a bit less than he had been willing to pay for it in the mid-1990s.

What happened? Most market analysts, like Cramer, fault Dow Jones management and shareholders for falling behind the times, and for failing to see how they could make money in the digital information age, for example allowing Bloomberg Information to muscle into its bond-reporting business and its wire service. So while business information has exploded over the last decade and Wall Street has boomed, the Dow Jones stock price moved nary an inch. Which made it a prime target for takeover by someone with money to burn and who thought it undervalued.

The irony of the *Wall Street Journal* is that it's such a great journalistic institution and yet it's been so poorly managed, according to Louis Ureneck,[3] a former editor at the *Philadelphia Inquirer* and now a professor at Boston University. "The double irony is that it's a newspaper about business," he says.[4] An irony indeed. But the *Journal* is without a doubt one of the top newspapers in the world. Its editorial page is probably the most influential in the world, its news division is stocked with top-shelf writers and editors, and the whole operation just reeks of credibility and respectability. Which is one reason Murdoch wanted it so badly.

It was probably only a matter of time before the Bancroft family had to make some kind of move. They had resisted suitors before, including the New York Times Company and the Washington Post Company, both of whom made inquiries in the past. The Dow Jones company prided itself on quality journalism above all else—even appointing journalists to executive positions within Dow Jones. In the past, according to the *Financial Times,* potential buyers were fended off by Roy Hammer, "the Boston lawyer who oversaw a web of Bancroft trusts and served as Dow Jones' patrician gatekeeper."[5]

But this time was different. Mr. Hammer had retired. The economics of the news business has changed in the digital age as newspaper circulation in general has plunged. And as Dow Jones's financial picture wobbled in recent years, younger members of the Bancroft family grew restless, perhaps thinking of their inheritances. There was also the possibility of a nasty fight among Bancroft family shareholders. The Dow Jones board could even have been sued for dereliction of their fiduciary responsibility if they had refused to seriously consider an offer from Murdoch. When news of Murdoch's offer reached Wall

Street, Dow Jones's stock surged more than 50 percent. What would have happened to the value of the stock if they had spurned Murdoch and held on to doing business the old way? How far would it have fallen? $25, $20?

The Dow Jones shareholders weren't likely to see an offer this good for a long, long time. Murdoch and News Corp. were following a familiar script. Overwhelm the sellers with an offer they can't refuse, in this case $60 per share. Remember, Murdoch paid an awful lot of money to launch Fox Broadcasting in the '80s, then a decade later offered cable carriers an exorbitant amount of money up front to carry Fox News.

Oh, they turned him down at first. In the initial Bancroft family meeting, about 80 percent of the votes, representing roughly 55 percent of the shareholders, were against selling to Murdoch. At the same time, a group of *WSJ* newsroom staffers signed petitions urging the family not to sell one of America's greatest newspapers to, as Joshua Chaffin of the *Financial Times* reported, "the man who gave the world Fox News."[6]

But a month later, the family was open to at least talking about it. A couple of things had happened to "broaden" their minds. Two of Dow Jones's major competitors in the financial information business, Thomson and Reuters, announced they were merging their operations. It was a move that blindsided most Dow Jones shareholders and illustrated the changing, hyper-competitive nature of the business of financial news. Also, Dow Jones's CEO, Rich Zannino, seemed to change the minds of some shareholders with a sobering financial assessment of where the company was and where it was likely to go if Murdoch's offer was rejected.

The family was divided. Two members, Christopher Bancroft and Leslie Hill, so wary of Murdoch's editorial style and tabloid past, frantically sought out alternative buyers. But no one else was prepared to offer the price that Murdoch was willing to pay. In the meantime, a couple of key Bancroft family shareholders had switched sides, based in part on the advice of Michael Elefante, the successor to Roy Hammer as lead trustee and family attorney.[7] A sizeable number of family members were now willing to go along with the News Corp. bid.

The last stumbling block was the family's concern over the journalistic integrity and independence of the *Journal*. Mr. Murdoch's reputation preceded him, and there was great concern that he would get hold of their beloved national treasure and take it "down market." When Murdoch met with the Bancrofts, he promised them that he would not interfere with the *Journal*'s news operation and editorial policy. But they wanted it in writing. The set of proposals the family attorneys submitted to News Corp. included a commitment on the part of Murdoch to safeguard the "independence" of the *Journal*.[8]

Many observers, however, believed such haggling over the integrity of the *Journal* was a waste of time. "Ultimately, the person who owns the paper in the long-term controls what happens," said John Morton, a longtime newspaper consultant. "I don't care what kind of editorial board you have . . . that's just the way it is."[9] Others believed that such broadly stated concerns over independence were nothing more than a "fig leaf," to give the Bancroft family cover in case Murdoch did follow his natural instincts and turns the *Journal* into a personal and political weapon.

In any case, ultimately it came down to price. Murdoch was confident all along that the offer would simply be too good to turn down, and he was right. In the end, facing economic reality, a majority of shareholders voted to accept Murdoch's offer.

It *is* a pretty strange story. The media mogul most known for racy tabloids, screaming headlines, and his topless "page 3 girls" at one of his British papers, the *Sun,* will now own one of the most respected and prestigious media franchises in the world. Does Murdoch crave respectability in his golden years?

Jon Friedman of MarketWatch.com, owned by Dow Jones, says that by aligning himself with Dow Jones, Murdoch "seems to be gaining instant credibility in the United States—something that has escaped him during his stewardship of the *New York Post* and Fox News, his most prominent American assets."[10]

Some of his friends and associates believe it's possible he may be thinking about how he will be regarded in the future. One longtime associate thinks Murdoch may be finally considering his legacy and wants to run a premier newspaper like the *Journal* to upgrade his reputation. "He's thinking about his obit," says an old friend.[11] But Murdoch scoffs at the very idea. He himself has said that craving respectability is the beginning of the end for a journalist. Media owners "can't be too worried about what they're told at their country clubs,"[12] he told one interviewer.

And of course there's more to the story than just looking for respect. There's money to be made. News Corp. has big plans for Dow Jones & Company, Inc. Like everything else Murdoch has done in building his media empire, acquiring the *Wall Street Journal,* even at an inflated price, makes good business sense. It fits into his long-term plans. For one thing, the new Fox Business Network, overseen by Roger Ailes and Neil Cavuto, will now inherit the resources and reputation of the *Wall Street Journal*. Most analysts believe Murdoch needed the *Journal* to provide professional, industry-respected content—business news, market analysis, and financial reporting—to his new business channel, Fox Business Network (FBN). And acquiring the *Journal* continues his enormously successful business model of producing content and then owning and controlling the "distribution" of that content.

Murdoch also has a businessman's feel for how integrated and universal the news and information business is becoming. Part of that has to do with the Internet. In 2005, he added the title "Internet visionary" to his résumé by acquiring MySpace, the fast-growing social networking site. Following the normal pattern, he bid more than any of the other potential buyers—$580 million. That was $30 million more than the next closest offer, which was made by Sumner Redstone of Viacom. In 2006 the site grew from a subscriber base of 20 million to 200 million, convincing Google to commit $900 million worth of advertising, which made Murdoch look like the very shrewd investor that he is. After all, he says, "A media company is basically anything that communicates with people—news, ideas, entertainment, advertising—and allows them to communicate with each other."[13] Good point.

Thomas Lifson of *American Thinker* claims Murdoch "sees how to exploit synergies among media properties" and is aiming at the affluent Americans (and others around the world) who are both investors and consumers. "He will use multiple professionally run and well-executed broadcast outlets, the Internet, and dead-tree publishing to increase his hold on this audience and the advertisers who want to reach it," Lifson said.[14]

In acquiring the *Journal,* Murdoch sees "the engine of a global, interactive, multiplatform business and finance network" that will drive his Fox business channel, power up his twenty-four-hour Sky News channel in Europe, and fuel a collection of online financial services. "We'll sell our business news and information in print, we'll sell it to anyone who's got a cable system, and we'll sell it on the web," he said.[15] The Fox business channel, which is going head-to-head with Roger Ailes's old stomping ground CNBC, makes spending the $5 billion for the *Journal* "an easy justification," according to Murdoch. "It almost ensures the price is worth paying." Added News Corp. president Peter Chernin, "There are millions of people throughout the world joining the financial class, and the *Journal* is the premier financial brand. We have the size and international strength to monetize it globally."[16]

News Corp. could tap into Dow Jones's other properties to help create an on-line platform for all of the company's news-gathering operations around the world. In addition to the *WSJ*, it owns the investing weekly *Barron*'s, Dow Jones Newswires, and the consumer-focused Web service MarketWatch.com. Assuredly, Murdoch would also use his Fox and Sky News video outlets as sources of video content on the new sites.

The *Wall Street Journal* has already been very successful at getting readers to migrate from the print edition to the electronic version on the Internet. The *Journal* has one of the most successful paid Internet sites in all of journalism, about a million paid subscribers, but it is not as profitable as the print edition. Advertisers just aren't willing to pay as much for digital ads as they are for print. Murdoch sees the potential, but no one is yet sure what the right money-making formula will be. Maybe a "hybrid model," he suggests. To him, one of the great business lessons of the Internet is that people have come to expect everything for free, so that an on-line product has to be advertising supported. He thinks it might work with free on-line users driving advertising sales and premium users willing to pay for higher-end content.

Make the *Journal* free on-line? Sure, says Jim Cramer. "A paid site can't generate anywhere near the eyeballs that a free site produces, and advertisers covet viewers. The additional ad revenue would dwarf the [on-line] subscription fees, which are puny to begin with. Dow Jones hasn't been able to afford to go free without corrupting the price of the print publication. News Corp could care less about that."[17] "It would be an expensive thing to do in the short term," according to Murdoch, but over the long term it would be a great thing to do.[18]

Making the *Journal* available for free on-line has certainly pressured rival publications to do the same or risk losing readership. For example, the *New York Times,* in anticipation of Murdoch's move with the *Journal,* beat him to the punch and dropped their on-line fees in September 2007. The *Financial Times,* based in London, announced in October 2007 that it would expand free access to FT.com, but not entirely abandon its fee-based service for unlimited use. Said one analyst, "If the *Wall Street Journal* goes free, the marginal buyer of the *Financial Times* is going to say 'hang on, why am I paying for a service I can get for free elsewhere?'"[19]

Sounds like another example of Murdoch's penchant for predatory pricing. In this case, he may be betting on News Corp.'s ability to absorb financial losses in the short term better than his competitors, either forcing them to jettison some of their services or reinstate paid on-line subscriptions at some point to generate revenue and accept a smaller share of the market. And of course, in the long term, News Corp. dominates the market and is able to generate a nice profit. The *Financial Times* doesn't sound worried. Market analysts say that any *FT* losses due to a free on-line *Journal* would be limited because the *Journal* has weaker European operations. And the *Financial Times* says it has been competing against Dow Jones for a very long time and beating them, and it believes it can go on beating them. Sounds an awful lot like something the folks at CNN said about Fox News in the late 1990s.

The execs at the *New York Times* may be more aware of what they are up against. Or at least they are more open to admitting it. A recent *NYT* article speculated that "based on his history, there is little doubt that Mr. Murdoch will directly aim at luring both readers and advertising away from the *New York Times* and the *Financial Times,* the *Journal*'s closest rivals. His strategy will probably include aggressively undercutting advertising and investing heavily in editorial content—particularly in Washington and international news—absorbing losses at first to win the long-term war."[20]

In his pitch to the Bancrofts, Murdoch promised to invest in the *Journal* and expand its reach. Sources say he is prepared to pump in "hundreds of millions" of dollars. He said he would expand the *Journal* both geographically and in terms of content. He wants to build the paper's presence in Europe, India, and other parts of Asia. He's pledged to enlarge the *Journal*'s Washington bureau, and he may increase the size of the paper by four or five pages.

Murdoch says his worry about the *New York Times* is that it's got the only position as a "national elitist general-interest paper . . . so the network news picks up its cues from the *Times*. And local papers do too. It has a huge influence. And we'd love to challenge it."[21] Roger Ailes put it another way: "The *New York Times* used to be the paper with all the news fit to put into the bottom of your dog kennel . . . Now, when their owners leave, the dogs are calling up and canceling their subscriptions . . . It's a dying asset."[22] Sometimes it's hard to tell if Ailes thinks he is going up against the *New York Times* or Dwayne "the Rock" Johnson in a cage-match at Madison Square Garden.

So Murdoch clearly wants to establish the *Journal* as the rival to the *NYT* in setting the daily news agenda of the country. Currently people tend to think of the *Journal* primarily as a business newspaper. Murdoch wants to broaden its audience and its appeal. And he thinks he can do it. He did it with Fox News at a time when many analysts said there wasn't room for another cable news channel.

Which brings us back to Roger Ailes. What role will he play in this new steroid-driven techno-media machine? According to the *Financial Times,* everyone is wondering what happens internally at News Corp. now; the most obvious question is, What happens to Chernin and Ailes? Ailes, whom News Corp. critics like to imagine as Darth Vader to Murdoch's Evil Emperor, has done what many thought impossible: built a new cable news operation from the ground up and eclipsed its rivals in the ratings.

And when Murdoch's son Lachlan walked away as president of the Fox Television Stations group, it was Ailes whom Murdoch appointed to take the reins. Ailes may be looking for new challenges anyway. He has been doing what he's doing for over a decade now, which, considering his rather nomadic history, is an eternity. It wouldn't surprise many to see him take on a larger role at News Corp., perhaps designing and managing the news operations of the "empire."

Jim Cramer thinks there's another reason Rupert Murdoch wants the *WSJ*—its editorial pages. In fact, says Cramer, "he's gaga over it . . . That was one reason he gave me back in 1996, and that's one reason why he wants it now. I think he would like to elect a president, [Citizen] Kane style, with it."[23] Everyone knows the editorial pages of the *Journal* are conservative; they always have been. So there wouldn't necessarily be an ideological shift with Murdoch taking the reins and Roger Ailes lurking in the background, but there might be a shift in emphasis on certain candidates and certain policies. For example, the *Journal*'s China policy may undergo a transition. It also wouldn't be too hard to imagine particular presidential candidates getting featured more often and in better terms.

During Murdoch's quest for Dow Jones, a group of reporters in the *Journal*'s Beijing bureau urged the company in an open letter to reject News Corp.'s offer, for fears Murdoch would meddle in the paper's China coverage. The *Journal* has won two Pulitzer Prizes for its often critical coverage of the economic and social policies of China's Communist leadership. In their letter, the reporters said Murdoch had "a well-documented history of making editorial decisions in order to advance his business interests in China and, indeed, of sacrificing journalistic integrity to satisfy personal or political aims."[24]

This is one of the main concerns many people have about Murdoch's taking control of the *WSJ*. Will he take one of the finest newspapers in the world and use it to bludgeon his opponents—both political and business adversaries? And worse, will he monkey with the news division? Will he try to make the *Journal* more appealing to the masses by dumbing it down and making it more glossy and gossipy?

Murdoch swears that he has no plans to alter its journalism. But by late summer 2007, he had already sent some signals about possible changes coming down the road in a News Corp.–owned *Journal*. For example, he sent shudders through its newsroom when he confessed to a reporter that he did not care for the long, front-page feature stories that are one of the paper's hallmarks.[25] In an interview with *Time* magazine, Murdoch admitted that he had little taste for the quirky stories that run in the center columns of the *Journal*. "To have these esoteric, well-written stories on page one every day is great, but I still think you want some hard news. I'd try to keep many more of them for the weekend. I'm sick of putting the *Journal* aside because I don't have time to get through these stories."[26] He also said he might relaunch the Saturday edition of the *Journal* with a glossy magazine section, a prospect that might make current readers a little nervous if they have seen some of the "special sections" in some of his other newspapers, such as the *Times of London*. Sure signs of change are coming, though, because in January 2008 sources confirmed that Murdoch is planning to move the *Journal* to Midtown Manhattan and away from Wall Street. According to the Associated Press, the *Journal* may wind up in the same building as News Corp. Maybe Mr. Murdoch wants to be as close as possible to his new toy? And that's not all. The *New York Times* reported that the *Journal* is making plans to start a sports page, which would help Murdoch make good on his goal to expand the *Journal's* nonbusiness coverage.[27]

Would Murdoch risk turning the *Journal* into another *Sun* or *Post*? Market analysts doubt it. Jim Cramer doesn't believe Murdoch will do anything that "fundamentally tarnishes the brand." He believes Murdoch is too good a businessman to let that happen. According to Murdoch, there's such a thing as a popular newspaper and an unpopular elite newspaper, and he claims that people understand the difference. "They play different roles," he says.

And what about Murdoch's agreement with the Bancroft family that he will preserve the *Journal's* independence and integrity? The agreement provides for a five-person committee of distinguished community and journal-istic leaders that must approve the hiring and firing of the *Journal* editor and the head of the opinion pages. This committee will also have the power to arbitrate any disputes where Mr. Murdoch is accused of interference, as well as the right to publish its rulings on the opinion pages of the paper.[28] But the agreement is vague on exactly what constitutes interference, and it gives the right to appeal to the committee only to the paper's top editors, and not to individual journalists. What's more, the members of the committee would have to be approved by News Corp.

The agreement specifically promises that Marcus Brauchi will stay in his post as editor after the takeover, and that Paul Gigot will remain as editor of the *Journal*'s editorial pages. Undoubtedly, the two think very highly of the arrangement. But a union representing 2,000 Dow Jones employees said the pact doesn't mean very much. It's the sort of agreement you might have with your dad, said Steven Yount, president of the union. "If there is love and trust on both sides, it can work . . . I am not sure that is the sort of relationship you have here."[29]

And the critics of Murdoch and News Corp. believe he just won't be able to help himself. "I've predicted that Murdoch will be a bad *Wall Street Journal* owner because of his instinct to foul every journalism nest in which he roosts," said Jack Shafer of Slate. "I need to reiterate my view that Murdoch fouls his nests not because he's a bad news man but because he is no sort of news man . . . He's an impresario, a politician, and empire builder who pushes the truth only when it serves his business interests."[30] Eric Alterman, media columnist for the Nation, is sure that Murdoch will "inevitably destroy the jewel of American journalism that the news pages of the *Journal* have long been . . . nothing, literally nothing, in his past indicates that he cares in the slightest bit for the journalistic quality of anything he owns."[31]

Murdoch's critics point to similar agreements he reached with newspapers he bought in the past, only in the end to get involved anyway, and transform them in his own image. Journalist David Olive, for example, says, "Few doubt that Murdoch will renege on an agreement made public last week to protect the autonomy of the *Journal*'s staff, just as he reneged on similar pledges of non-interference soon after acquiring the U.K. tabloid *News of the World,* the formerly liberal *New York Post* and the *Times of London.*"[32] Slate's Jack Shafer adds that Murdoch loves to make promises but loves even more to break them. "The day will come," he says, "that Murdoch decides that the newspaper and parent company no longer fit in the colossus' ever-shifting plan to straddle all the world's media. After extracting a bit of the *Journal*'s prestige value for his forthcoming cable business news channel, I predict he'll grow tired of the criticism and sell it off."[33]

Richard Zannino, the CEO of Dow Jones—the man who brokered the sale to Murdoch—is gone. The Dow Jones company announced in December 2007 that he was leaving the firm. It will likely be only the first of perhaps many changes in personnel and in corporate philosophy. Zannino disputed speculation that he was pushed out, saying he and Mr. Murdoch had reached an "amicable and friendly" agreement for his departure.[34]

The thing is, business is business. And Murdoch has played his business cards and his political cards masterfully. He will push it as far as he can. He'll try to make the *Journal* less "elitist," as he sees it, which may mean shorter stories and more of a focus on the bottom line. There is little doubt he will use the news pages of the *Journal* to "go after" his enemies, which are around every corner. And Cramer is probably right, he undoubtedly will try to elect presidents and will try to sway elections and policy discussions in Europe as well. But the *WSJ* is unlikely to become the *New York Post*. If he feels that the credibility and long-term interests of the *Journal* as a political institution are at stake, Murdoch will back off. He's too smart to overplay his hand in such a public arena.

Murdoch's feelings are apparently hurt over all of this nonlove. "We're very proud of what we do at all our papers," he told *Time,* "and we just feel insulted by the coverage . . . we make mistakes here and there, but there's nothing wrong with the *Post*—most people would prefer to read it before they go to the Times."[35] This author's feeling is that Murdoch could not care less about what his critics, or most other sources, say about his empire as long as it shows a profit. It's good to be the king.

16

Murdoch's Money Honey

Who needs a Money Honey, when you have a veritable Money Hive?

—Variety

The original "Money Honey," Maria Bartiromo, was Roger Ailes's creation. When Ailes took over at CNBC in 1993, it was a pretty battered group of people. The channel was struggling in the ratings, the NBC brass was getting frustrated, and the future didn't look very bright. Then Roger Ailes turned on the lights, literally. As told by Ken Auletta in his book *Backstory: Inside the Business of News,* he "placed a neon sign on the building," ordered fresh coats of paint and new furniture, and brought an attitude that treated "business news as a sport."[1]

And in typical Ailes fashion, he found a way to brighten up the "made-for-black-and-white-TV" floor of the New York Stock Exchange by putting the energetic Bartiromo, CNBC's stunningly attractive female anchor, there in the midst of the action, instead of in a studio behind a desk. Thus the Money Honey was born, and financial news was never quite the same. And of course Ailes repeated this pattern at Fox News later in the '90s, with his selection and placement of a number of attractive female reporters and anchors.

In 1993, Bartiromo, then an assistant producer with the CNN business desk, sent a videotape of her on-air appearances with CNN to Ailes. She was perfect for what Ailes thought CNBC needed. "What I saw in Maria was a fast-talking New York street kid who was fearless when it came to dealing with powerful business people," he said.[2] She went on to help change business news reporting by instilling in it some glamour and style, and she has won numerous awards and credits. She is part of a long line of people that Ailes helped make into a star.

At the time of this writing, it seems that the two may end up working with each other again. The real Money Honey that Rupert Murdoch and Roger Ailes have their eyes on is their newest project, the Fox Business

Network. And some current CNBC employees could end up moving over to Fox if the circumstances are right. When Ailes moved to Fox in 1996, he took a fair number of CNBC staff with him. He had earned their loyalty in the two years he had been there by providing leadership and a winning game plan, and by supporting them as a team.

According to the *New York Observer,* some CNBC staffers are "pining for Ailes."[3] Why? Because of their experience with him back in the '90s. "I watched him transform CNBC," one source told the *Observer.* "The guy is a genius. Before I leave this business I want to work for him again." Other CNBC staffers have talked about the "excitement" of building something new from the ground up, similar to what Ailes did with the Fox News Channel. "The general feeling is that Fox will crush CNBC," one pessimistic staffer said. Feelings like that are based on Fox's come-from-behind ratings win over CNN and the David and Goliath subtext.

One of those CNBC performers who followed Ailes to Fox News was Neil Cavuto, a founding father of business news television. He oversees editorial content at FBN and is involved in programming decisions. Cavuto was already a major presence at Fox. His business program on Fox News, *Your World with Neil Cavuto,* has been a consistent ratings leader on cable. He also has an inspiring personal story, having survived Hodgkin's disease, a form of cancer; then a decade later he was diagnosed with multiple sclerosis. He is known as a cheerleader for Republicans and is often accused by his critics of dragging politics and ideology into discussions about business issues.

There has been quite a bit of buzz about Fox's raiding CNBC's on-air talent, as well as their production staff and marketing reps. The highest-profile "steal" so far is probably Liz Claman, former anchor at CNBC, who brings star appeal to FBN. Her significant fan base at CNBC appreciated her "optimism, cheerfulness, and journalistic instincts," says Jon Friedman of MarketWatch.com.[4] And even better, she brings a good bit of journalistic credibility, which Roger Ailes needs if FBN is going to make a serious run at CNBC.

Another former CNBC anchor, Eric Bolling, joined FBN at its launch. And there will undoubtedly be more high-profile hires in the future. Sources also say that Ailes himself made a run at getting the animated, high-strung CNBC superstar Jim Cramer, whose show brings in high ratings numbers if for no other reason than to see if he will have a stroke on the air. Cramer seems comfortable staying right where he is at CNBC. In fact, he seems downright combative. "We have a competitor now in Fox and it's really important to destroy and humiliate them," he told *Broadcasting & Cable*'s Ben Grossman.[5] He even called Liz Claman a "turncoat"[6] for jumping ship and going to FBN.

Maria Bartiromo would seem like a natural candidate for Ailes and company to acquire, but her contract doesn't expire until 2009. However, chances are pretty good she will make the jump at that time—she and her agent have reached out to Roger Ailes in the past, according to *TV Newser*, "after she whined about how desperate she was to leave CNBC."[7] In previous interviews, Bartiromo has called Ailes a "terrific programmer" and said, "I would take a call from Roger any day of the week."[8]

And CNBC has yet another rising star, a new Money Honey, or "Street Sweetie" as she's being called. Erin Burnette, who also got her start in broadcasting with CNN, has gained quite a following over the last two years as host of *Street Signs* and appearing on other CNBC programs, as well as *NBC Nightly News* and the *Today* show. As with Bartiromo, Burnette has become known for her looks as much as for her talent. Her notoriety was cinched when she was lampooned by Jon Stewart on Comedy Central's *The Daily Show*. So if Roger Ailes is interested in snagging a big-name on-air talent from CNBC who can help continue to pull in Fox's big numbers with male viewers, he has two "Sweeties" to choose from.

And don't think he doesn't know it. In a maneuver of which Machiavelli would be envious, it has been suggested that Ailes and Co. managed to manufacture a fight between Bartiromo and Burnette that, as best anyone can tell, doesn't even exist. As reported by Nat Worden in TheStreet.com, "the blogosphere is buzzing with speculation that Bartiromo is peeved about the rising star of Burnette, and the rivalry may lead one or both of them to leave" CNBC. There are some media analysts who believe that for Fox to compete head-to-head with CNBC, they are going to need a high-profile "face" for the network. Bartiromo "has her own network of relationships and she can get to people where a lot of other reporters cannot," said Porter Bibb, a managing partner with Mediatech Capital Partners. [9]

And where did all this "buzz" originate? Why, Rupert Murdoch's *New York Post*, of course. A series of pieces in the *Post*'s gossip pages that, according to TheStreet.com's Worden, were "laced with sexist innuendo and loosely sourced information," claimed there was growing friction between the two stars and that CNBC might be losing its grip on one or both of them. The *Post*'s "Page Six" stories are known for their hype and celebrity gossip, and the speculation on the Money Honey and the Street Sweetie launched a torrent of commentary on the Web.

Don't forget, Roger Ailes is one of the most successful political consultants of the last twenty-five years. He knows how to lay land mines, and Rupert Murdoch has shown he is more than willing to use his newspapers to further his political and business goals. At least, the folks at CNBC seem to think so. Their spokesman Kevin Goldman suggested that the *Post* stories were a setup: "It's clear to everyone why the News Corp.-owned *New York Post* is trying to manufacture something that doesn't exist."[10] News Corp. denies it. A spokesman for Mr. Murdoch said that News Corp. has "better ways to compete with CNBC than by coming up with plot lines like that."[11] But anyone that has been around political campaigns long enough knows that if you can sow dissension in the ranks of your opponents, or even raise private questions in their minds, then you can create problems for them down the road. And goodness knows, Roger Ailes loves to get "into the minds" of his opponents.

After all, this is the man who, after threatening to sue Paula Zahn and her agent when she left Fox for CNN, put a movable Fox News billboard across from CNN's Atlanta headquarters on the very day that Zahn debuted her new CNN program. "I heard it was available and that everyone who walks in the building has to look at it," he said.[12] When a Fox show would outperform a CNN show, Ailes would put updated ratings numbers on the billboard to remind CNN. Turner Broadcasting's Jamie Kellner remembers it as a strange experience: "It's not nice . . .You're in the news business—it should be a higher playing field."[13]

But everyone dealing with Roger Ailes and Rupert Murdoch should always remember that they're not so much in the "news" business as they are in the "winning" business. As his old political campaign partner from the 1980s, Lee Atwater, once said of Ailes, "Roger has two speeds, attack and destroy."[14] Ailes enters any competition as if it were a political campaign—that's his nature.

Consider this from Rupert Murdoch's head "news-man," who, in an interview with *Newsweek* shortly after News Corp. acquired Dow Jones, said that to keep CNBC guessing about the makeup of the FBN, he'd been floating "disinformation" for months.[15] One result, according to Ailes, was that CNBC changed its slogan to "America's Business Channel" because, he said, "they thought I might be patriotic" on FBN. He went on to say that CNBC's highest-rated program is a "game-show" called *Deal or No Deal.* And he joked that most of CNBC's revenue comes from weekend infomercials for "nose tweezers and Body by Jake."[16] The billboard thing with Paula Zahn and CNN, and the put-downs of CNBC—that's the kind of thing an aggressive political consultant would do—intimidate the enemy, get into their heads.

That's what makes the launch of the Fox Business Network such an interesting public spectacle. Based on Roger Ailes's history and the example of Fox News's ratings triumph over CNN, everyone is waiting to see how Ailes and Co. will do it this time.

When Murdoch and Ailes first announced their plans to launch a new business channel back in the summer of 2005, it seemed to many like some kind of suicide mission. Providing business information to investors and financial services companies is one thing, but starting a business news network in a field already crowded with competitors is an uphill battle. Two business news channels already exist. CNBC is the king of the hill, but it continues to fight for an audience, particularly in the evenings and on weekends when the stock market is closed. Then there is the much smaller Bloomberg Television, pretty much just a video equivalent of their business information service with a few interviews sprinkled in. Then, of course, there used to be CNNfn, the financial news channel of CNN, a project so exciting that, according to NBC's Bob Wright, "even its original founder Lou Dobbs after awhile didn't want to be a part of it."[17] Television news analyst Andrew Tyndall questioned whether the TV market for financial news is big enough for two titans. "I'm not so sure that there is an audience that is not being served by CNBC . . . The niche isn't that big."[18]

So what's going on here? How are profits going to be made? Well, if Rupert Murdoch is involved, rest assured there are going to be profits—somewhere along the food chain of his global empire. Obviously Murdoch; his president, Peter Chernin; and Roger Ailes see a market opportunity here, just as they did with Fox News over a decade ago. Sources say Ailes at first was reluctant to go in the direction of a new business channel, thinking the odds were stacked against them and they might not be able to match the success of Fox News. That view is seconded by NBC's Wright, who doubts that Ailes was particularly interested in an all-business channel. "It's got to be Murdoch," said Wright. "He's like a supernova—it's in his nature to keep expanding his holdings, he doesn't know how to do anything else."[19] As one longtime Fox executive told *BusinessWeek*, "Nothing turns on this company like taking on the other guy."[20] And it also makes Murdoch and News Corp. more confident knowing they have the man at their side (Ailes) who ran CNBC in the '90s during the time it built an audience and drove up its profits. And Fox is quick to point out that the Neil Cavuto–led business programs on Fox News passed CNN and CNBC to grab the top five spots in cable news, including the Saturday morning business-news block.

But when CNBC was doing relatively well in the '90s, it was feeding off the dot.com boom, as well as the burgeoning stock market in general, and it was also before the advent of Blackberries and Wi-Fi allowed anyone interested in business news to get market updates and stock quotes quickly and easily without turning on the TV. But the world has changed since then, and the market for business news has changed with it. CNBC's viewer numbers have dropped as consumers gained more options for getting news, and as the gyrations of Wall Street (from 2000 to 2007) have made investors and market-watchers more selective. According to Nielsen ratings for CNBC, average daily viewers fell from almost 400,000 on average to about half that from the late 1990s to early 2000s. However, CNBC points out that Nielsen numbers don't reflect the "multitude" of analysts, investors, and businesses that have their channel on at work during the day. And the Nielsen numbers for CNBC were up in 2007, partly due to the success of *Mad Money* with Jim Cramer.

But even though the ratings numbers aren't where they used to be in the halcyon days, the advertisers still line up at the CNBC trough because, until FBN came along, it was essentially the only game in town that reached the consumers they're interested in—high-income, highly educated white males. And as Murdoch, Chernin, and Ailes will tell you, advertising revenue is where the profits are. CNBC brings in $245 million a year in advertising—it has a 57 percent operating margin and operating profits of $335 million, according to *BusinessWeek*.[21] News Corp. and Rupert Murdoch want some of that action. Advertisers have long said they would welcome a competitor to CNBC. The vice president of one large ad-space-buying company said, "We would all still love a viable option to CNBC," reasoning that CNBC's ad rates of nearly $30 per household are too high given its relatively small audience.[22]

But looking strictly at the numbers, it's still an uphill battle. Fox business news, in 2008, is seen in just over 30 million homes, which is about one-third of CNBC's audience and even less than Bloomberg Television. And many analysts believe this specific viewing audience is finite—the number of people craving business news will not increase by very much. If that's true, it means Fox is going to have to take away a significant share of current CNBC and Bloomberg viewers—a challenge when one considers that consumers of business information tend to be creatures of habit.

So how do General Ailes and Chairman of the Joint Chiefs Murdoch go into battle? Look for clues in how they outmaneuvered CNN. They didn't simply copy what CNN does and then turn on the cameras. They had a marketing plan that involved identifying its core audience, then creating programming and finding on-air talent that would attract and hold the viewers they were after. The result is a more raucous, freewheeling entertainment-oriented style that emphasizes political commentary more than straight news, and with an ideological edge.

Some parts of that approach will no doubt characterize the Fox Business Network. Judging from its early months, it is certainly more raucous and entertainment-oriented than CNBC. And it will likely feature more personalized commentary and opinion than CNBC or Bloomberg currently offer. But whether it will be more ideological or political is an open question. Part of the Fox News formula was to go after conservative white males who felt disenfranchised by the Big Three networks and CNN. But that formula may have limited utility in this situation. CNBC is already pretty conservative. After all, it is a business news network catering to the business world, which tends to be right-of-center to begin with. So is there enough room on the right for Fox to try to outflank them? Maybe. And they may try, but they won't make that their main appeal.

Jon Friedman of MarketWatch.com, a Dow Jones company now owned by Rupert Murdoch, of course, anticipates that FBN will strive to look and sound like what he calls the "anti-CNBC." When it comes to CNBC, he said, "there is no middle ground: people either love it or hate it. Its fans appreciate interviews with newsmakers, its ability to report a breaking story quickly, and the familiarity of 'Squawk Box' every morning."[23] But that familiarity and safety can also be its weakness. Familiarity, as they say, breeds contempt, reminds Friedman. Part of Ailes's strategy will rely on the perception, pushed by Fox and News Corp., that CNBC has gotten dull and complacent—perhaps similar to Murdoch's characterization of CNN in the 1990s. Certainly, CNBC hasn't had to face any kind of direct competition, at least since CNNfn folded in 2004. And Ailes will come at them with everything he has got, with Murdoch making sure he has a lot to throw.

For starters, Murdoch and Ailes have said that FBN will be more "business friendly" than CNBC. Yes, as incredible as it may seem, Fox is going to go after CNBC as being "antibusiness." Ailes laid out the battle strategy when he said in an interview, "Many times I've seen things on CNBC where they are not as friendly to corporations and profits as they should be . . . We don't get up every morning thinking business is bad."[24] At a media conference in New York, Mr. Murdoch accused CNBC of being quick to "leap on every scandal" reported in the business community. And apparently, with a straight face, Fox News business editor Neil Cavuto said, "We're going to be a channel for America, not for old white men with money."[25]

One has to hand it to them. This is classic political strategy: define your opponent before they have a chance to define themselves. It's what Ailes and George H. W. Bush did to Michael Dukakis in 1988—that's what the tank ride was all about. And Ailes has successfully adapted political lessons to business use before. In 1996, Ailes and Murdoch characterized CNN and the mainstream media and then, later, all of Fox's critics, as hopelessly left-wing. That worked out pretty well for them. Now they are saying their main business news competitor is antibusiness.

For their part, CNBC doesn't sound worried. Their spokesman Kevin Goldman answered the criticism saying, "It doesn't surprise me that our alleged competition is already starting with its usual lies and propaganda."[26] CNBC's president, Mark Hoffman, took a jab at Fox's reputation for ideologically based reporting when he said CNBC will continue to do what it is doing successfully and that they will be the "unbiased" business news channel. Jeff Zucker, chairman and CEO of NBC Universal, the parent company of CNBC, said that his network will be defined by what it delivers on the air every day and not by Fox. "When you don't have a product," he said, "it's easy to throw darts . . . We're not concerned at all."[27] Well, the folks at CNBC had better hope he wasn't serious about those last five words: "We're not concerned at all." Publicly, that's fine. But behind closed doors, they'd better be building an ark.

When Fox News was launched, the CNN brass wasn't too concerned either. The truth is, Fox News and Roger Ailes weren't taken seriously by their competitors back then. But then, why would they have been? What Murdoch was attempting to do seemed as if Don Quixote was tilting at a large CNN windmill. Rick Kaplan, president of CNN from 1996 to 2000, typified the response of most to Fox News's sloganeering approach, such as calling CNN the Clinton News Network, and calling itself the Fair and Balanced news network. "I thought that people weren't going to buy that argument," he said.[28] But CNN has learned. Now they counterpunch. And CNBC seems poised to fight. Maybe that's an advantage CNBC has now that CNN didn't have in the late '90s: You can see them coming. You know the tactics. And most of all, you know that what they're doing and saying isn't merely words and slogans, but is a well-designed marketing strategy.

Part of that strategy is to continue to emphasize the Fox "brand" and do in business news what it has done successfully in covering national and international news. The first personnel announcements made by Roger Ailes concerning FBN anchors and correspondents included David Asman, host of *Forbes on Fox;* Rebecca Gomez and Cheryl Casone, both Fox News business correspondents; Dagen McDowell, a Fox News journalist; and Stuart Varney, a business news veteran of both CNN and CNBC. MarketWatch.com's Jon Friedman asked, "Do you detect a pattern here? Fox intends to build on what has previously succeeded." Friedman anticipates that Fox will add a number of names and faces from outside the company. "By all indications," he said, "the network was deluged with job seekers . . . Even I was getting calls from fellow journalists and friends asking me for advice on how to apply for positions."[29]

Fox's mostly middle-aged-male audience is undoubtedly happy to see that Fox Business Network is continuing at least one tradition that has helped make Fox News a ratings winner: attractive female journalists reporting the news. Led by coanchor Alexis Glick, the FBN team will give the regular Fox News channel a run for its money in the "media babe" department. *New York* magazine, in an article called "Fox Business Network: Full of Foxes!" reported that FBN's new Web site, launched in September 2007, "lends a little insight" into the network's strategy: "Namely, foxy young broads," according to the magazine. The reporter goes on to say that "almost all of the on-air talent that's plugged on the site are skinny, youthful beauties like Shibani Joshi (a former model in India), Cheryl Casone (a former flight attendant), Jenna Lee (she played Division One softball in college), and Nicole Petillades (she loves slalom waterskiing!)."[30]

Not to be outdone, *Variety* speculates that Roger Ailes has taken a page from GLOW—the Gorgeous Ladies of Wrestling—and given us GLOB, the Gorgeous Ladies of Business. "Who needs a Money Honey when you have a veritable 'Money Hive?'" asks its reporter, Brian Lowry. "Realizing that the heavy hitters interviewed on FBN would be mostly old white guy CEOs," said Lowry, "the channel has conspicuously adorned its talent roster with eye candy for the predominantly male audience to tune in."[31] But here again, this mirrors the Fox News strategy of adapting the flash of local television news to cable.

And Ailes's penchant for bringing radio talent into TV news is on full display, as one of the featured programs on FBN is a show hosted by Dave Ramsey, the popular host of a syndicated radio program. Ramsey's niche is counseling consumers to reduce debt and make smart personal financial decisions. This plays well into Murdoch and Ailes's marketing strategy of positioning FBN as a channel that focuses on "Main Street" instead of only on "Wall Street."

Fox's strategy is to ignore the analysts who say that there is no more room for another business news channel and that the audience and the market can't be grown very much larger than what it currently is. Fox intends to appeal to a wider audience than CNBC's by providing programming that appeals to average consumers, not just to Wall Street, and by making their news coverage less reliant on business "lingo" and jargon. FBN anchor David Asman says that "nine times out of ten, when you listen to another channel on TV talk about business . . . they use a kind of claptrap terminology, or they use a kind of lingo that is unapproachable by the man on the street."[32] Asman goes on to say that FBN will make business and financial news "accessible" to everybody.

Just as he did with CNBC and America's Talking, Ailes is shaking it up by trying to generate crowd-pleasing original programming to build an audience. As Ailes has said, cable is an "edge" business, and his style is to always push his programming toward that edge. For example, a show called *Happy Hour* actually takes place in a bar. Its host dresses casually and has long hair, looking like the typical middle school student of today, and hangs out in the Bull & Bear (in the Waldorf Astoria Hotel) after hours, interviewing stock traders and other bar patrons. Depending on your point of view, it's either edgy or just plain goofy.

In a way, this mirrors Fox's strategy in its competition with CNN. Fox News appealed to the "average American" and played up the nation's "resentment" at the elitist, East Coast liberalism of CNN and network news. So with FBN they will try something similar—broaden its appeal to more people and brand it as the "people's business channel." If this is successful and translates to high ratings, it will vindicate Fox's marketing strategy. For example, the ticker that rolls at the bottom of the screen on FBN doesn't have just the stock symbol, but spells out the name of the company. There is also less business jargon on FBN to make it more accessible to more people. Whether these marketing techniques aimed at a "broader" audience will pan out is too early to tell at the time of this writing.

In the long term, they will try to marry this appeal to "average" consumers with the higher-income demographics that are drawn to financial news at CNBC. Media analysts note that one reason CNBC can charge high ad rates is that their audience is a highly sought-after demographic. And it is much the same with CNN. As the Financial Press reports, while Fox has long outpaced CNN in total viewers, they have never really captured the more desirable demographic groups. Therefore, Fox doesn't charge nearly as much as CNN does for advertising time. One advertising executive said, "Fox viewers are more Chevy buyers than BMWs."[33] That's probably one reason why Murdoch wanted a business channel in the first place, to go after that upscale advertising market.

And there's one more piece to the puzzle: the *Wall Street Journal*. This is the other part of the formula that Murdoch and Ailes will use to try to push FBN to the top of the ratings. It's no secret that one of the reasons Murdoch wanted the *Journal* was to provide news content, market analysis, interviews with business leaders, and other resources to the new Fox business channel. Analysts agree that the *Journal* name and association with Fox will bring tremendous clout and "cachet" to FBN. J. Max Robins of *Broadcasting & Cable* says, "Whatever happens, you can bet Murdoch will use his far-flung resources to cross-promote the *Journal* and FBN, hoping to graft the blue-chip newspaper brand on his newbie network."[34] Robins even suggests, probably with tongue firmly implanted in cheek, that as soon as it is legally possible, Murdoch should change the name of the Fox Business Network to the Wall Street Journal Network.

Rupert Murdoch had first mentioned the possibility of a business news channel to compete with CNBC several years ago. He had originally projected the launch sometime in 2006, then postponed it to early 2007, then to the fall of 2007. "I keep telling him to stop announcing launch dates," Ailes once said.[35] But it is no accident that FBN was launched around the same time that News Corp. and Murdoch had secured the *Wall Street Journal*.

One can envision *Wall Street Journal* reporters appearing on the Fox business news channel for news updates and commentary, and FBN feature stories that use the *Journal*'s resources and contacts. Owning the *Journal* could give a competitive advantage to FBN when vying with CNBC for a relatively small pool of interviewees; for example, CEOs of companies who seek favorable coverage in the *Journal*.

But of course there is one problem. The *Wall Street Journal*, a Dow Jones company, is under contract to provide business news content exclusively to CNBC until 2012. But that's a potential fly in the ointment with which

Murdoch and Ailes are willing to contend. "Rupert has a knack for getting those things ironed out,"[36] said Eric Boehlert, a senior fellow at Media Matters, an advocacy group. Many speculate that Murdoch will attempt to find a way out of the dilemma. Several reports indicate that he may try to buy his way out of the potential problem—a cash settlement is a possibility.

But without question, Murdoch wants to capitalize on the *Wall Street Journal* brand name now, rather than later. He has suggested that the *Journal* contract with CNBC doesn't prevent Fox from using the *Journal*'s reporters for most kinds of stories—only for business news. "There is no reason we could not have *Wall Street Journal* coverage of politics, international affairs, lifestyle, travel, you name it," he said at a media industry event.[37] And there is absolutely nothing to stop FBN and Murdoch from using Dow Jones's other business news entities, such as *Barron's*, the Dow Jones Newswires, and MarketWatch.com.

CNBC's Hoffman has made it clear that the network has an ironclad agreement with the *Journal,* and that it has four more years to go. And NBC's Bob Wright said it is a major advantage that CNBC will use to stay in front of Fox. But even if Fox is forced to wait until 2012 to use business content from the *Journal,* that's probably okay with Murdoch. He's used to planning for the long term anyway, and he has shown that he can be very patient while his strategy takes shape.

Industry analyst Porter Bibb believes sooner or later the *Wall Street Journal* will give Fox the upper hand. He calls it their "ace in the hole." He said that when Murdoch gets his hands on the *Journal,* then the competition will really begin. "When he starts the WSJ Network or something with that brand," said Bibb, "then he can go head-to-head with CNBC—and kick butt."[38]

One of the reasons that Fox's launch of the business network was delayed was so they could be assured they had a large enough audience to be competitive. Roger Ailes insisted on this. "I did not want to do it until we had at least 30 million homes," he told Joshua Chaffin of the *Financial Times.* "I was dragging my feet until we had the distribution piece."[39] Some of those pieces fell into place in 2007 as News Corp. was pursuing the *Wall Street Journal.* Fox completed negotiating cable distribution deals with major carriers in 2007, including contracts with Comcast, Time Warner, and Charter Communications. And naturally, FBN will be carried on the News Corp.–owned Direct TV satellite service. It was crucial to strike a distribution deal with Time Warner, due to its access in Manhattan, the center of the business world. Fox is continuing to seek deals with carriers in other parts of the country in order to fill gaps in its distribution.

One aspect of the competition between FBN and CNBC that hasn't received much attention is their Web presence. That's surprising, given the increasing importance of the Web as a platform for news and commentary as well as for generating advertising revenue. The major news outlets, both print and broadcast, have been gravitating to the Internet in recent years anyway, and without question, much of the competition for business news and information will be fought in cyberspace. MarketWatch.com's Jon Friedman suggests that CNBC has some catching up to do on-line. CNBC has revamped its Web presence a few times, says Friedman, "but it still looks slapped together . . . It lacks vision and has an extremely busy look to boot . . . It's anything but sleek."[40] By contrast, the *Wall Street Journal*'s Web site is the envy of many in the news business. In Friedman's opinion, it reflects the *Journal*'s commitment to excellence in every phase of its operations. "The *Journal*'s site features some of the most sophisticated blogs and graphics anywhere . . . Shrewdly, it stresses interactivity, one of the keys to success in the Internet world." Reminder: MarketWatch.com is a Dow Jones company, now owned by Rupert Murdoch.

The early reviews have been mostly favorable. *BusinessWeek* says FBN "ain't your grandfather's business channel, and that's the point."[41] Like Fox News, FBN has a certain swagger to it, and plenty of attitude. They may have a swagger, but as of this writing, the ratings are anemic. Nielsen ratings in January 2008 show that Fox Business attracts only about 6,000 viewers a day.[42] That's lower than most local television stations. Compare that to CNBC's average viewership of 283,000 over the same period, and the scope of Ailes and Murdoch's challenge is clear—they have a very long way to go.

CNBC seems ready for the battle. They're trying to stay on the cutting edge. Just after FBN launched, CNBC announced their "Investor Network," the installation of "next generation web cams" on trading floors. This allows traders and analysts to appear on the air instantly, as a business story is breaking. In a bid to become more user-friendly, their Web site now features thousands of video clips and tools that allow users to model their stock portfolios. Their ratings are up from where they were a couple of years ago, and they have revamped their after-market programming. CNBC president Mark Hoffman believes they are in an excellent position. "Bring it on," a CNBC spokesperson said.[43]

17

The Fox Follies

*Any candidate for high office of either party who
believes he can blacklist any news organization
is making a terrible mistake about journalists.*

—Roger Ailes[1]

There's an old saying in show business: "Dying is easy, but comedy is hard." Peter O'Toole said it in the movie *My Favorite Year,* but its origin appears to go back to vaudeville days. Whoever said it first, Roger Ailes proved it again in 2007 when the Fox News Channel tried its hand at comedy. Apparently inspired by the success of *The Daily Show with Jon Stewart* on the Comedy Central network, in February 2007 Fox News launched a comedy program called the *1/2 Hour News Hour.*

Actually, if one is going after ratings (and Roger Ailes is *always* going after ratings—remember, this is the network that had a correspondent whose only apparent job, as far as this author could tell, was to update viewers on the Anna Nicole Smith controversy), a comedy show isn't really a bad idea. It's especially true if a network is trying to attract younger viewers—a perennial problem for a news programming network. In recent years, more than one survey has shown that younger viewers get most of their political information from watching entertainment programming, for example *The Tonight Show* with Jay Leno, David Letterman, Jon Stewart's *Daily Show,* and the bane of politicians and government officials everywhere, Stephen Colbert's *The Colbert Report.*

But—and here's the thing—all of those programs are funny. The *1/2 Hour News Hour* on Fox News wasn't. At least, not often enough to build much interest in the show. A review of the show by the *Washington Post*'s entertainment writer said the program "isn't terrible."[2] Not exactly a ringing endorsement. Airing on Sunday nights—normally a soft spot for the news anyway—the show was built around a phony newscast, sort of like "Weekend Update" on *Saturday Night Live.* The "anchors," Kurt Long and Jenn Robertson, sat behind a desk and gave a conservative look at the day's news, skewering liberals in the process. The show also included skits and interviews: a segment with a T-shirt salesman, trying to take advantage of the current popularity of Che Guevara T-shirts, hawking Adolf Hitler T-shirts fell with a thud.

And the context of a comedy show on a news channel is far different from the popular comedy shows Fox News wanted to emulate. Stewart and Colbert are on Comedy Central, not on CNN. Many entertainers have proved that it's possible to be topical and funny, and political humor has long been a staple of stand-up comics and television variety shows. But not many viewers (not even conservative ones) are used to tuning in to a news network for laughs—that's not what the audience is looking for or they would tune in to one of the comedy programs that are already out there. The senior vice president of programming for Fox News, Bill Shine, acknowledged the difficulty, saying at the time that it was a "risk." But, he said, "we have a whole history here of doing risky things."[3]

But Roger Ailes must have been thinking that there are no "conservative" comedy programs out there, and that conservatives were being underserved when it comes to political humor. Well, he may have had a point there, but if so, there's probably a pretty good reason for it. For one thing, there aren't many conservative comedians out there. Dennis Miller comes to mind—actually he's a libertarian. And Fox already has him anyway—he appears from time to time on the Bill O'Reilly program. Miller can be pretty funny; at least when O'Reilly allows the comedian to get a word in. Miller also provided video "rants" for the *1/2 Hour News Hour*. But let's face it, there aren't many artists of any kind that are politically conservative—comedians, actors, musicians, what have you. The world of performing arts normally just isn't a "conservative" thing. And except for Stewart and Colbert, political humor is a very small part of most entertainers' bag of tricks anyway. It's not that interesting to most of them. And it's not that interesting to most audiences either.

The creator and executive producer of the *1/2 Hour News Hour* was Joel Surnow, who produces the popular program *24* on the Fox Network. Surnow is a conservative—he referred to himself as a "right wing nut job" in a February 19, 2007, *New Yorker* magazine interview.[4] He also happens to be a good friend of Roger Ailes's and was a Rudy Giuliani for President supporter.[5] Surnow first pitched the comedy program to the executives at the Fox television network, but they turned it down. So he turned to Ailes, who agreed to give it a shot on the Fox News Channel. Another of the show's producers,

Manny Coto, told the *Los Angeles Times*, "We thought it would be fun to have some unabashedly conservative entertainment . . . Our audience will be the millions who tune in to Rush Limbaugh and like-minded people who want that same kind of acerbic commentary and liberal bashing they get on his radio show everyday."[6] Indeed, the show's premiere featured a skit with special guest Rush Limbaugh, along with anything-but-comedienne Ann Coulter.

The show ran for about six months, the last episode airing in September 2007. Officials at the Fox News Channel said it was just too expensive to produce, with scripts, actors, sets, studio audiences, and the like. Apparently, the ratings were not there to justify the expense.

Perhaps a conservative comedy show just feels too "forced" to viewers. But so would a liberal comedy show. If it's funny, it's funny; if it's not, it's not—regardless of politics. Trying to force comedy through an ideological megaphone isn't natural, and there's no market to support it. Not many people will tune in to see a "conservative" or a "liberal" comedy program. People tune in to see a comedy show, period. And when the show turns to political humor, most of it will typically be left-of-center; it's just the nature of the beast.

It's a little bit like political protests—those on the political left will show up in droves for liberal and progressive causes, depending on the circumstances and the issues involved. But conservatives are lousy protesters, with the possible exception of those on the "right" on abortion. They're just not into it; it's not their thing.

Maybe Roger Ailes figured that if the show was a success, they could generate a lot of jokes at Democrats' expense, and if they could draw in younger viewers, they could teach them to think of Democratic Party icons with derision and laughter. But wait a minute, if Fox News is Fair and Balanced, shouldn't their comedy show have featured conservative comedy *and* liberal comedy?

The show's creator, Joel Surnow, warned against using the show's cancellation as proof that conservatives aren't funny. And some conservatives agree. The folks at the right-of-center Media Research Center now have a twice-weekly comedy show on its on-line "NewsBusters" blog. According to its Web site, the show is about "politics, Hollywood, and media bias."

Around the same time as the debut of the *1/2 Hour News Hour*, Roger Ailes had a very public, and what he must have considered a decidedly unfunny dustup with the Democratic Party. This may become known as the Great Debate Debacle of 2007. And it may have long-term consequences.

Potentially, it could influence how mainstream television viewers look at the Fox News Channel—is it a legitimate source of news or is it an unofficial organ of the national Republican Party? Right now it's pretty black and white—or red and blue would be more accurate. Republicans say it is absolutely a legitimate source of news, and that it has fair, insightful commentary and analysis of the day's events. Most Democrats are convinced, and will probably always be convinced, that it is simply a mouthpiece for the GOP. It is the middle ground, the independents, that are in play—just like in an election.

It all started in Nevada with a Democratic presidential candidate debate scheduled for August 2007, sponsored by the Nevada Democratic Party and the Fox News Channel. Fox News had cosponsored and broadcast Democratic presidential debates in 2004, so there was nothing particularly groundbreaking about this event. Initially, even Harry Reid, the Democratic senate leader, a proud Nevadan, thought it was a good idea. But a good many Dems, particularly on the left of the party, began criticizing the Nevada state party for partnering up with what they consider the primary source of evil in America, Fox News.

Led by the liberal advocacy group MoveOn.org, a number of Democratic activists and opinion leaders urged the Nevada Democratic Party to drop Fox News as a cosponsor of the debate. Several thousand Democrats e-mailed the headquarters of the state party, and MoveOn.org claimed they had over 260,000 people supporting an on-line petition urging that Fox be dropped from the debate. The chair of the Nevada state Democrats, Tom Collins, defended the decision to go with Fox News, saying it would give Democratic presidential candidates an opportunity to reach out to voters who normally wouldn't be listening to Democratic candidates. But the criticism from Democrats around the country intensified, and some Nevada Democrats also began to have second thoughts and to second-guess how the state party made its decision in the first place.

The critics of the debate scored their first victory when Democratic candidate John Edwards said he would not attend because of Fox News's participation. That set in motion a chain of events that led to the outright cancellation of the entire Nevada debate. And to believe the Democrats, it was Roger Ailes himself who struck the deathblow. Speaking to the Radio and Television News Directors Association at an event in Washington, Ailes was irritated. He complained about "pressure groups" trying to force candidates to appear only on those TV networks that "give them favorable coverage." He talked about the long tradition of news organizations sponsoring debates in the past and resisting pressure to organize them in certain ways and ask only certain questions.

> This pressure has been successfully resisted, but it's being tried again this year with the added wrinkle that candidates are being asked to boycott debates because certain groups want to approve the sponsoring organizations. This pressure must be resisted as it has been in the past. Any candidate for high office of either party who believes he can blacklist any news organization is making a terrible mistake about journalists. And any candidate of either party who cannot answer direct, simple, even tough questions from any journalist runs a real risk of losing the voters.[7]

There he goes again, defending journalists, even though he has probably attacked more journalists in the last forty years than any person alive. But that's not the comment that caused the problem. After getting the Nevada thing off his chest, he moved on to lighter topics. In a series of jokes about various public officials, he mentioned the similarity of Democratic senator and presidential candidate Barack Obama's name to that of Osama bin Laden. "And it is true that Barack Obama is on the move," he said. "I don't know if it's true that President Bush called Musharraf [the president of Pakistan] and said, 'why can't we catch this guy?'"[8]

The next day, the Nevada Democratic Party canceled the debate. Whether it was a fit of pique over Ailes's joking comments about Barack Obama, or whether it was simply one bridge too far in their willingness to take more fire from Democratic Party activists, it is hard to say. "Comments made last night by Fox News President Roger Ailes in reference to one of our presidential candidates went too far," explained Tom Collins, the Nevada Democratic chair. Senator Harry Reid joined Collins in saying, "We cannot, as good Democrats, put our party in a position to defend such comments." MoveOn.org declared victory: "We hope this sets a precedent for all Democrats, that Fox should be treated as a right-wing misinformation network, not legitimized as a neutral source of news," said its executive director.[9]

Ailes and Fox News reacted predictably. A Fox spokesman said, "News organizations will want to think twice before getting involved in the

Nevada Democratic caucus which appears to be controlled by radical, fringe, out-of-state interest groups, not the Nevada Democratic Party."[10] On his program, Bill O'Reilly compared the "radicals" in Nevada to "Nazis."[11]

This is one skirmish in Fox News's larger battle in defending its integrity and journalistic values against the Democratic Party and left-of-center advocacy groups that seek to "de-legitimize" Fox as a news organization. A senior advisor to one of the 2008 Democratic contenders said, "The more they can be de-legitimized the better . . . They are in business to promote the Republican Party and to hurt the Democratic Party, and they have every right to do that, but to the extent their pretense of objectivity can be challenged, it should be."[12]

Political reporter Ron Brownstein of the *Los Angeles Times* wonders if "with this precedent established, Democratic leaders may increasingly view the network less as a megaphone than as a foil . . . They may try to demonstrate their toughness to their own activists by appearing on Fox to denounce it, the way Bill Clinton did on Fox News Sunday."[13] Liberal columnist E. J. Dionne said that Ailes knows "the campaign to block Fox from sponsoring Democratic debates is the most effective liberal push-back against the network" since its inception in 1996. Dionne said his "hunch is that Ailes, one of the toughest and smartest in a generation of Republican political consultants, sees his adversaries as playing the kind of political hardball he respects . . . It's why he's angry."[14]

Some opinion leaders suggest that this simply puts Democrats on a level playing field with Republicans, who have been throwing stones at the "mainstream media" for years amid accusations that network news and major newspapers are biased against conservative causes. Brownstein believes that this may be the legacy of the 2007 debate debacle: "One of the premier conservative media institutions [Fox News] now faces the likelihood of a sustained siege from Democrats using the same fluid tactics many conservatives have long applied"[15] against their adversaries in the media.

As some of the previous chapters have demonstrated, as time has gone by, Rupert Murdoch has put more and more faith in Roger Ailes's ability to get results. Since Ailes went to News Corp. in 1996, his responsibilities and presence at the company have grown and multiplied. For example, when Murdoch's son Lachlan abruptly resigned as president of the Fox Television Stations group in 2005, Murdoch turned to Ailes to pick up the pieces. He was appointed by Murdoch to take over its operations in addition to his stewardship of Fox News.

The Fox TV Stations division oversees its thirty-five broadcast TV stations and a production studio, Twentieth Television. All told, this division represents approximately 30 percent of News Corp.'s operating income. And the TV Stations group is strategically crucial as the main outlet for the Fox broadcast network. The stations are also useful for promoting Fox's other businesses, such as its cable networks and programming.

The departure of Lachlan Murdoch stunned the media world and caused major tremors at News Corp. and throughout Fox. For some time, he had been considered the heir apparent to the Murdoch empire. Rupert Murdoch had not openly dwelled on the topic of who would succeed him, but made no secret that he would like to pass the baton to one of his children. "I think it is a very, very human motive to see your work carried forward by one of your own," he told the *New York Times* in 2003.[16]

Family businesses can produce difficult situations, and this was no different. Lachlan, being the oldest, was considered the front-runner. But by December 2007, with Lachlan no longer in the picture, it was clear that his younger brother, James, would inherit the keys to the kingdom. James, thirty-four, was named chairman of News Corp.'s European and Asian operations. He will take charge of the broadcasting, print, and Internet divisions including Hong Kong–based Star TV, Britain's *Sun* newspaper, and Sky Italia. This move appears to address the much-publicized speculation about who will succeed Rupert Murdoch. "This is grooming James for a larger role longer term at News Corp.," said Pali Research analyst Richard Greenfield. "He has proved himself beyond a doubt over the last several years" at British Sky Broadcasting.[17]

Some media reports have suggested that Lachlan Murdoch didn't feel that he had his father's complete confidence in his ability to manage News Corp. properties. And some of these reports have Lachlan in direct conflict with Roger Ailes. According to the *Australian*, "Everyone knows Ailes and Lachlan just do not get on . . . Ailes was one of the senior thorns in the paw of the young lion . . ."[18] Admittedly, some publications in Australia and Britain have taken a certain amount of joy in Rupert Murdoch's business and family dramas, but publications such as the *Wall Street Journal* have reported similar findings in the past—of course, presumably the *WSJ* will no longer dwell on such things.

At the time, Lachlan was technically above Ailes in the News Corp. food chain, but Ailes's relationship with Rupert was such that he could go directly to him with whatever was on his mind. That apparently caused some difficulties.

According to *New York* magazine, the final straw came when Rupert Murdoch backed Ailes over Lachlan in a dispute about a police crime series called *Crime Line* that Ailes wanted to put on Fox News. Reportedly, the elder Murdoch told Ailes to go ahead and do it, and "don't listen to Lachlan."[19] The *Guardian* reported in 2005 that "it is an open secret that Lachlan has felt "out of the loop, partly due to Ailes's close relationship with Rupert.[20] The *Wall Street Journal* also reported that Lachlan had developed a sense that his father was "undercutting his work at News Corp."[21] Ailes denies there was any such tension between himself and Lachlan Murdoch. He said the *WSJ*'s characterization of their relationship was "just flat-out incorrect."[22]

The *New York Times* reported that the relationship between Lachlan and his father was badly frayed. "In one example of their deteriorating relationship," according to the *Times,* "Lachlan told someone in close contact with the family that his father dressed him down in a meeting with other top company executives." Lachlan reportedly tried repeatedly to express his dissatisfaction to his father, according to a person close to the family.[23]

Other analysts have pointed to family and financial issues causing strains in the father–son relationship. The *Knight Ridder Tribune* reported that "disagreements over the family trust fund, the relocation of the business [News Corp. headquarters] from Sydney to New York, and Lachlan Murdoch's 10-week vacation contributed to his resignation" from News Corp. *Knight Ridder* suggested that the two had "crossed swords" over a family trust that holds News Corp. shares: "Murdoch's 1999 divorce settlement with his second wife Anna is believed to include a stipulation for assets to be held in trust for their children . . . But Murdoch's current wife, Wendy Deng, wants their two young children to be cut in—something Lachlan is said to oppose."[24]

Whatever the manifold causes of Lachlan's departure, his father said he was "deeply saddened" by his son's decision. Lachlan retains a seat on the News Corp. board, and his father reportedly has not given up hope that one day he may return and take up a senior post in the business once again. Lachlan and his wife, former model Sara O'Hare, spoke of their desire to return to Australia to bring up their young son. He also said it was time to apply what he had learned from his father in business on his own. Upon returning to Sydney, Lachlan set up a media and entertainment production company called Illyria. But relations with his father and with News Corp. are still apparently strong enough for him to list News Corp.'s Sydney offices as the principal place of business for Illyria.

Ailes took over the Fox TV Stations group at a crucial time. The division's performance was under a microscope due to programming weaknesses and slower than expected revenue growth. Some programming decisions simply weren't working out. A talk show with *American Idol* host Ryan Secrest was an expensive flop, according to industry publications. And the attempt to revive *A Current Affair,* one of the Fox programs that Ailes worked on as a consultant in the early '90s, didn't catch on with viewers. One of the first changes Ailes made was to replace *A Current Affair* with a news and talk show hosted by Geraldo Rivera, who through the years has proven to be an Ailes favorite— Rivera also worked for Ailes at CNBC.

Taking the helm of the TV stations has put Ailes in a different environment from what he was accustomed to at Fox News. Some industry analysts say his go-it-alone style and authoritative management have not gone quite as smoothly when dealing with TV stations, programming personnel, and executives at other networks who run content on Fox TV stations. The *Wall Street Journal,* for example, reports that he was used to "operating his own fiefdom," and that he "has ruffled feathers among other executives."[25] The *Journal* and others suggest that as Rupert Murdoch has allowed Ailes to carve out a larger power base at News Corp., it has sparked tensions within the executive suite. Ailes says such reports are overblown. "There are lots of things you can say about me—but not playing for the full team is not one of them," he told the *Journal.*

Ailes set about making the Fox TV Stations' operation more closely resemble the franchise of Fox News. For example, he informed CNN that the Fox local TV stations would no longer use the CNN feed for international news coverage, a move that some local Fox TV executives questioned. He also transplanted the iconic red-and-blue Fox logo to each of the Fox-owned TV stations to give them a standardized Fox look. Transferring the base of operations from Los Angeles to New York also changed the culture of the Fox TV Stations group somewhat. In a throwback to his days as a communications consultant, Ailes had local Fox anchors, reporters, and editors flown to New York for training sessions—sort of a "this is how we do it at Fox" education. He has, in effect, grafted the Fox network identity onto the local Fox TV stations. But even though he has taken control of the management and standardized operations to a degree, he has said that each station will retain its editorial independence.

Thus far, the changes haven't increased viewership for Fox TV properties or led to increased revenue. But part of the problem is that the industry suffered through a slump throughout 2006 and into 2007 as local TV continued to fight off competition from the Internet and cable television programming. And another part of the difficulty may be that he is dealing with a different demographic in local television markets—one far less interested in national issues and one far younger in age. The average age of the Fox News viewer is sixty, compared with an average age of thirty-eight for the viewers of the programs on the Fox broadcast network.

Now, heaven knows that Ailes can multitask. In the early and mid-'70s, he consulted for political campaigns, television specials, and Broadway shows. And in his television career, he has often juggled numerous balls in the air at once. But in a possible case of spreading oneself too thin, Ailes was caught off guard when CBS, which owned the UPN network, decided to merge with the WB network, owned by Time Warner. The new arrangement was called the CW network.

The Fox-owned TV stations had been relying on the UPN network for programming content. But the UPN-WB merger left at least ten of the Fox-owned stations out in the cold with no network programming. According to the *Wall Street Journal,* CBS executives felt that Ailes and the rest of Fox management were "dragging their feet" about renewing its contract with UPN, and therefore wanted to move forward with a new deal. "We weren't dragging our feet," Ailes insisted, "we just weren't in a hurry." He said CBS president Les Moonves had called him from his car "on his way into the press conference" announcing the formation of the new CW network in partnership with Time Warner.[26]

The development left Ailes and News Corp. scrambling to come up with programming for its affiliates that had no network affiliation. The result was My Network TV, a new network meant to patch together the Fox TV stations and provide programming content. The odd-sounding My Network moniker is likely an attempt to capitalize on News Corp.'s recent acquisition of the MySpace.com social networking Internet site. Launched in the fall of 2006, just months after the CBS–Time Warner deal, My Network had to move fast. They revived an idea that had been kicked around by a few producers. The "telenovela," a soap opera–like serial, had proved very popular on Spanish-language television and in parts of Asia and Europe. So Twentieth Television, the production studio owned by Fox, kicked into overdrive and produced two hour-long dramas, *Desire* and *Fashion House.* In a News Corp. statement, Ailes said at the time, "Backed by the strongest media company in the world, My

Network TV is a viable alternative brought to you by proven winners who know quality programming."

But the telenovela dramas performed very poorly, and by early 2007, Fox was revamping the My Network TV lineup to appeal to younger men by including martial arts fights, action movies, and a special on Anna Nicole Smith, which was one of its highest-rated programs. Even though Ailes and Peter Chernin (the number two at News Corp.) were "disappointed" with the ratings and revenue generated by My Network through 2007, they were optimistic that their producers and programmers would be able to grow the network's audience in the near future. With Ailes's background—*Mike Douglas, A Current Affair, The O'Reilly Factor,* etc.—they probably have a shot.

Closing

Roger Ailes seems to have long viewed himself as an "advisor to the king." He really does remind one of Niccolo Machiavelli—the title of chapter 4 really isn't as much of a joke as it may seem. He would have very much enjoyed playing that role in the Nixon White House, but after the revelations of Joe McGinniss's *The Selling of the President 1968,* Ailes's political star was tarnished, at least for the time being. In the '70s and '80s he relished his role as communications consultant to the stars—the stars of corporate America, that is. And then, of course, the ultimate star turn for Ailes came in 1984 with his "coaching" of an aging Ronald Reagan.

His mastery of the universe became complete with the Bush campaign's come-from-behind destruction of the Democrats in 1988. But like a shooting star, the light dimmed soon after, when the repercussions of the 1988 campaign ushered him away from politics and back toward his first love, television production. But even after leaving the political stage, he played the role of Machiavelli—advising the George H. W. Bush administration every so often, helping Bush with his 1992 convention speech, and so on.

Even after he was a media executive with NBC he dispensed political advice to those he deemed worthy, aspiring 1996 presidential candidate Steve Forbes, for example. In 2002 a major ruckus erupted over a memo Ailes had sent to the George W. Bush White House. In Bob Woodward's book *Bush at War,* Woodward writes that shortly after the 9/11 attacks, Ailes sent a confidential note to Karl Rove. According to Woodward, the note was supposed to be a "back-channel message" to President Bush, offering public relations–type advice about how to respond. Ailes's advice to Bush was reportedly something along the lines of "convey to the American public that you are taking the harshest possible actions—if you do so, the public will be patient about when to retaliate."

This is consistent with Ailes's actions in the past and his self-image as an "advisor." But Woodward's point in relating this story is that it was improper for Ailes to do this—"Ailes was not supposed to be giving political advice,"[1] he notes, because he was now running Fox News. With the publication of Woodward's book and the firestorm of criticism of Ailes's actions that followed, Ailes erupted in anger, as usual. He compared Woodward's book to the work of fiction novelist Tom Clancy, saying, "only Tom Clancy does better research."[2] Ailes claimed that Woodward's characterization of his memo was "incorrect."

He said it was simply an American showing his nonpartisan support of the president. "I wrote a personal note to a White House staff member as a concerned American expressing my outrage about the attacks on our country. I did not give up my American citizenship to take this job."[3]

Of course Ailes is right that any American should be able to write the president and express their solidarity with the nation. But that doesn't seem to be what Ailes did. He was apparently offering strategic advice to the president of the United States about how to handle public opinion. And he isn't just any American, he's the president of a news network, with, presumably, a journalistic responsibility. Now he has moved beyond advising mere presidents and kings. He has the ear of someone truly powerful on an international stage: Rupert Murdoch.

Roger Ailes is probably not a bad person. His friends and coworkers adore him—some of them would follow him into hell. He is funny, smart as a whip, and he professes to love his country. But it does seem that he is playing a con game. And he plays it well.

Contrary to the conclusions some may have drawn about him due to his complicity in Nixon's Southern Strategy, various race-themed political campaigns, and Willie Horton–style politics, Roger Ailes is not a racist. He's too smart for that. But in his long career, he has placed himself in the service of those who have a callous attitude toward race relations and a conveniently dismissive attitude about race in America.

The biggest problem with Roger Ailes is that he takes us all for fools. True to his political consulting roots, he believes that if he uses the right slogan, repeats it often enough and loud enough, and aggressively shouts down his critics, he can do whatever he wants and rush off to victory. Well, maybe we are fools. His approach certainly worked for his political clients, at least until the Willie Horton albatross. And it has worked brilliantly for Rupert Murdoch and Fox News. In the face of a mountain of evidence to the contrary, Ailes continues to insist that his network is not biased in any way, that he is fair to all sides, and that he is just practicing "good journalism."

"So what?" one might say. So he refuses to admit that his news network has a built-in conservative bias, what's the big deal? It's not doing any harm; it's just giving a large core of right-of-center Americans a more conservative alternative to the "mainstream media." The big networks and the other major media have a reputation for being liberal, so isn't it the same thing? Not really. And it *could* be doing some harm in the long run.

There is a difference between the Fox News approach and the news procedures at most other media organizations. Yes, most reporters probably are liberal. That's just who they are as individuals. It has been pretty well established by communications scholar Doris Graber and others that professional journalists tend to view government activism as constructive and generally support its various missions and objectives. They usually view the role of journalism as an instrument of democracy, something that can help lead to a better society. That kind of social orientation, more often than not, produces someone who is left-of-center politically. Paul Friedman, a network executive with years of producing experience with NBC and ABC, recognizes that traditional broadcast media have a "slightly left-of-center bias . . . It's not so much in what is said. It's in the choice of what to cover."[4]

But given that reality, the end product of most news organizations is much closer to the political middle than Roger Ailes, Rupert Murdoch, or Newt Gingrich would have you believe. Yes, a liberal perspective will creep into their reporting from time to time—some more often than others. But it is not a grand conspiracy, regardless of what Bernard Goldberg (*Bias*) and other conservative media critics say. The heads of the major TV networks do not get together somewhere at a convention hall and plot how they can "screw" George Bush. Andy Lack, the former president of NBC News, said of overt political bias, "I never saw it, I never participated in it, and I think it's very rare."[5] Most major newspapers do not direct their reporters to "bring down" Republican officials, although their editorial boards may cheer for that outcome. What liberal bias does come through is the product of the values and shared assumptions held by individual journalists about government and public policy—and those values are normally going to be more liberal than conservative.

If those journalists are professionals, though, and if they care about their reputations in the industry, they will rarely place personal political belief over reporting the news. And in a competitive business such as the news industry, one that depends on following breaking events and understanding their significance, there rarely is adequate opportunity for a political agenda anyway.

It's very convenient for Ailes to "defend" journalists from the likes of Bill Clinton and the Democratic candidates who boycotted the Fox News debate in Nevada. But the truth is, few people in the world have attacked and criticized journalists and journalism more in the last forty years than Ailes himself—first from the pulpit of politics, then from the pedestal of Fox News. Many who have been around Ailes find that he appears to actually "disdain" journalism. Senior executives he has worked with at Fox say that he seems to "hate" journalists as a group. "I've never seen him use the word 'journalism' and smile at the same time" said one.[6]

Roger Ailes complains that journalism schools teach their students to be negative, to look for bad news first, and to hate America. Well, he's only partially right, in this author's view. Traditionally, in reporting the news, journalists *are* taught to look for conflict because it provides a useful frame for telling the story. Conflict and drama are compelling and so will interest the public enough to pick up a newspaper or tune in to the news. Conflict also provides two or more sides to a story, which enables a reporter to focus in on the issues that provide that conflict. Ailes is probably also right that journalists look for bad news—Thomas Patterson at Yale University has coined the term Bad News Syndrome to describe the journalistic appetite for death, destruction, and scandal. But there is no support anywhere for Ailes's contention that journalists are trained or encouraged to hate America. First of all, they would be hating themselves. And second, when he says "hating America" he means that it seems to him that they hate the particular conservative policy agenda or goal that he and his clients advocate.

As for conflict and bad news, it is there year after year, through Republican administrations and Democratic ones. A lot of reporters admired Bill Clinton as a candidate in 1992, but the mainstream media went after him pretty hard—not just during the Monica Lewinsky ordeal, but before that—during Whitewater and even early on in the first Clinton administration when his policy team seemed confounded and halting. In the Democratic administration before that one, the Jimmy Carter years, there was some pretty brutal reporting and analysis about his "ineptitude" and the lack of confidence that many international leaders had developed in America's ability to lead the world.

But Fox News is different. There is a grand conspiracy to politicize the news, and it is orchestrated by Roger Ailes and Rupert Murdoch. Perhaps Ailes learned from his experiences with Joseph Coors and Jack Wilson at Television News Inc. in the 1970s. This time around, so this theory goes, most of the news hires would be conservative. "There was a litmus test," say some of the early Fox employees from the 1990s. From the early morning to the late evening, most Fox News broadcasters exhibit a right-of-center approach to covering the news. And similar to TVN, there is evidence to indicate that the coverage and flow of the news is steered in a political direction by management—in this case, the executive vice president for news, John Moody.

Just as his client George H. W. Bush did in 1988, Ailes uses the word *liberal* as some sort of weapon to beat over the heads of his critics. He dismisses any criticism as the product of "liberals." He malevolently casts his news organization as the one in the political middle—the one doing it the right way, the fair way—and the others, his competitors, as the ones with the political bias. He ignores evidence of his own organization's political bias and accuses those that produce such evidence of wrongdoing. When a 2005 Pew Foundation study showed that in covering the Iraq war, 73 percent of Fox stories included opinion from anchors and reporters compared with 29 percent on MSNBC and just 2 percent on CNN, Ailes dismissed the Pew Foundation as a "liberal lobbying organization."[7]

So in essence, Roger Ailes has created at Fox the very thing he accuses other media organizations of doing—political management of the news. Only there is significantly more evidence of it at Fox News than at almost any other news organization. As the journalist Stanhope Gould said about the work of the Coors-funded TVN, there's nothing wrong with producing news programming with a political slant—*as long as it is labeled as such.*[8] Labeling something as objective and fair, when it is consistently and intentionally anything but, is misleading and dishonest.

But Roger Ailes the businessman is a true genius. He parlayed his experience in television and politics into a very successful consulting business, active in many different fields: entertainment, corporate communications, and political consulting. He then went to work for one of the big networks and turned CNBC into a successful, profit-generating operation. But when he met Rupert Murdoch, that's when the earth moved. The two of them together have proved to be an unstoppable force.

Everyone in the world of business and media bows their heads in admiration of what Ailes and Murdoch have accomplished at Fox. The niche market positioning, the branding of Fox News as the "one" network that plays it down the middle, the careful cultivation of its right-of-center audience, the casting of its on-air talent, its flashy, tabloid-style production values—it's really quite a cultural phenomenon.

Bob Wright of NBC thinks they redrew the map as far as what works on television:

What Roger did at Fox is to prove you can take a print media theme and make it work in television news. We've had print vehicles that have been conservative and liberal and had points of views and have become known for that. But it wasn't done in television before Fox came along. Everybody was thinking they were down the middle—PBS and the networks—I don't think anyone tried intentionally to be anything but down the middle, and Roger carved a niche out to be something else. That's been done in entertainment programming since day one. It's smart business. It's good marketing. Before Fox, broadcast media tried to be in the political middle and stay committed to that, but Roger showed you can mimic newspaper strategies, as far as being considered liberal or conservative.[9]

Andy Lack believes Ailes is known for creating an "incredibly valuable asset" for Rupert Murdoch and News Corp. that didn't exist before. "From a pure business standpoint that's quite an achievement." Now, of course, Ailes and Murdoch will try to take it a step further with Fox Business Network, and the acquisition of the *Wall Street Journal* will catapult them into the highest ranks of journalism.

A maverick, a renegade, a showman, a political hatchet man? He's all of these things: just don't bet against him.

News Corporation Holdings

Television
FOX Broadcasting Company
Fox Television Stations:

> WNYW—New York City
> WWOR—New York City
> KTTV—Los Angeles
> KCOP—Los Angeles
> WFLD—Chicago
> WPWR—Chicago
> KMSP—Minneapolis
> WFTC—Minneapolis
> WTXF—Philadelphia
> WFXT—Boston
> WTTG—Washington, D. C.
> WDCA—Washington, D. C.
> KDFW—Dallas
> KDFI—Dallas
> WJBK—Detroit
> KUTP—Phoenix
> KSAZ—Phoenix
> WUTB—Baltimore
> WRBW—Orlando
> WOFL—Orlando
> WOGX—Ocala
> WAGA—Atlanta
> KRIV—Houston
> KTXH—Houston
> WJW—Cleveland
> WTVT—Tampa
> KDVR—Denver
> KTVI—St. Louis
> WITI—Milwaukee
> WDAF—Kansas City
> KSTU—Salt Lake City
> WHBQ—Memphis
> WGHP—Greensboro
> WBRC—Birmingham
> KTBC—Austin

FOX Sports Australia
FOXTEL
MyNetworkTV
STAR

DBS & Cable
FOXTEL
BSkyB
FOX Business Network
Fox Movie Channel
FOX News Channel
Fox College Sports
Fox Sports Enterprises
Fox Sports En Espanol
Fox Sports Net
Fox Soccer Channel
Fox Reality
Fuel TV
FX
National Geographic Channel United States
National Geographic Channel Worldwide
Speed
Stats, Inc.

Filmed Entertainment
20th Century Fox
20th Century Fox Espanol
20th Century Fox Home Entertainment
20th Century Fox International
20th Century Fox Television
Fox Searchlight Pictures
Fox Studios Austrailia
Fox Studios Baja
Fox Studios LA
Fox Television Studios
Blue Sky Studios

Newspapers
Australasia:
      Daily Telegraph
      Fiji Times
      Gold Coast Bulletin
      Herald Sun
      Newsphotos
      Newspix
      Newstext
      NT News
      Post-Courier
      Sunday Herald Sun
      Sunday Mail
      Sunday Tasmanian

Sunday Territorian
Sunday Times
The Advertiser
The Australian
The Courier-Mail
The Mercury
The Sunday Mail
The Sunday Telegraph
Weekly Times

United Kingdom:

News International
News of the World
The Sun
The Sunday Times
The Times
Times Literary Supplement

United States:

New York Post

International:

The Wall Street Journal
Dow Jones

Magazines

InsideOut
donna hay
SmartSource
The Weekly Standard
TV Guide (partial)

Books

HarperCollins:
Access
Amistad
Avon
Caedmon
Collins
Ecco
Eos
Fourth Estate
Greenwillow Books
HarperAudio
HarperCollins Children's Books
HarperBusiness
HarperEntertainment
HarperFestival
HarperLargePrint

HarperOne
HarperResource
HarperTempest
HarperTorch
HarperTrophy
Joanna Cotler Books
Katherine Tegen Books
Laura Geringer Books
Perennial
Quill
Rayo
William Morrow
William Morrow Cookbooks
Zondervan
HarperCollins Australia
HarperCollins Canada
HarperCollins India
HarperCollins New Zealand
HarperCollins Publishers
HarperCollins UK

Other Assets

Broadsystem
Fox Interactive Media
MySpace
IGN Entertainment
Rotten Tomatoes
AskMen
FoxSports.com
Scout
WhatIfSports
kSolo
Fox.com
AmericanIdol.com
Spring Widgets
Milkround
National Rugby League
NDS
News Digital Media
News Outdoor
News.com.au
FoxSports.com.au
CARSguide.com.au
careerone.com.au
truelocal.com.au

Source: News Corporation Web site

Notes

CHAPTER 1

1. Botelho, Greg, CNN.Com, "JFK, Nixon Usher in Marriage of TV, Politics," September 24, 2004.
2. Ibid.
3. Ailes, Roger, *You Are the Message,* New York: Dow Jones-Irwin, 1988, p. 11.
4. *Television and the Presidency,* video documentary, 1984. Produced by Ailes Communications.
5. Ailes, p. 11.
6. Bianco, Robert, "Mike Douglas, Former TV Show Host, Dies," *USA Today,* August 13, 2006.
7. Collins, Scott, *Crazy Like a Fox,* New York: Portfolio, 2004, p. 25.
8. Swint, Kerwin, *Political Consultants and Negative Campaigning: The Secrets of the Pros,* University Press of America, 1998. Lanham, MD; p. 89
9. Sella, Marshall, "The Red State Network," *New York Times,* June 24, 2001.
10. McGinniss, Joe, *The Selling of the President 1968,* New York: Trident Press, 1969, p. 33.

CHAPTER 2

1. McGinniss, Joe, *The Selling of the President 1968,* New York: Trident Press, 1969, p. 111.
2. CNN/Time *All Politics* transcript from 1984 presidential debates.
3. Rollins, Ed, *Bare Knuckles and Back Rooms: My Life in American Politics,* New York: Broadway Books, 1996, p. 145.
4. Ailes, *You Are the Message,* p. 16.
5. Ibid., p. 19.
6. Jamieson, Kathleen Hall, *Packaging the Presidency,* 2nd ed., New York: Oxford University Press, 1992, p. 269.
7. McGinniss, *Selling of the President 1968,* Trident Press, 1969, p. 103.
8. Weinraub, Bernard, "TV Battlefield Tests Presidential Strategies," *New York Times,* October 8, 1980.

9. McGinniss, *Selling of the President 1968,* p. 64.

10. Ibid., p. 73.

11. Ibid., p. 97.

12. Ibid., p. 108.

13. Ibid., p. 111.

14. Ibid., p. 149.

15. Stengel, Richard, "The Man Behind the Message," *Time,*
    August 22, 1988.

16. Ibid.

17. Rollins, *Bare Knuckles,* p.193.

18. Devroy, Ann, "Candidate Quayle Recalled Harshly in New Book,"
    Washington Post, July 16, 1989.

CHAPTER 3

1. McGinniss, *The Selling of the President 1968,* p. 99.

2. Ibid., p. 101.

3. Memo dated April 1, 1969, quoted in AP wire story: "Buchanan's
   Positions ... In His Own Words," *Charleston Gazette,* March 3, 1996.

4. Hass, Nancy, "Roger Ailes: Embracing the Enemy," *New York Times
   Magazine,* January 8, 1995.

5. Alterman, Eric, "GOP Chairman Lee Atwater: Playing Hardball,"
   New York Times, April 30, 1989.

6. West, Darrell, "Independent Ads", InsidePolitics.org.

7. Schwartz, Maralee, and Howard Kurtz, "Giuliani Turns to Ailes to Boost
   His Mayoral Bid," *Washington Post,* July 30, 1989.

8. Barbanel, Josh, "Roger Ailes: Master Maker of Fiery Political Darts,"
   New York Times, October 17, 1989.

9. Ibid.

10. Kurtz, Howard, "With Ailes's Aid, Convict Becomes 'Willie Horton'
    of N.Y. Campaign," *Washington Post,* October 20, 1989.

11. Ibid.

12. Ibid.

13. Ibid.

14. Ibid.

15. Ibid.

16. Ibid.
17. Kurtz, Howard, "Time Running Out, Giuliani Steps Up Attacks,"
    Washington Post, November 3, 1989.
18. Wald, David, "Courter Defends TV Commercial as Truthful,"
    Newark Star-Ledger, September 28, 1989.
19. Ibid.
20. Ibid.
21. Purdum, Todd, "Rudolph Giuliani and the Color of Politics in New York,"
    New York Times Magazine, July 25, 1993.
22. Ibid.

CHAPTER 4

1. Whalen, Bill, "He Taught George Bush Telegenics," *Insight on the News,*
    June 27, 1988, vol. 4, p. 21.
2. Ibid.
3. Stengel, Richard, "Bushwacked!" *Newsweek,* February 8, 1988.
4. Ibid.
5. Garcia, Robert, "Was It an Assault?" ABCNews.com,
    September 28, 2006.
6. Stengel.
7. Ibid.
8. Ibid.
9. Crawford, Craig, transcript of Crawford's conversation on air with Keith
    Olbermann on MSNBC, October 2, 2006
10. Garcia.
11. Stengel.
12. Whalen.
13. "Fox News Sunday with Chris Wallace", Fox News transcript,
    September 24, 2006.
14. "Fox News Chief: Clinton Hatred for Journalists Is Showing,"
    Associated Press, September 27, 2006.
15. Olbermann, Keith, "Countdown with Keith Olbermann," MSNBC
    transcript, October 2, 2006.
16. Jamieson, Kathleen Hall, *Packaging the Presidency,* New York: Oxford
    University Press, 1992, p. 467.
17. Ibid., p. 468.

18. Alterman, Eric, "GOP Chairman Lee Atwater: Playing Hardball,"
    New York Times, April 30, 1989.
19. Hinerfeld, Daniel, "How Political Ads Subtract," *Washington Monthly,*
    May 1990.
20. *Advertising Age,* November 14, 1988, p. 87
21. Jamieson, p. 479.
22. Jamieson, Kathleen Hall, *Dirty Politics,* New York:
    Oxford University Press, 1992, p. 7.
23. Hinerfeld.
24. Sourcewatch, Center for Media and Democracy.
25. Ibid.
26. Ibid.
27. Opensecrets.org
28. Sourcewatch, Center for Media and Democracy

CHAPTER 5

1. Gould, Stanhope, "Coors Brews the News," *Columbia Journalism Review,*
    March/April 1975, p. 29.
2. Baum, Dan, *Citizen Coors,* New York: Perennial, 2000, p. 111.
3. Gould, p. 19.
4. Ibid., p. 23.
5. Ibid.
6. Baum, p. 111.
7. Ibid.
8. Ledbetter, James, *Made Possible By . . .,* New York: Verso, 1997, p. 99.
9. Ibid.
10. Isaacs, Stephen, "Coors-Backed Unit Seeks Defeat of Hill 'Radicals,'"
    Washington Post, May 6, 1975.
11. Isaacs, Stephen, "Coors Beer and Politics Move East," *Washington Post,*
    May 4, 1975.
12. Ibid.
13. Weyrich, Paul, "Faith is a Right, Not a Theocracy, Senator Schumer,"
    www.renewamerica.us/columns/weyrich/060724, July 24, 2006.
14. Crawford, Alan, "When Paul Weyrich Speaks, Conservatives Listen Up,"
    Los Angeles Times, May 19, 1991.
15. Gould, p. 27.

16. Baum, p. 112.
17. Gould, p. 24.
18. Ibid p. 26.
19. Ibid.
20. Media Matters for America,
     www.mediamatters.org/items/200407140002
21. Sella, Marshall, "The Red State Network," *New York Times,*
     June 24, 2001.
22. Ibid.
23. *Inside Media,* December 11, 1996.
24. *New York,* November 17, 1997.
25. Hickey, Neil, "Is Fox News Fair?", *Columbia Journalism Review,*
     March 4, 1998.
26. Ackerman, Seth, "The Most Biased Name in News," *FAIR,*
     July/August 2001.
27. *Huffington Post,* November 14, 2006, www.huffingtonpost.com
28. Goldstein, Bonnie, *Slate,* November 17, 2006.
29. Gould, p. 24.
30. Ibid.
31. Ibid.
32. Ibid.
33. Baum, p. 113.
34. Ibid.
35. Ibid.
36. C-SPAN transcript December 19, 2004.
37. Gould, p. 28.
38. Carmody, John, "Coors to End Television News Effort," *Washington Post,*
     September 30, 1975.
39. Ledbetter, p. 101.
40. Ibid., p. 102.
41. Isaacs, Stephen, "Coors Beer and Politics Move East."
42. Ledbetter p. 103.
43. Carmody, John, "Senate Panel Tables Coors Nomination 11-6,"
     Washington Post, October 31, 1975.
44. Ledbetter, p. 101.

CHAPTER 6

1. Richardson, John, "Okay Ailes, Fix Me!" *Communicator's Journal,* November/December 1983, p. 39.
2. Collins, *Crazy Like a Fox,* p. 29.
3. Ailes, *You Are the Message,* p. 2.
4. Richardson, "Okay Ailes, Fix Me!" p. 35.
5. Krucoff, Carol, "And Creating an Image," *Washington Post,* May 17, 1983.
6. Richardson, p. 44.
7. Ibid.
8. Ibid.
9. Ibid.
10. Ibid.
11. Morganthau, Tom, and James Doyle, "The Prime Time Players," *Newsweek,* January 28, 1980.
12. Lynn, Frank, "A G.O.P. Panel Backs D'Amato," *New York Times,* September 25, 1980.
13. Diamond, Edwin, and Stephen Bates, *The Spot,* Cambridge, Mass.: The MIT Press, 1988, p. 323.
14. Ibid.

CHAPTER 7

1. Telephone conversation with author, November 8, 2006.
2. West, Darrell, "Independent Ads," www.insidepolitics.org.
3. Alterman, Eric, "GOP Chairman Lee Atwater: Playing Hardball," *New York Times,* April 30, 1989.
4. Stengel, Richard "The Man Behind the Message," *Time,* August 22, 1988
5. West.
6. Ibid.
7. Conason, Joe, "The Vast Right Wing Conspiracy Is Back in Business," Salon.com, March 9, 2004.
8. Tapper, Jake, "The Willie Horton Alumni Association," Salon.com, August 5, 2000.

9. Conason.

10. Sweitzer, Thomas, "Kill or Be Killed," *Campaigns & Elections,* September 1, 1996.

11. Conason.

12. Tapper.

13. Ibid.

14. Jamieson, Kathleen Hall, *Packaging the Presidency,* 2nd ed., New York University: Oxford Press, 1992, p. 471.

15. Jamieson, *Dirty Politics,* New York: Oxford University Press, 1992, p. 19.

16. Ibid., p. 25.

17. West, "Independent Ads."

18. Ibid.

19. Jamieson, *Dirty Politics,* p. 23.

20. West.

21. Ibid.

22. Mendelberg, Tali, "Executing Hortons: Racial Crime in the 1988 Presidential Campaign," *Public Opinion Quarterly,* vol. 61, 1997, p. 151.

23. West.

24. Babcock, Charles, "FEC Split over Horton Ad Investigation," *Washington Post,* January 16, 1992.

25. McCarthy, Larry, affidavit, Federal Election Commission, Certified Administrative Record Under Review 3069, August 1, 1990.

26. Ibid.

27. Ailes, Roger, affidavit, Federal Election Commission, Certified Administrative Record Under Review 3069, August 1, 1990.

28. McCarthy.

29. "Inquiry of Willie Horton Ad Ends without FEC Reaching Judgment," *Los Angeles Times,* January 17, 1992.

30. Babcock.

31. Ibid.

32. Tapper.

33. Babcock.

34. Ibid.

35. Tapper.

CHAPTER 8

1. Taylor, Paul, "Consultants Rise via the Low Road," *Washington Post,* January 17, 1989.
2. Reid, T. R., "Media Consultant Fights 'Bad Boy' Image," *Washington Post,* July 29, 1989.
3. Ibid.
4. Reid, T. R., "Negative Ad Wizard Becomes Part of the Issue," *Washington Post,* May 9, 1998.
5. Reid, "Media Consultant Fights . . .".
6. Ibid.
7. Barbanel, Josh, "Roger Ailes: Master Maker of Fiery Political Darts," *New York Times,* October 17, 1989.
8. Reid, "Media Consultant Fights . . . "
9. Schwartz, Maralee, and Howard Kurtz, "Giuliani Turns to Ailes to Boost his Mayoral Bid," *Washington Post,* July 30, 1989.
10. Ibid.
11. Barbanel.
12. Perry, James M., and David Shribman, "The Negative Campaign Ad Comes of Age in Eastern Races, Stealing the Limelight," *Wall Street Journal,* November 2, 1989.
13. Ibid.
14. Barbanel.
15. Ibid.
16. Kurtz, Howard, "Time Running Out, Giuliani Steps Up Attacks," *Washington Post,* November 3, 1989.
17. Ibid.
18. Barbanel.
19. Ibid.
20. Taylor, Paul, "Campaigns Take Aim Against Consultants," *Washington Post,* February 15, 1990.
21. Ibid.
22. Ibid.
23. Ibid.
24. Oreskes, Michael, "High Hopes of Defeating Simon Are Being Deflated," *New York Times,* October 19, 1990.
25. Ibid.

26. Schwartz, Maralee, and David Broder, "Ailes Levels Attack on Simon in Illinois," *Washington Post,* October 10, 1990.
27. Hertzberg, Hendrick, "Making Tracks toward '92," *Los Angeles Times,* October 10, 1991.
28. Ibid.
29. Ibid.
30. Myers, Steven Lee, "Presidential Election of 1992," *New York Times,* December 13, 1991.
31. Rothenberg, Randall, "Political Consultants May Be Election's Big Losers," *New York Times,* November 9, 1990.
32. Collins, Scott, *Crazy Like a Fox,* New York: Portfolio, 2004, p. 37.
33. Nichols, Max, "Negative Campaigning: People Absorb the Information," *Journal Record,* Oklahoma City, October 10, 1990.
34. Taylor, Paul, "The New Political Bosses," *Washington Post,* January 1, 1989.

CHAPTER 9

1. Welch, Mary Alma, "Cable Exec's Joke Bombs at the White House," *Washington Post,* March 12, 1994.
2. Roberts, Roxanne, "The Yellow Ribbon Special," *Washington Post,* April 4, 1991.
3. Toner, Robin, "Political Memo: Show Dulls Democrats' View of '92," *New York Times,* April 5, 1991.
4. Ibid.
5. Ibid.
6. Schwartz, Maralee, "Strong Denials from Ailes," *Washington Post,* August 19, 1992.
7. *Crain's New York Business* 9 (13) March 23, 1993, p. 14.
8. Fries, Charles, The Caucus for Television Producers, Writers, and Directors, Summer 1994.
9. Auletta, Ken, *Backstory: Inside the Business of News,* New York: Penguin, 2003, p. 251.
10. Robichaux, Mark, "GE's CNBC Cable Unit Names Ailes As It's President,"

Wall Street Journal, August 31, 1993.

11. Ibid.
12. Telephone Interview with Bob Wright, September 13, 2007.
13. Robichaux.
14. Ibid.
15. Fabrikant, Geraldine, "Ex-Consultant to Bush Named to Head CNBC," *New York Times,* August 31, 1993.
16. Hall, Jane, "CNBC Chief No Stranger to Tube Television," *Los Angeles Times,* October 18, 1993.
17. Telephone interview with Andy Lack, October 11, 2007.
18. Hall.
19. Ibid.
20. Wright.
21. Moore, Frazier, "Trying to Cure What Ailes You," *Los Angeles Times,* August 6, 1995.
22. Ibid.
23. Ibid.
24. Wright interview.
25. Broder, Jonathan, and Murray Waas, "The Road to Hale," *Salon.com,* March 17, 1998.
26. Von Drehle, David, and Howard Schneider, "Foster's Death a Suicide," *Washington Post,* July 1, 1994.
27. Grossman, Karl, "Koppel Covers for Limbaugh's Rumor-Mongering," FAIR, www.fair.org, August 1994.
28. Ibid.
29. Transcript of Don Imus radio program, March 10, 1994.
30. Welch.
31. Ibid.
32. Ibid.
33. Ibid.
34. Mundy, Alicia, "Guessing Where Roger Ailes Will Go," *Mediaweek,* January 29, 1996.
35. Welch.

CHAPTER 10

1. Telephone interview with Bob Wright, September 13, 2007.
2. Collins, Scott, *Crazy Like a Fox,* New York: Portfolio, 2004, p. 18.
3. Ibid.
4. Ibid.
5. Auletta, Ken, "The Race for a Global Network," *New Yorker,* August 3, 1993.
6. Lesly, Elisabeth, and Kathy Rebello, "Network Meets Net," *BusinessWeek,* June 14, 1997.
7. Telephone interview with Andy Lack, October 11, 2007.
8. Auletta, Ken, *Backstory: Inside the Business of News,* New York: Penguin, 2003, p. 253.
9. Collins, p. 15.
10. Ibid., p. 18.
11. Wright interview.
12. Mundy, Alicia, "Guessing Where Roger Ailes Will Go," *MediaWeek,* January 29, 1996.
13. Ibid.
14. Carter, Bill, "Ailes Steps Down as Head of CNBC Cable Channel," *New York Times,* January 19, 1996.
15. Ibid.
16. Jensen, Elizabeth, "Bolster will Succeed Ailes as President of General Electric's CNBC Cable Unit," *Wall Street Journal,* January 19, 1996.
17. Mundy.
18. Ibid.
19. Wright.

CHAPTER 11

1. Colford, Paul D., *The Rush Limbaugh Story: Talent on Loan From God,* New York: St. Martin's Press, 1993.
2. PBS Transcript, *NewsHour with Jim Lehrer,* October 13, 2003.
3. ESPN.com News Service, October 2, 2003.
4. Naureckas, Jim, "50,000 Watts of Hate," *FAIR,* Jan/Feb 1995.
5. Ibid.
6. Egan, Timothy, "Talk Radio or Hate Radio?" *New York Times,* January 1, 1995.

7. Grant, *FAIR* archive, www.fair.org.
8. Rowland, Kara, "Talk Radio Award Revoked" *Washington Times,*
    January 17, 2008.
9. Cornell University School of Law, Supreme Court Collection,
    Case 418 U.S. 241, www.law.cornell.edu.
10. Henninger, Daniel, "Rush to Victory," *Wall Street Journal,* April 29, 2005.
11. PBS transcript.
12. Ibid.
13. Ibid.
14. Hartmann, Thom, "The Battle Hymn of the New Liberal Media,"
    Common Dreams News Center, October 16, 2003.
15. "State of the News Media 2007," Project for Excellence in Journalism,
    http://www.stateofthenewsmedia.org/2007.
16. Arbitron, "Radio Today: How Americans Listen to Radio, 2006 Edition,"
    February 14, 2006.
17. "State of the News Media 2007".
18. Polster, Sandor, "Perception of Truth Rules on Talk Radio,
    Bangor Daily News, Bangor, Maine, December 16, 1995.
19. Bolton, Alexander, "GOP Preps for Talk Radio Confrontation,"
    The Hill, June 27, 2007.
20. Shafer, Jack, "Talk Television," *Slate,* April 5, 2005.
21. Wallace, David Foster, "Host," *Atlantic Monthly,* April 2005.
22. Shafer.
23. Ibid.

CHAPTER 12

1. Auletta, Ken, *Backstory: Inside the Business of News,* New York, Penguin, p. 254.
2. *Hollywood Reporter,* October 22, 2007.
3. Baker, Russ, "Murdoch's Mean Machine," *Columbia Journalism Review,*
    New York: May/June 1998, , pp. 51–56.
4. Stecklow, Steve, Aaron Patrick; Martin Peers; and Andrew Higgins,
    "In Murdoch's Career, A Hand on the News," *Wall Street Journal,*
    June 5, 2007.
5. Ibid.

6. Shawcross, William, *Murdoch: The Making of a Media Empire,* New York: Touchstone, 1997, p. 188.
7. Chenoweth, Neal, *Rupert Murdoch: The Untold Story of the World's Greatest Media Wizard,* New York: Crown Business, 2001, p. 158.
8. Baker.
9. Tumulty, Karen, "When Rupert Met Newt," *Time,* January 1, 1995.
10. Auletta, p. 271.
11. Alterman, Eric, *What Liberal Media? The Truth About Bias and the News,* New York: Basic Books, 2003, p. 235.
12. Stecklow.
13. Alterman, p. 237.
14. Shawcross, William, *Vanity Fair,* October 1999.
15. Kahn, Joseph, "Murdoch Has Flattered Communist Party Leaders and Done Business with Their Children," *New York Times,* June 26, 2007.
16. Stecklow.
17. Gleick, Elizabeth, "The Murdoch Chill Factor," *Time,* March 9, 1998.
18. Blumenthal, Sidney, "Rupert Murdoch's Debasing Taste," www.thesmirkingchimp.com, November 30, 2006.
19. Stecklow.
20. Kahn.
21. Ibid.
22. Ibid.
23. Baker, as quoted from Andrew Neil's book, *Full Disclosure,* London: Macmillan, 1996.
24. Collins, Scott *Crazy Like a Fox,* New York: Portfolio, 2004, p. 96.
25. Ibid., p. 97.
26. *Time,* "The Battle of New York," January 17, 1977
27. Siklos, Richard, "In Murdoch's Past, Clues to the Journal's Future," *New York Times,* August 1, 2007.

CHAPTER 13

1. Carr, David, "From Start-Up to Upstart," *New York Times*, April 18, 2004.
2. Collins, Scott, *Crazy Like a Fox*, New York: Portfolio, 2004, p. 24.
3. Brock, David, *The Republican Noise Machine,* New York: Crown Publishers, 2004, p. 313.

4. Lichter, Robert; Stanley Rothman; and Linda Lichter, *The Media Elite,* Bethesda, MD.: Adler & Adler Publishers, 1985, p. 54.
5. Auletta, Ken, *Backstory,* p. 254.
6. Goldstein, Bonnie, *Inside Fox News,* November 17, 2006.
7. Auletta, p. 261.
8. Ibid, p. 262.
9. Noah, Timothy, "Fox News Admits Bias," *Slate,* May 31, 2005.
10. Auletta, Ken, "Vox Fox," *New Yorker,* May 26, 2003.
11. Hickey, Neil, "Is Fox News Fair?" *Columbia Journalism Review,* March/April 1998.
12. Ibid.
13. Ketcham, Diane, "About Long Island; Liberal or Conservative, both are from L.I.," *New York Times,* March 1, 1998.
14. FoxNews.com.
15. "Susan Estrich, Fox's Pet Democrat, Attacks Elizabeth Edwards Again", *Daily Kos,* September 23, 2007.
16. Estrich, Susan, "Fox News is Under Attack Again," FoxNews.com, May 21, 2006.
17. Collins, p. 140.
18. Ibid., p. 142.
19. Ibid.
20. Ibid.
21. Ibid., p. 144.
22. Telephone interview with Bob Wright, September 13, 2007.
23. Auletta, p. 255.
24. Wright.
25. Collins, p. 212.
26. Fallows, James, *Breaking the News: How the Media Undermine American Democracy,* New York: Vintage Books, 1997, p. 14.

CHAPTER 14

1. Siegel, Joel, Greg B. Smith; and Jere Hester, "Clobbered in Cable War, Judge Rips Rudy for Trying to Aid Rupe", *New York Daily News,* November 7, 1996.

2. Giuliani, Rudolph, *Leadership,* New York: Hyperion, 2002, p. 112.
3. Buettner, Russ, "In Fox News, Giuliani Finds a Friendly Stage,"
   New York Times, August 2, 2007.
4. Collins, Scott, *Crazy Like a Fox,* New York: Portfolio, 2004, p. 98.
5. Grossman, Lawrence, "Bullies on the Block," *Columbia Journalism Review,*
   Jan./Feb. 1997, pp. 19–20.
6. Collins, p. 95.
7. Carter, Bill, "ABC and NBC Look Ahead to Rival All-News Channels",
   New York Times, December 6, 1995.
8. Grossman.
9. Swanson, Carl, "Fox Battles Time Warner for a Parking Place on
   Manhattan Cable," *Salon.com,* October 18, 1996.
10. Collins, p. 100.
11. Ibid.
12. Levy, Clifford, "An Old Friend Called Giuliani and New York's Cable
    Clash Was On," *New York Times,* November 4, 1996.
13. Swanson.
14. Buettner.
15. Grossman.
16. Collins, p. 105.
17. Ibid., p. 106.
18. Ibid.
19. Buettner.
20. Ibid.
21. Collins, p. 111.
22. Ibid.
23. Graham, Tim, "Journalists Slam *New York Times* for 'Paranoia',
    Light Proof on Ailes-Giuliani Expose", newsbusters.org, August 4, 2007.
24. Ibid.
25. Koppelman, Alex, "Did Fox News Chief Ailes Try to Protect Rudy
    Giuliani?" *Salon.com,* November 16, 2007.
26. Buettner, Russ, "Giuliani-Kerik Angle in Suit by Ex-Publisher,"
    New York Times, November 14, 2007.
27. Koppelman.
28. Ibid.
29. Buettner, "Giuliani-Kerik Angle."
30. Koppelman.

31. MSNBC transcript from Barrett interview on "Countdown with Keith Olbermann" November 14, 2007.
32. Rich, Frank, "What That Regan Woman Knows," *New York Times,* November 18, 2007.
33. Ibid.
34 News Corp. press release, January 25, 2008.
35 Goldstein, Bonnie, "Murdock and Regan, Best Friends 4-Ever", slate.com, January 29, 2008.

CHAPTER 15

1. Roberts, Johnnie, "Forward Into Battle," *Newsweek,* August 13, 2007.
2. Cramer, James, "Rupert's Eleven Year Hunt, *New York Magazine,* June 11, 2007.
3. Chaffin, Joshua, "Dow Jones Deal: Murdoch's Defining Moment," *Financial Times,* July 31, 2007.
4. Ibid.
5. Ibid.
6. Ibid.
7. Ibid.
8. Ibid.
9. Ibid.
10. Friedman, Jon, "Above All, Murdoch Is a Businessman," *MarketWatch.com,* August 6, 2007.
11. Pooley, Eric, "The Fox in the Henhouse," *Time,* July 9, 2007.
12. Ibid.
13. Ibid.
14. Lifson, Thomas, "Rupert Murdoch vs. Pinch [sic] Sulzberger: Let the Match Begin," *American Thinker,* August 2, 2007.
15. Pooley.
16. Ibid.
17. Cramer.
18. Haycock, Gavin, "Murdoch Free wsj.com Plan Raises Risks for Pearson," *Reuters,* August 10, 2007.
19. Ibid.

20. Siklos, Richard, "In Murdoch's Past, Clues to the Journal's Future," *New York Times,* August 1, 2007.
21. Pooley.
22. Roberts.
23. Cramer.
24. "WSJ Says Murdoch Won't Affect Coverage," *Associated Press,* August 8, 2007.
25. van Duyn, Aline, and Joshua Chaffin, "What Next, Now that Murdoch Has Won the Prize?" *Financial Times,* August 1, 2007.
26. Pooley.
27. Sutel, Seth, "Dow Jones Plans to Move to Midtown New York", *Associated Press,* January 28, 2008.
28. "Staff Support Pact with Murdoch," *The Statesman,* New Dehli, July 5, 2007.
29. Ibid.
30. Shafer, Jack, "The Murdoch Journal Watch," *Slate,* July 31, 2007.
31. Catts, Tim, "Murdoch, Dow Jones: 'The Unholy Union,'" *BusinessWeek,* July 31, 2007.
32. Olive, David, "Grand Delusion," *Toronto Star,* August 26, 2007.
33. Shafer.
34. MacMillan, Robert, "Dow Jones CEO Zannino to Leave Company," *Reuters,* December 6, 2007.
35. Pooley.

CHAPTER 16

1. Auletta, Ken, *Backstory: : Inside the Business of News,* New York: Penguin, 2004, p. 252..
2. Sauer, Patrick, *Success* magazine, September 12, 2006.
3. Gillette, Felix, "Roger and Me," *New York Observer,* September 18, 2007.
4. Friedman, Jon, "Wall Street Had It Easy On Black Monday", *Marketwatch.com,* October 19, 2007.
5. Grossman, Ben, "Cramer's War of Words," *Broadcasting & Cable,* October 29, 2007.
6. Ibid.

7. Daily TV Newser Feed, MediaBistro.com, November 22, 2005.

8. Ibid.

9. Worden, Nat, "Bartiromo-Burnette: Feud or Corporate Dust-Up?" TheStreet.com, September 12, 2007.

10. Ibid.

11. Ibid.

12. Auletta, p. 267.

13. Ibid.

14. Stengel, Richard, "The Man Behind the Message," *Time,* August 22, 1988.

15. Roberts, Johnnie, "Forward into Battle," *Newsweek,* August 15, 2007.

16. Ibid.

17. Telephone interview with Bob Wright, September 13, 2007.

18. James, Meg, "CNBC Confronted with a Formidable Challenger," *Los Angeles Times,* August 2, 2007.

19. Wright.

20. Grover, Ronald, and Diane Brady, "Fox vs. CNBC: Countdown to War," *BusinessWeek,* October 8, 2007.

21. Ibid.

22. Angwin, Julia, "Fox Quietly Gears Up its Business Channel to Challenge CNBC," *Wall Street Journal,* June 20, 2005.

23. Friedman, Jon, "Fox Business Network Opens a Window," MarketWatch.com, September 17, 2007.

24. Wyatt, Edward, and Geraldine Fabrikant, "Fox to Begin a 'More Business-Friendly' News Channel," *New York Times,* February 9, 2007.

25. Friedman, Jon, "Fox's Neil Cavuto Will Key New Business Channel," MarketWatch.com, February 8, 2007.

26. Bauder, David, "Fox Opens Competition with CNBC," *Associated Press Financial Wire,* February 19, 2007.

27. "Fox Opens Competition with CNBC with Jab," *Associated Press,* February 18, 2007.

28. Ibid.

29. Friedman, Jon, "Fox Business Network Opens a Window," MarketWatch.com, September 17, 2007.

30. Fox Business Network: Full of Foxes! *New York* magazine, October 2, 2007

31. Lowry, Brian, "Fox Business Network," *Variety,* October 17, 2007.

32. Gershberg, Michele, "Fox Business Says to Lure Viewers with Less Jargon." *Reuters,* October 1, 2007.

33. "Fox Business News vs CNBC," *Financial Press,* February 9, 2007.

34. Robins, J. Max, "Rupert's Gambit," *Broadcasting & Cable,* August 6, 2007.

35. Angwin.

36. James.

37. Learmonth, Michael, "Rupert Murdoch Takes Aim at CNBC," *Variety,* September 18, 2007.

38. *Associated Press,* October 14, 2007.

39. Chaffin, Joshua, "Fox Channel's Business is Finding an Audience", *Financial Times,* February 10, 2007

40. Friedman, Jon, "News Corp. Puts CNBC on the Defensive," MarketWatch.com, May 7, 2007.

41. Grover, Ronald, "Fox Business Channel: A Great Start", *BusinessWeek,* October 17, 2007

42. Steinberg, Jacques, and Brian Stelter, "Few Viewers for Infancy of Fox Business," *New York Times,* January 4, 2008.

43. Greppi, Michele, "Ailes: Fox Biz Network Must Limit Infomercials," *Television Week,* February 12, 2007.

CHAPTER 17

1. "Fox News Boss Hits Edwards' Boycott," CBS/AP, March 9, 2007.

2. Shales, Tom, "Fox News Channel's Half-Hour News Hour: Right Funny in Spots," *Washington Post,* February 17, 2007.

3. O'Hare, Kate, "And Now for the Jokes," McClatchy-Tribune News Service, August 7, 2007.

4. Miller, Martin, "Two Liberals Walk into a Bar. . .," *Los Angeles Times,* February 17, 2007.

5. McCain, Robert, "'24' Chief Scoffs at Hillary," *Washington Times,* November 12, 2007.

6. Miller.

7. Media Bistro, March 9, 2007.

8. Phillips, Kate, "Stung by Remarks, Nevada Democrats Cancel Debate on Fox," *New York Times,* March 10, 2007.

9. Ibid.

10. Ibid.

11. "Fox News CEO Ailes: 'The Candidates That Can't Face Fox Can't Face Al Queda,'" *Think Progress,* June 6, 2007.

12. Brownstein, Ron, "Fox Hounded," *Los Angeles Times,* March 16, 2007.

13. Ibid.

14. Dionne, E. J., "Saying No to Fox News," *Washington Post,* April 13, 2007.

15. Brownstein.

16. Kirkpatrick, David, "Murdoch Gets a Jewel, Who'll Get His Crown?" *New York Times,* December 28, 2003.

17. Holton, Kate, "James Murdoch Steps Up as News Corp Heir Apparent," *Reuters,* December 7, 2007.

18. Stevens, Matthew, "Lachlan Rumors Storm in a Tea-Cup," *The Australian,* October 5, 2006.

19. Fishman, Steve, "The Boy Who Wouldn't Be King," *New York* magazine, September 11, 2005.

20. Huck, Peter, "'Someone gets in my face, I get in their face': One clear winner has emerged from the Murdoch family split," *The Guardian,* August 29, 2005.

21. Peers, Martin, Julia Angwin, and John Lippman, "Strained Relations: At News Corp., a Bitter Battle Over Inheritance Splits Family", *Wall Street Journal,* August 1, 2005.

22. Huck.

23. Siklos, Richard, "Behind Murdoch Rift, a Media Dynasty Unhappy in Its Own Way," *New York Times,* August 1, 2005.

24. Steiner, Rupert, "Trust Fund and Holiday Rows Caused Lachlan to Step Down," *Knight Ridder Tribune Business News,* July 31, 2007.

25. Angwin, Julia, "After Riding High with Fox News, Murdoch Aide Has Harder Slog," *Wall Street Journal,* October 3, 2006.

26. Ibid.

CLOSING

1. Carter, Bill, and Jim Rutenberg, "Fox News Head Sent a Policy Note to Bush," *New York Times,* November 19, 2002.

2. Ibid.
3. Transcript from CNN's *Crossfire,* "Fox Chief Too Cozy with White House?" November 19, 2002.
4. Auletta, Ken, *Backstory: Inside the Business of News,* New York: Penguin, 2004, p. 270.
5. Telephone interview with Andy Lack, October 11, 2007.
6. Auletta, p. 277.
7. Johnson, Peter, "Fox News's Ailes Takes Jab at Competitors, Blasts 'Biased' Polls," *USA Today,* April 7, 2005.
8. "Coors Brew the News", *Columbia Journalism Review,* March/April 1975, p. 22
9. Telephone interview with Bob Wright, September 13, 2007.

Bibliography

NEWSPAPERS

The Australian
The Charleston Gazette
The Christian Science Monitor
The Denver Post
Financial Times
The Guardian
The Los Angeles Times
The Newark Star-Ledger
The New York Daily News
The New York Observer
The New York Post
The New York Times
The Philadelphia Inquirer
The Statesman, New Delhi
The Hill
The Orlando Sentinel
The Rocky Mountain News
Roll Call
The Toronto Star
USA Today
Variety
The Wall Street Journal
The Washington Times
The Washington Post
The Weekly Standard

MAGAZINES

Advertising Age
American Thinker
Atlantic Monthly
Brill's Content
Broadcasting & Cable
BusinessWeek
Life
MediaWeek
Newsweek
The New Yorker
New York

The New York Times Magazine
Success
Talkers
Time
Vanity Fair
Washington Monthly

NEWS SERVICES

Associated Press
Associated Press Financial Wire
Bloomberg News
Knight Ridder Tribune Business News
McClatchy-Tribune News Service
Reuters

ONLINE MEDIA

ABCNews.com
Arbitron.com
Center for Media and Democracy
CNN.Com
Common Dreams News Center
C-SPAN
FAIR
FoxNews.com
FT.com
Huffington Post.com
MarketWatch.com
MediaBistro.com
Media Matters
Media Resource Center (MRC)
MSNBC.com
NBC.com
Opensecrets.org
PBS.com
Salon.com
Slate.com
TheStreet.com
Townhall.com

BOOKS AND JOURNAL ARTICLES

Ailes, Roger, *You Are the Message,* New York: Dow Jones–Irwin, 1988

Alterman, Eric, *What Liberal Media? The Truth About Bias and the News,* New York: Basic Books, 2003

Arbitron, "Radio Today: How Americans Listen to Radio, 2006 Edition," February 14, 2006

Auletta, Ken, *Backstory: Inside the Business of News,* New York: Penguin, 2003

Baum, Dan, *Citizen Coors,* New York: Perennial, 2000

Brock, David, *The Republican Noise Machine,* New York: Crown Publishers, 2004

Chenoweth, Neal, *Rupert Murdoch: The Untold Story of the World's Greatest Media Wizard,* New York: Crown Business, 2001

Collins, Scott, *Crazy Like a Fox,* New York: Portfolio, 2004

Crain's New York Business, 9 (13) (March 23, 1993)

Crawford, Craig, *Attack the Messenger,* New York: Rowman & Littlefield, 2005

Diamond, Edwin, and Stephen Bates, *The Spot,* Cambridge, Mass.: MIT Press, 1988

Fallows, James, *Breaking the News: How the Media Undermine American Democracy,* New York: Vintage Books, 1997

Fries, Charles, *The Caucus for Television Producers, Writers, and Directors,* Summer 1994, www.caucus.org/archives/94sum_whoowns.html

Friendly, Fred, *The Good Guys, The Bad Guys, and the First Amendment,* New York: Random House, 1976

Goldberg, Bernard, *Bias,* Washington, D.C.: Regnery Publishing, 2001

Gould, Stanhope, "Coors Brews the News," *Columbia Journalism Review,* March/April 1975

Grossman, Lawrence, "Bullies on the Block," *Columbia Journalism Review,* Jan/Feb 1997

Giuliani, Rudolph, *Leadership,* New York: Hyperion, 2002

Hickey, Neil, "Is Fox News Fair?" *Columbia Journalism Review,* March/April 1998

Jamieson, Kathleen Hall, *Dirty Politics: Deception, Distraction, and Democracy,* New York: Oxford University Press, 1992

Jamieson, Kathleen Hall, *Packaging the Presidency 1968,* 2nd. ed., New York: Oxford University Press, 1992

Ledbetter, James, *Made Possible By . . .,* New York: Verso, 1997

Limbaugh, Rush, *The Way Things Ought to Be,* New York: Pocket Books, 1992

Mayer, Jeremy, *American Media Politics in Transition,* New York: McGraw-Hill, 2008

McGinniss, Joe, *The Selling of the President,* New York: Trident Press, 1969

Mendelberg, Tali, "Executing Hortons: Racial Crime in the 1988 Presidential Campaign," *Public Opinion Quarterly,* vol. 61, 1997

Phillips, Kevin, *The Emerging Republican Majority,* New Rochelle, N.Y.: Arlington House Publishers, 1969

Richardson, John, "Okay Ailes, Fix Me!" *Communicator's Journal,*
        Nov./Dec. 1983
Rollins, Ed, *Bare Knuckles and Back Rooms: My Life in American Politics,*
        New York: Broadway Books, 1996
Shawcross, William, *Murdoch: The Making of a Media Empire,* New York:
        Touchstone, 1997
Swint, Kerwin, *Political Consultants and Negative Campaigning: The Secrets of the Pros,*
        Lanham, Md.: University Press of America, 1998
West, Darrell, *Air Wars,* Washington, D.C.: CQ Press, 1993
Whalen, Bill, "He Taught George Bush Telegenics," *Insight on the News,*
        June 27, 1988
White, Theodore, *The Making of the President 1960,* New York: Pocket Books, 1961

Acknowledgments

I'd like to express my appreciation and gratitude to those in the fields of politics and media who helped me with this book, whether it was through personal interviews, off-the-record chats, or just helpful suggestions. Some are mentioned in the book and some are not, but all were extremely valuable. A big thank-you goes to my agent Scott Mendel of Mendel Media Group for his faith in me and for his very helpful suggestions and guidance. And I can't say enough about Philip Turner of Union Square Press. In helping me put this project together, he has been thoughtful, patient, and supportive. And his team at Union Square/Sterling has been great, especially Iris Blasi. I very much appreciate the contributions made by Keith Wallman, who edited the manuscript and provided some helpful insight. And thanks also to Justin Woelk, who helped me track down some of the research.

About the Author

Kerwin Swint is a professor of Political Science at Kennesaw State University, a frequent political commentator, and a former campaign consultant. He is also the author of *Mudslingers: The 25 Dirtiest Political Campaigns of All Time.*

Index